# On Deadline

## Managing Media Relations

## Carole M. Howard
## Wilma K. Mathews

WAVELAND

PRESS, INC.

Long Grove, Illinois

For information about this book, contact:
Waveland Press, Inc.
4180 IL Route 83, Suite 101
Long Grove, IL 60047-9580
(847) 634-0081
info@waveland.com
www.waveland.com

10-digit ISBN 1-57766-440-X
13-digit ISBN 978-1-57766-440-6

Printed in the United States of America

8   7   6   5   4   3   2

FOURTH EDITION

# On
# Deadline

This book is dedicated
to all the bright young students and professionals
who are following in our footsteps and branching out beyond.

**CAROLE M. HOWARD**, PRSA, ABC, is an award-winning author, speaker and public relations counselor. She is the retired vice president of public relations and communications policy for The Reader's Digest Association in New York, where she had worldwide responsibilities and staff in 15 countries. She also was president of the Reader's Digest Foundation and served on the corporate Management Committee. A former reporter, she worked for AT&T in Seattle, New York and New Jersey for 18 years in various public relations and marketing positions. She has written scores of magazine articles on global PR, employee communications, marketing and management, and has contributed chapters to eight other books. She is a frequent speaker, primarily to university students and corporate audiences, and her speeches have been published in *Vital Speeches* and in three textbooks. She is a contributing editor of *Public Relations Quarterly* and serves on the editorial boards of several other magazines. An accredited member of the Public Relations Society of America and International Association of Business Communicators, Howard is a past member of Women in Communications, Inc. and National Press Women. She has a BA from the University of California-Berkeley and an MS in management from Pace University, New York City. She is listed in the *Who's Who of American Women* and the *World's Who's Who of Women*. In 1990 she was named one of the top 40 "Corporate PR Superstars" by *Public Relations Quarterly*. With experience on the Board of Directors of a public company and several nonprofit organizations, as well as 40 years in communications and marketing, she brings a broad perspective to the practice of media relations. She lives in southwest Colorado with her husband Bob and cats Mac and Molly. E-mail: *tailwinds1@aol.com*

**WILMA K. MATHEWS**, ABC, has 35 years in domestic and international public relations management including media relations, marketing communication, crisis communication and planning. She is director of constituent relations for Arizona State University and also continues to provide consulting services and media coaching to a variety of clients. Mathews worked for AT&T for 15 years in various public relations and media relations positions. She also has directed programs in nonprofit organizations and began her career with magazine and newspaper experience. A Fellow and accredited member of the International Association of Business Communicators, Mathews has received the association's Gold Quill Award of Excellence for Media Relations. She is author of *Effective Media Relations: A Practical Guide for Communicators* and a contributor to *Inside Organizational Communication* and *The Communicator's Guide to Marketing*. She has spoken before numerous audiences in the U.S., Canada, China, Malaysia, Australia, New Zealand and England. Mathews is an inductee in the Rowan University Public Relations Hall of Fame and is listed in several recognition publications including *Who's Who of American Women*. She serves on the advisory board of *communication briefings* and is active in several local organizations including the Valley of the Sun United Way, United Blood Services and the Phoenix Public Library. E-mail: *wkm23@asu.edu; wmathews1@cox.net*.

# Contents

# Foreword

It is unusual for strong audience demand for a public relations textbook to warrant a fourth edition. *On Deadline: Managing Media Relations* has achieved that special distinction because its experienced authors have communicated the breadth and depth of media relations in a straightforward, practical and original way.

All too often we hear that media relations isn't really public relations; it is "merely" publicity. But Carole M. Howard and Wilma K. Mathews explain why media relations must be preceded by policy determination, issue analysis, counseling and the like. They demonstrate that solid planning skills are necessary to practice successful media relations.

Howard and Mathews believe that media relations, properly practiced, has great value to clients and organizations as a strategic management function. And it is in the counseling role that media relations professionals make their greatest contributions to their companies and clients, be they global enterprises or nonprofit charities. But instead of suggesting the counting of clips, column inches and ad equivalencies, they focus on changing opinions and behaviors. That's the real purpose of public relations. And by limiting this book to media relations and enlarging its definition, the authors restore media relations to its proper position.

The authors know from their own careers that you do not get a seat at the proverbial management table without having thoroughly mastered the basics of your craft. For that reason, *On Deadline* also covers all the fundamentals, starting with tools like the basic news release.

They also have added new information on how the Internet has affected media relations. Not only has technology changed the way media relations is conducted; it also has changed the way people get their news. Think blogs, for example, a medium virtually unheard of by all but the most technologically sophisticated before the American presidential election of 2004. The proliferation of new media has dramatically increased the need for up-to-the-minute, online directories as well as tighter planning and identification of target audiences.

After all the research has been done and the organization has set its policies, after the news releases have been written, after management has approved them and the lawyers have cleared them, there remains the "small" task of distributing them to the news media.

If the news release has been soundly conceived and professionally prepared, chances are reasonably good that editors will accept it for publication in one form or another. But alas for all of us in public relations, a large percentage of media contacts are handled poorly. Milliseconds after most news releases have arrived electronically or on paper, editors hit the delete key or toss the paper in the "Big Round File." For the most part, those releases will concern events or information of no interest to the medium receiving them.

No form of media contact—phone call, hand-written note, e-mail, fax, video news release or whatever—will provide a return on the investment if it conveys the wrong message or has been sent to the wrong medium, or to the wrong person at the right medium, or has been sent in the wrong format or at the wrong time.

Wasted effort, wasted time, wasted money! It is no wonder, therefore, that editors who screen such material form a low opinion of media relations and its practitioners. Public relations professionals know that news releases may be only the tip of the iceberg. But certainly we deserve to be judged by how well or how poorly we perform this essential function.

Few professionals actually have directed and participated in so many precedent-setting and successful worldwide public relations activities as the authors, so their recommendations are sound. Readers will benefit from their experiences on behalf of The Reader's Digest Association, AT&T, Arizona State University and other clients, as well as the new case histories and material on international public relations from additional organizations that they include in this fourth edition.

Their practical advice can be put to use immediately whether you work for a huge corporation or a smaller nonprofit association, whether you are a novice or an experienced professional. For the authors' unstinting sharing of this information, the entire public relations profession is in their debt.

The fourth edition of *On Deadline: Managing Media Relations* is virtually an encyclopedia of media relations. This book will help those who must "meet the press" (or interviewers from television, radio, magazines or cyberspace) and provide useful guidance to those helping to steer their organizations through the complex issues facing them today.

Whether you are responsible for calling an editor, posting news on your organization's Web site, managing a full media relations program or advising management in a crisis, you will discover that Howard and Mathews have provided you with sound counsel.

Chester Burger
Life Member, Counselors Academy
Founding President, College of Fellows
Public Relations Society of America
New York
January 2006

# Preface

We were in the midst of training a new person who had transferred into our media relations group when a colleague mentioned a similar situation at his company. "He's pestering all of us for hints on how to do his job," our friend said. "Why isn't there some book I can give him to read?"

"It sure would have been nice if someone had written it all down for us," we joked. And then, "One of us really ought to write that book." But even two robins do not make a spring. The conversation veered off in another direction, and writing the book became a dormant topic.

Shortly thereafter we responded to a late-night query from *The Wall Street Journal* after the leak of a layoff announcement. We had to coordinate responses to internal and external queries with spokespersons in 20 locations across the country. At one point a public relations manager in a manufacturing plant remarked, "You really ought to write this up—it would make a perfect case history."

Some time later we canceled plans for dinner together, one to write a speech on corporate media relations to a Public Relations Society of America chapter in Louisiana, the other to plan a workshop on media relations at the International Association of Business Communicators annual conference. At each of these functions we heard similar comments from members of the audience: "You have had so many different experiences with the news media you really ought to write a book." Thus, the idea came to life again.

The fundamental tools of our trade are words. How flattering—and how humbling—to be told there is a need to sit down at your computer and bang out the story of how you spend your working life.

Successful sales of this book's first edition, initially in hardcover and later in paperback, led to another request—to produce a second edition updating the book and including a separate chapter on international media relations because of its growing importance to our profession.

Five years later it was time for a third edition. The Internet had rapidly changed the way we communicate with each other, and e-business was transforming entire industries. Measurement had become more sophisticated than merely counting press clippings or Web site hits; rather, it involved tracking changed opinions and modified behaviors. And globalization had become even more important for almost all organizations, large and small, in our worldwide, interdependent economy.

## Technology Changes Prompt the Fourth Edition

Now, 21 years after the first edition and six years after the third, continuing strong sales and ongoing dramatic changes in technology have prompted us to publish a fourth edition. You will find new case histories. And you will see how technology continues to transform the media world and our jobs. Just one example: Only a few years ago blogs were unknown. Yet today bloggers and staffers on dot-com desks are interviewed on mainstream television news shows for their unique insights into world events. And CEOs are using blogs to communicate with their employees and other key audiences, including journalists.

Education and training, even of a very high magnitude, are not enough. You also need experience. As cosmetics tycoon Helena Rubinstein put it, "First you've got to get educated—and then you've got to get smart."

Our approach in this book is to cite anecdotes and case studies from our combined eight decades as public relations practitioners in the corporate and nonprofit worlds and from the experiences of others who have graciously shared their stories with us. We hope you will find in them a freshness of vision that will enrich your own insights. Our goal is to provide direction, not directives.

We will talk about the media relations job from both a strategic and a tactical point of view. We also will temper our advice with knowledge gained from our days as working reporters.

The fourth edition of *On Deadline: Managing Media Relations* gives an overview of how the new media and the current focus of traditional media are affecting how you communicate your organization's news events. We delve into the critical first step of planning a media relations program. There is nothing so wasteful of our resources or our energies than activity without insight. We also include a detailed description of setting goals and measuring results, for only with such operational systems in place will you be treated as equal members of the business team by others in your organization. We offer tips on how to get your management's approval *before* you begin and keep them informed of your progress and any changes in external or internal conditions as you proceed, so that your contributions are appreciated by the decision makers of the organization.

## Building Relationships with the Media and Your Management

Architect Mies van der Rohe once said, "God is in the details"— and this is no less true of our profession than it was of his. With that in mind we offer specific suggestions on how to improve your relationship with reporters—including hints for ensuring that reporters can reach you 24/7; keeping your news release distribution lists up to date; creating interest in your organization with regular Web site updates and background mailings; deciding whether to announce your news in the morning or the afternoon, in New York or Hong Kong; modifying your office coverage to match the media's needs; getting the most mileage out of clipping and electronic monitoring services; and deciding when to be responsive and when to say no.

We also provide detailed instructions on how to background both your organization's spokesperson and the reporter before a major interview, because the preparation you put in before they meet often makes the difference between success and failure. As well, we guide you in becoming a part of the decision-making process within your organization. You can take advantage of the instantaneous public opinion polls you can get from your ongoing contacts with reporters and from the Internet to counsel your organization's officers and board before practices and policies are set.

We have written the fourth edition of *On Deadline* for a broad audience. Students of journalism and public relations should find insight into their fields no matter which side of the profession they choose. Chief executive officers and other key spokespersons for organizations may find that parts of the book offer valuable background on how the media operate. It could be useful as a handy reference before an interview with a reporter. Perhaps even reporters will find it interesting to glimpse the inner workings of the world of media relations. It may make them understand why we practitioners view ourselves— when we are doing our job well—as performing a valuable service that makes us not barriers to information but rather indispensable translators of the needs of both reporters and our organizations.

Most of all, the fourth edition of *On Deadline* is written for those people who are, or plan to be, responsible for an organization's or client's day-to-day relations with the news media. Whether you work for a bank wanting to publicize expanded financial services, a utility explaining the complexities and benefits of deregulation, a social service agency desiring to generate attendance at a new job-counseling clinic, a trade association lobbying for legislation or a large corporation marketing a new product, the media's coverage—or lack of coverage— of your news will be an important factor in getting the desired results.

## Influence Decisions as Well as Report Them

A natural avenue into the world of public and media relations is to join a company or organization after a few years of experience as a reporter. For those of you who fell victim to the siren's song of journalism, the transition should not be difficult. Dealing with the media from this side can be just as stimulating as chasing after a story and a byline. Indeed, we would argue it is more so, because you now have the opportunity to influence decisions and activities rather than just report them. You will have the same almost instant feedback as the media cover your organization's news on that evening's newscast, in tomorrow morning's newspaper, in the next issue of a magazine or in an online article.

On the other hand, for people who have not spent time as reporters, producers or editors, a move into the media relations position can be an abrupt change, requiring flexibility not only in *your* lifestyle but also in your family's as you strive to adapt to the media's sense of urgency. The workday's planned activities are forsaken when a reporter asks for information on your agency's fundraising expenses, as it takes you several hours to gather the facts, arrange an interview and brief a spokesperson. A dinner party is interrupted when you receive word that there has been a chemical spill at the plant and reporters are clamoring for information. A weekend outing is canceled when you must move up your planned news conference by a week because of a leak that has surfaced on the Internet. A night's sleep is lost when the clock is stopped during union bargaining as your organization works to negotiate a contract and avoid a walkout.

If you like order and predictability and prefer to take a great deal of time to enunciate your views orally or in writing, media relations is not the job for you. But if you are stimulated by being at the center of action, enjoy responding to stimuli from several directions at once, can rapidly formulate thoughts and clearly articulate positions, and find it exhilarating to bring definition to ambiguity, then media relations may be the field for you.

Your energy and your ability to learn will be tested. The job requires people who can remain calm and focused in a crisis—and above all, keep a sense of humor and perspective. Your reward comes from the people you meet and the events you influence.

We hope the fourth edition of *On Deadline* will help all present and future media relations practitioners to do a better job of walking the tightrope as you strive to balance a reporter's demand for fast and accurate information with the organization's need to guard competitive secrets and avoid violating the privacy of employees; to become as adept at bringing valuable information into the organization as at getting the news out.

For the beginner, *On Deadline* will serve as a textbook; for the more experienced person, a reference book. For neither should it be dull. Media relations is an exhilarating field. If our prose reflects the excitement of being part of news events as they unfold—and contributes to more accurate coverage of the activities of corporations and other organizations—then we will have adequately achieved our objectives and served our profession.

# Acknowledgments

Deciding whom to thank when you work with colleagues and journalists who are so willing to share ideas and experiences is a very difficult task. However, there were some who were especially helpful with editorial advice, manuscript reviews and unflagging interest from the time we got the initial idea for the book to the day the first edition of *On Deadline: Managing Media Relations* was published. These include Chester Burger, Bob Burke, Hal Burlingame, Bill Cooper, Bob Ehinger, Roy Foltz, David Manahan, Brian Monahan, Bill Mullane, Elizabeth Park, Jack Sauchelli, Deb Stahl, Mike Tarpey, Al Wann and Candy Young. We also want to pay tribute to Mary Sokol, whose magic fingers kept us on our toes as well as on schedule.

For support and suggestions on the second edition we gratefully acknowledge the contributions of Stephanie Carpentieri, Carol Cincola, Lesta Cordil, Helen Fledderus, David Fluhrer, Chris King, Craig Lowder, Linda Milone, Martha Molnar, Lynn Munroe, Tara Phethean and Don Ranly. Valuable assistance for the third edition came from Barbara Griswold, Chris King, Lynn Munroe, Debbie Tully and the staff of the Pagosa Springs, Colorado, library. As well, Mac and Molly provided close and much appreciated supervision of the manuscript.

For insight and information for the fourth edition, we thank Bish Mukherjee, Katie Paine, Fraser Seitel, Dr. Melvin L. Sharpe and his public relations graduate student committee for the 25th anniversary Vernon C. Schranz lectureship event at Ball State University, and Ed and Pat Nieder from the Arthur Page Society.

As always, special thanks to Bob Howard, who is our greatest supporter and most constructive critic. We also very much appreciate the ongoing counsel and contributions of the Waveland Press editorial and marketing team—Tom Curtin and Jeni Ogilvie—who have become both publishing partners and good friends over the years.

# 1

# Technology, Tabloids and Trends

## How the New Media World Is Changing Your Job

$A$s the world has become more complex, business and financial journalism has changed. It used to be relegated to the back pages of newspapers or to filling airtime on slow news days. Then increased consumer involvement in the stock market, significant advances in research, dramatic corporate mergers and acquisitions, as well as massive organizational restructuring, layoffs and billion-dollar frauds put economics, finance, technology and business subjects on the front pages.

Economic issues have also become personal issues—and thus, news. They are frequently covered in specific sections of print and online newspapers, such as the real estate section's inclusion of an article on the intrusion of big-block stores in your neighborhood, instead of in the business section. Those of us who make our living

1

by helping reporters translate such news into terms the general public can understand often feel as if we are living in an enormous clothes dryer—events are tumbling around us and we around them in a frantic, haphazard way. It is, after all, somewhat scary to see the words you spoke yesterday to a reporter on the phone set in type in this morning's Asian *Wall Street Journal* or the *New York Times*.

## The Trend Toward Infotainment Journalism

Unfortunately, business journalism suffers from the same trend toward shallow reporting and sound bite editing that has afflicted the general consumer media. The traditional double-source rule is fast disappearing if not gone, with rumors and gossip too often masquerading as news.

Grant N. Horne, retired vice president–public relations of Pacific Gas and Electric Co., says "TV/radio news formats and much of the print press increasingly take their reporting cues—especially a harsh, confrontational style—from the psycho-babble of their talk show cousins." As a result, Horne points out, "Increasingly, people recognize that the media business, and especially television, is more about entertainment, provided by entertainers, than it is about fact."[1]

Veteran PR executive and teacher Fraser Seitel reinforced that concern when he said, "Leaks and lies and innuendo no longer become the province only of the tabloids. Journalistic survival, even for mainstream media, means a greater willingness to stretch the truth to become more categorical and controversial."[2]

Even respected journalists are joining in the criticism. Calling her 1999 autobiography the story "of my ride on the decline of network news," CBS correspondent Lesley Stahl spoke harshly of the drop in TV news standards: "There was a new ethic at CBS . . . going for the buck was first, second and third priority," she wrote. She felt that management "was downgrading us to some second-rate tabloid." Stahl added, "The lines between tabloid shows and us were blurring, and it wasn't just how we looked. More and more we were covering their subject, the world of personality. The private lives of famous people were becoming our territory too, as the competition for ratings heated up."[3]

Meanwhile Robert MacNeil, famous for his nearly 40 years in broadcasting, wrote a blistering, behind-the-scenes novel in 1998 about network news today—a world in which crazed competition drives serious journalists into the tabloid feeding frenzies Americans increasingly see on their screens. In a promotional piece Walter Cronkite wrote, "MacNeil calls it a novel but here, in delightfully readable style, may be the best explanation yet of that which ails television news."[4]

As *60 Minutes* creator and executive producer Don Hewitt put it, "I would like to believe that the [networks'] founding fathers, were they still around, would have stood fast on what was, for them, an article of faith: News is news and entertainment is entertainment, and crossing the line between them is often dishonest and always bad broadcasting."[5]

What appears on the Internet, then, has great impact on what we will see on our TV news that night and read in our newspapers the next morning. As the editor of the *American Journalism Review* put it, "One thing is clear: The phenomenon is not going to go away no matter how much journalism purists and reformers decry it. The day when the elite media could make the call on whether something comes to light is far behind us." [6]

## The Internet and Blogs Transform Our Lives

Many journalists look first to an organization's Web site—or its competitor's Web site—before calling the media relations contact for information. They also search for blogs—pro and con—on the specific topic in question.

The number of Web sites and blogs increases exponentially each day. The ease with which any individual anywhere in the world can set up and maintain either a Web site or a blog—or both—clearly places individuals in charge of what they perceive as news.

And with the advent of the portable, wireless devices that can be used to access the Internet, such as the BlackBerry, of satellite (subscriber) radio, and of other technology spin-offs, those organizations disseminating news must now look to multiple venues for that dissemination in order to reach those audiences who can easily self-select the news or information they want.

"The problem isn't so much the ability to communicate," says Michael Bloomberg, founder of Bloomberg L.P. and mayor of New York City. The company he founded provides a wealth of information on financial markets and activities around the world. The company's "Bloomberg News" offers a full range of business and financial stories reported by Bloomberg journalists. Said Bloomberg about the delivery of information: "It's the ability to find the one piece of information you need amid all the clutter. I don't think that there's a lack of information out there. Quite the contrary: There's so much information nobody can find anything."[7]

Jonah Bloom, executive editor of *Advertising Age* and former *PR Week* writer, believes that "the Internet and PR were made for each other." He says, "They are both about making a connection, about establishing one-on-one relationships."[8]

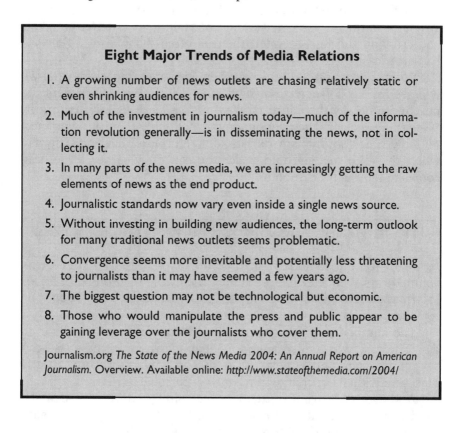

### Eight Major Trends of Media Relations

1. A growing number of news outlets are chasing relatively static or even shrinking audiences for news.

2. Much of the investment in journalism today—much of the information revolution generally—is in disseminating the news, not in collecting it.

3. In many parts of the news media, we are increasingly getting the raw elements of news as the end product.

4. Journalistic standards now vary even inside a single news source.

5. Without investing in building new audiences, the long-term outlook for many traditional news outlets seems problematic.

6. Convergence seems more inevitable and potentially less threatening to journalists than it may have seemed a few years ago.

7. The biggest question may not be technological but economic.

8. Those who would manipulate the press and public appear to be gaining leverage over the journalists who cover them.

Journalism.org *The State of the News Media 2004: An Annual Report on American Journalism*. Overview. Available online: *http://www.stateofthemedia.com/2004/*

## Print Is Not Dead

Publishers of print publications are not about to cede their entire future to cyberspace. *American Journalism Review* editor Rem Rieder reminisces with a chuckle about Ted Turner's prophecy in 1981, shortly after the launch of CNN, that newspapers were dinosaurs and in 10 years or so they would be a fond memory. As it turns out, he was wrong. Readership among the larger daily papers might be shrinking, but the print media are still competitive and willing to take steps to adapt to today's readers. The 157-year-old *Chicago Tribune* publishes the *RedEye* in a tabloid format, featuring shortened versions of Tribune stories and other columns geared toward a youthful audience.

There has been a proliferation of weekly/semiweekly local newspapers that thrive in defined communities, whether a small town or a suburb of a larger city. The national trend towards community is reflected in these papers, which cover the local high school, city ordinances, village board meetings and the opening of a new flower shop—none of which appear in the larger daily newspaper. Readership is high and advertisers are pleased.

Ethnic print media is on the rise with newspapers and magazines focused entirely on their audiences' events, heritage, opportunities and businesses. Here, too, readership is high. Additionally, specialty magazines continue to increase. Some magazines have been borne from their cable TV counterpart, other magazines have been spawned from a hole in media coverage. A check at any major bookstore clearly demonstrates the ever-expanding shelf needs for magazines and special publications. These magazines offer numerous opportunities for the media relations specialist who has a clearly defined audience.

Sadly, there are some additions in the print media not so welcome. These are local free dailies whose advertisers are the only paid customers. Many of these publications have advertising people writing restaurant and art reviews, masquerading as journalists while plugging businesses. In other papers, the advertisers themselves write columns disguised as editorial pieces.

Print isn't dead but is taking on life-support in multiple ways. A vast majority of newspapers and magazines have corresponding Web sites. As print readership decreases, online readership increases. Major newspapers also have reporters hosting their own blogs in order to gain more input from readers, as well as story ideas, public concerns and issues.

## Changes in Media Mix

Although newspapers remain an important information source, they have been disappearing at an alarming rate. Major U.S. cities have changed from multi-paper towns to one-paper towns. Other papers like *The Wall Street Journal, USA Today* and *The New York Times* are becoming truly national papers.

Cable television, or narrow casting TV, continues to grow as audiences want more specific viewing rather than the traditional, one-size-fits-all viewing offered by traditional, noncable networks. The Public Broadcast System also is reinventing itself with programming designed for viewers with multiple interests for quality programs.

Radio stations, now often owned by nonmedia companies, are looking for ways to cut costs. Many are turning to plug-and-play programming, which allows them to air several hours of preprogrammed material with no need for DJs or newscasters. Satellite radio is rapidly becoming popular for those who want specific types of audio programming, whether it's all-Elvis all the time, or all-talk or all-country. This subscriber-based system more clearly matches audience and programming and keeps overhead to a minimum.

Special interest magazines are making serious inroads into the circulation of traditional news and general readership magazines. Wire services are proliferating and/or expanding services to meet the needs of niche or specialty media.

Major media organizations have come to find out they are mortal too, as corporate raiders invade their lives. The convergence of news media—with one company owning newspapers, radio and television stations—brings with it concerns of news management shifting from an objective news perspective to a business perspective. Already there is evidence of owner-based decisions affecting editorial coverage. Evidence of staff cuts to cut costs is seen in the slow disappearance of beat reporters.

Video and audio news releases supplied to the media by companies are often not acknowledged as such and are seen or heard as news rather than as merely publicity for the company. Both TV and radio stations use them to fill the void in their newscasts.

## Other Technological Changes

A live video "feed" from the other side of the world is seen in true-to-life color and real time many thousands of miles away. Cell phone cameras allow citizens to report the news live as they are experiencing it, even in disasters. Thanks to video or radio satellite tours, spokespersons can "travel" to scores of cities in one day to publicize a new book or to drum up support for a political campaign without leaving their hometowns. Annual meeting speeches can be uploaded to a company's Web site for download to your iPod.

Truly, the information age is here and the information highway is well developed. We are only beginning to realize the opportunities and benefits for the exchange of information and news. In fact, possible applications are limited only by the imagination of the users of these technologies and of those who would serve us with interconnected networks, sophisticated terminals, expanded databases and software programs.

The public's thirst for information never seems to be quenched. As Dan Rather opined, "In a world where it seems we're inundated with news, I think we're only inundated with . . . well, mutations of the news, imitations of the news, variations on the news. When it comes to real and serious and important reportage we're not glutted. We're starved."[9] And Robert MacNeil wrote in his autobiography; "In most of the stories television cares to cover, there is always 'the right bit,' the most violent, the most bloody, the most pathetic, the most tragic, the most wonderful, the most awful moment. Getting the effective 'bit' is what television news is all about. . . ."[10] Although both Rather and MacNeil stated their observations over 20 years ago, they hold true today, as well.

## Changes in Media Relations Jobs

Demands on the people responsible for relations with the news media also are increasing. If we have not changed with the requirements of the job, then we have no doubt lost opportunities to serve our organizations, clients and the profession. It was not so many years ago that the press job in an organization was a seat-of-the-pants, reactive position. All we had to do was keep up friendships with reporters at local press association functions, keep our sense of humor when they phoned with tough questions, and keep the company's name *out* of the newspapers. Many corporations and organizations believed their decisions and actions were none of the media's— or the public's—business.

Today that has changed. For one thing, the name of our job has changed. It is *media* relations now, reflecting the ever-increasing importance of television, radio, the Internet, including blogs, as sources of news. For another thing, today's management expects more of us: Not only must we be able to get the organization out of a mess, we also are expected to *keep it from ever getting into the mess in the first place.* Our work has become accepted as a valued management and strategic function.

## Media Relations in the Twenty-first Century

Media relations people, like all public relations professionals, are moving rapidly into the more complex—and more ambiguous—world of issues and issues management. Not that we have moved out of the fire-fighting, news-releasing, question-answering business. That will be as important a part of what we do tomorrow as it is today. But it will not be the major thing we do, and it cannot be the only thing we let consume our time. It no longer is enough that we be good communicators with a broad knowledge of our organization and its product lines. Now we must be familiar with everything from equal-opportunity laws to environmental-protection legislation, from workers' compensation to antitrust actions, from global issues and corporate social responsibility, to regulations governing the buying and selling of stock on Wall Street. Our knowledge of a broad base of information, our skill in assessing its effects on our organization, and the guidance we provide based on that assessment are a large part of the work we do. In short, our skills and our work are expected to make a positive, measurable contribution to the organization's goals.

Former Eli Lily CEO Randall L. Tobias believes that "most effective functions [in corporations] are becoming increasingly more *virtual* than functional. To be valuable to your CEO," he advises, "you need to spend your time focusing on issues—not trying to preserve your traditional function as it was practiced in the past."[11]

Walter K. Lindenmann, formerly head of research at Ketchum, the New York-headquartered multinational PR consulting firm, describes the substance of media relations in the past. His words serve as a reminder of another significant change in our function. For years our focus had been "almost exclusively on the communications of key messages to selected target audience groups," he said.

> If we could somehow appropriately disseminate the messages and themes that organizations were interested in conveying to others, if we could somehow begin to show that the appropriate audience segments were indeed being exposed to the messages, were receiving them, understanding them, and retaining them, and finally, if we could somehow prove that the messages that were sent had changed public opinion, then most of us felt that we could argue that [media] relations has value.[12]

Today the job of a media relations professional is more complex and more difficult to achieve; we now go beyond delivering the message; our goal is actually to *change behaviors*—or to preserve the behaviors that we want to continue.

Of course, media relations is not a stand-alone function. It is one part of your organization's arsenal to meet customer needs and increase shareholder value. Good media relations requires thoughtful plans and targeted strategies. It is much more than churning out news releases on new products or services. It is searching for other opportunities and news events that can be turned into positive media coverage. It is taking time to develop a rapport with key reporters in order to sell them on the news value of your organization's activities.

Some argue that to serve well we must be retained as outside counsel *of* the organization rather than *in* it. In fact, we must be both. We must be able to explain to a reporter why we may *not* be able to give out certain information, and a few minutes later argue equally convincingly with an organization officer as to why we *should* disclose it. Representing at different times the perspective of the reporter, the public and the organization, we become the official split personality—a much more difficult yet fascinating role.

# 2

# Getting Started

## Setting Up Your Program

Getting started in media relations means understanding your role and your objectives and sticking to both. But what is your role? Referee? Propagandizer? Shuffler of news releases? Senior counsel? One fact that few executives or organization leaders seem to appreciate is that your role is to make a reporter's job easy, to help that reporter meet his or her objectives and, at the same time, to help your organization meet its objectives.

This tightrope-walking exercise means that when you speak to a reporter you are representing the organization; when you speak to the people in your organization you are representing the reporter. You do not need a split personality to achieve the balance, but you do need a sound understanding of everyone's goals and objectives. The reporter's objective is to get a story to help his or her editors meet a goal of having a newspaper that will sell or a television newscast that will attract viewers or a Web site marked "Favorite." Now, what are your goals and objectives?

## What Kind of Program?

There are two possible kinds of media relations programs: (1) passive or reactive and (2) active or proactive. A passive program means that your organization has determined, for whatever reason, not to seek the attention of the public eye. A passive posture may be initially frustrating to reporters. Once the word gets around, however, the organization generally is left alone, except in crises. Any other mention in the media about the company often is speculation. Privately held companies sometimes engage in this practice and can do so because they are not required by law or regulation to divulge earnings or other financial data.

Even an organization obligated to divulge information to the public can still have a passive program. In this case, nothing beyond what must be reported is given out. This stance does not win friends among the media, but respect from journalists is probably not a goal. There is no need for a media relations person in such an organization because attorneys and accountants can prepare the basic required releases for the public.

If, however, your organization wishes to have an *active* media relations program, you need to know that active does not mean: churning out a release a day; taking reporters to lunch frequently; holding a news conference at the drop of a hat; scheduling all of your subject-matter experts on every radio and television talk show in your area; counting inches of copy or seconds of air time as the sole measurement technique; or creating glitzy video news releases.

Active means that you plan, implement and measure a well-conceived media relations program that supports your organization's goals and objectives. The way to do this is to set up your own media relations goals, objectives, strategies and timetables.

## Developing a Communications Policy and Media Rules

Media scholar Harold Lasswell has said the communications process must be considered in terms of "who says what to whom, through what channel, with what effect."[1] This applies most significantly in media relations where you need to know—before the telephone rings—who will speak on behalf of your organization and to what purpose.

Dr. Amanda Hamilton-Attwell concurs, defining communication policy as "The rules that will determine the behavior of the communication specialists and the management of the flow of information."[2]

Beyond designating the official spokespersons, a communications policy can set the tone of all your media activities. The policy needs to be endorsed by and disseminated from the leadership of your organization. Early in his tenure, Theodore Vail, the first president of AT&T, wrote a communications policy that has withstood the test of time:

> The only policy to govern the publicity [of AT&T] is that whatever is said or told should be absolutely correct, and that no material fact, even if unfavorable but bearing on the subject, should be held back. When we see misstatements, make it certain that those making them have the correct facts. This will not only tend to stop the making of them, but will lessen the influence of them by decreasing the number of misinformed, and any excuse for misstatements. Attempted concealment of material fact cannot but be harmful in the end.[3]

## Rules for Responding to Media Queries

Organizations with more than one employee should have a clearly written media policy that spells out who may respond to media inquiries, what kinds of information can or should be released to reporters and what must be kept confidential. A good media policy should include most or all of the following elements:

1. List who in the company may respond to media inquiries, and to whom others should direct media inquiries.
2. Be familiar with the publication or broadcast that the reporter represents.
3. Treat reporters courteously. Their impression of each person in your organization affects how they perceive the entire organization and may influence how they report about it.
4. Return reporters' calls within an hour, if possible. They are usually on tight deadlines.
5. Briefly explain to the media who you are and what you do. Prepare a short statement for authorized representatives to refer to.
6. Speak in a way that average readers and listeners can understand. Avoid industry jargon or bureaucratic language.
7. Your media relations policy should indicate what data or information must remain confidential.
8. Feel free to ask the reporter questions about the story—the theme, the point of view, who is being interviewed.
9. If information is already a matter of public record, don't hesitate to share it. Withholding such information will only reinforce the reporter to develop other sources.

10. Always be truthful and accurate. Never exaggerate or inflate. Understatement usually works better than hyperbole. Trust is key to good media relations.

11. Discuss with reporters only what is in your area of expertise. Do not speculate. If you don't have personal knowledge about a subject, suggest a reliable source.

12. When you talk to a reporter, remember that you're really talking to the public.

13. If you need time to research or think about how to answer a question, it's fine to say so. Just arrange a deadline for providing the additional information to the reporter.

14. Avoid disparaging other companies or defaming other people. Not only is it actionable, but it also makes you appear unprofessional.

15. Refer media questions about your firm's policies or political views to the firm's designated executive or spokesperson.

16. If you cannot answer a question, make sure the reporter understands why.

17. Keep it simple. If you finish answering the question and the reporter remains silent, don't feel pressured to elaborate. It may only serve to dilute your message.

18. If a reporter asks about a pending lawsuit or criminal action, it's normally not advisable—and in many cases it's improper—to discuss it.

19. Take notes on the interview and promptly send them on to a designated executive, allowing for additional information or clarification. If you plan to record the interview, ask the reporter's permission.

20. Assume that everything you say to a reporter is on the record. If you don't want to see it in print or on the air, don't say it.

21. Don't argue with the reporter. You can be persuasive, but never confrontational.

22. Don't ask the reporter if you can review the story before it's published. If the story is highly controversial, ask the reporter to read back your quotes to confirm accuracy.

23. Don't infringe on a reporter's right to report on and photograph newsworthy events or statements made in public.

24. Ignore minor factual errors or omissions in the published story. If it seriously misrepresents your position or misstates an important fact, politely request a correction.

Reprinted by permission from David M. Freeman, writer and editor

You should not be creating your communications policy while the reporter is waiting at the door. If your organization does not have a clear communications policy that covers publicity, it is your responsibility to write that policy.

The basis for your communications policy can be found in the guiding tenets of your organization, such as its code of conduct, mission statement or rules of ethical behavior and business principles. It can also be found in communication disseminated by management to employees, as well as in CEO speeches and advertising.

Your policy should address—in clearly understood words (skip the legalese here)—your organization's proactive or reactive stance, guidelines for disclosure (what is proprietary and what is not) and who will be authorized spokespersons for the organization.

The communications policy must be understood, approved and endorsed by the senior management of your organization. More important, the policy must be adhered to at *all* times. The strength of a communications policy will be tested during a crisis or negative coverage.

With a policy in hand and mind, you now can focus on more detailed guidelines and plans.

## Writing It Down

First, thoroughly know and understand what your organization is and does. What is its purpose? Its history? Is it regulated? By whom and for what? Who are its customers, clients, shareholders, competitors? What is its structure, temperament, philosophy? Finally, what is its overall growth strategy and goals?

Look at each of the organization's goals carefully. Then, write down all the ways in which you can help your organization meet those goals. For example, if your organization is like most, it will have a goal concerning finances. It may be a declared statement about the amount of return on investment, or it may be a desire not to have to raise members' dues. Your support could include a series of briefings for financial analysts, placement of articles relating to organizational growth in magazines that reach investor audiences or making sure the public knows of the many services your organization provides.

Another organizational goal probably relates to human resources: the intention to maintain a well-trained, well-paid, employee universe with a low percentage of turnover. If you think this is an internal matter only, ask yourself where the employees come from. They come from the public at large. Your role in this area can be to make sure the public is aware of your organization's hospitable environment by issuing announcements of promotions, long-term service anniversaries, suggestion award winners, employee service projects in the community, plant/office improvements, corporate donations, tuition reimbursement programs, on-site day care centers and travel opportunities.

This exercise of writing down ideas helps you marshal your thoughts, ensures that you truly do understand your organization's key objectives and helps you recognize how you can fit into the overall structure. Put aside your list of ideas; they will be used later.

Next, gather the work plans and goals/strategies from other departments, such as marketing, community relations, product development, labor relations and legal affairs.

Your media relations plan also should support—directly or indirectly—these departments. You may find it helpful to create a separate media plan for each department so that individual departments and you know what is expected and who will do it.

Even if you're not in a position to provide direct support to each department, having their plans helps you anticipate possible issues, schedule media events around key activities or serve as an advisor to the department. At a minimum, knowing what is in these plans prevents you from unknowingly causing harm or conflict.

## The Formal Structure

There are numerous ways to structure your media relations program. Select the way that best suits the day-to-day management techniques, language and operations of your organization. The following example may be of help, as will the case study at the end of this chapter.

### Media Relations Program: XYZ COMPANY

**GOAL I.** To support the company's goal to attain financial stability through increased investments by the public.

*First Objective:* To help financial media have a better understanding of the organization's future.

*Tactics:*

1. Select three key financial writers who reach an influential target audience.

2. Arrange for each writer to interview a selected specialist in the finance department; each interview should occur at separate times, covering separate topics.

3. Send undated information to all financial journalists on the distribution list.

4. Develop a special "Financial Information" section on the XYZ Company "News" Web site.

**Second Objective**: To provide the financial media with timely, accurate earnings information.

*Tactics:*

1. Develop a "Financial Information" section on the XYZ Company News Web site.

2. Establish contact with a key person in the finance department who will provide information to the media relations department on prearranged schedule.

3. Create a checklist of financial reporters in general, also business and trade publications that reach targeted audiences.

4. Prepare questions and rehearse answers in advance to inquiries by journalists about the organization's finances.

5. Issue earnings announcement each quarter.

6. Provide detailed briefings for financial reporters at the annual meeting.

**Third Objective**: To help encourage targeted audiences to invest in the organization by making them aware of the solvency and growth of the company.

*Tactics:*

1. Determine the key investor audiences by working with the investor relations department.

2. Determine which publications or types of publications those audiences are likely to read.

3. Attempt to place six articles, which reflect the growth of the company, in those publications.

**GOAL II.** To support the organization's goal of hiring and maintaining a well-trained employee body with a low percentage of turnover.

**First Objective**: To inform targeted audiences of the employment opportunities and benefits of XYZ Company

*Tactics:*

1. Work with the personnel department to make sure the "Working at XYZ Company" Web site is both functional and attractive.

2. Notify industry media of the employment Web site.

3. Pitch specialized stories to specialized newspaper sections, such as "Living," "Education," and "Business."

**Second Objective**: To show the organization as a good corporate citizen.

*Tactics:*

1. Compile a list of all employees involved in civic and volunteer activities.

2. Develop a list of all organizations benefiting from XYZ Company employee service and support.

3. Work with service organizations to have them include XYZ Company in their news releases on corporate support.

4. Create and link the "XYZ Company Community Service" Web site to the company's News Web site.

5. Develop data profile of company's community activities (number of employees involved, number of hours in service, dollars saved for service organizations, etc.); distribute to media and place on the company's News Web site.

While the XYZ Company example is somewhat simplistic and altruistic, it does show that a media relations program can be planned by writing concise goals, objectives and tactics. Of course, each tactic should have a specific time frame and budget included with it, as well as the name of the person responsible for that tactic.

When the plan is completed, send it to the key executives in your organization for review and comment. This action serves several purposes. First, it shows your top management that you are attuned to the workings of your organization because your departmental activities are geared to support the entire organization and its objectives. Second, it allows each person the opportunity to have some input to the plan. Everyone likes to be asked his or her opinion of something; most people like to respond with a suggested change or two. A word of caution: Do not automatically incorporate all suggestions into your plan. Look at each suggestion and, as objectively as possible, consider both its source and what happens to related activities if it is incorporated.

The reason to take some time with these suggestions is that not everyone sees the world in the same way. The vice president of labor relations will have concerns quite different from those of the vice president of financial relations who, in turn, will focus on different issues than the vice president of marketing, who will see things very differently than the general attorney.

Understanding each person's viewpoint will help you understand the suggestion he or she made. At that point, you can see what the implications might be if you automatically incorporate that person's suggestion about your media program. You may find that all suggestions are actual improvements on your plan; you may find that none of the suggestions will improve the plan but that they reflect territorial concerns rather than overall organizational issues.

Of paramount importance is making sure you and your organization's legal counsel have a clear understanding of your individual roles, and a good working relationship. You need cooperation and mutual respect to be effective.

After incorporating any new data, make sure these same people see the final document labeled as your "working document." This is the plan from which you will work day by day. This also is the basis for the measurement of your program and your individual performance.

Each person on the media relations staff should have a copy of the final plan as well. It should be referred to often and updated regularly.

Provide quarterly updates to your key executives, including progress, challenges, delays, deletions, etc. Also plan to provide a year-end report based on your plan.

## Getting the Office Prepared

Generally speaking, not enough effort is spent outfitting a media relations office. Much time and frustration could be saved if more preparation were put into the physical items needed in your working area. If you were a dentist, would you open up shop without the proper equipment? And a lawyer would not think of hanging out a shingle without making sure the necessary reference books were nearby.

The physical equipment for media relations may be determined by the way in which your business operates. You may need the latest in computer software, graphics support, Web site development and video production, if that is how your company thinks. You may need plenty of filing space and workspace, or you may be able to work from a cubbyhole, or from your home office.

How reporters reach you is key. They should never be frustrated in their attempts to contact you because your office telephone is busy or unanswered. Ditto your cell phone. You need more than one line to your office, successive lines that automatically reroute to an assistant's or subordinate's line when your line is busy, and/or a cell phone. Whatever system you select, remember that the objective is to make sure a reporter can reach you when he or she wants to—not when it is convenient for you.

Make sure your e-mail system has all the bells and whistles it can provide such as lots of storage space and broadcast e-mail capability. If you can't be in your office, carry your e-mail with you in the form of a BlackBerry or other personal communication device.

You will still need a fax machine, preferably one with memory, multiple distribution capability and plain paper feed. Direct-line access to public relations news lines or even newsrooms is an important plus.

Your office should be a veritable library of resource information. Among the books, software and other materials that should be readily accessible to you are:

- An up-to-date dictionary
- Style manual (your own or one such as the *AP Stylebook*)

- Thesaurus
- Your organization's annual reports for the past five years
- Professional/academic journals/books relating to media relations
- Company-produced material, such as recruitment brochures, product promotion material, benefits booklets
- Copies of your organization's internal publications
- Media directories, including online and industry-specific directories
- Organization charts
- History of the organization (if one doesn't exist, consider writing it)
- Company data/statistics
- Calendar of events for the organization (earnings releases, product announcements, speeches to be given by the president, trade shows, annual meeting, seminars, fund drives)
- Hard copy and online information kits consisting of, for example, the most recent annual report, a fact sheet about the company's products or services, the president's most current or best speech
- Business cards
- Corporate goals and objectives/media goals and objectives
- Atlas
- Editorial calendars

All of this material will be used in some way at various times. Reporters can ask obscure questions, and you have to be ready to reply as quickly as possible. In adding to the above, you should subscribe to the publications with which you'll be dealing and set up a monitoring service for broadcast media and a clipping service for print.

Of key importance is the compilation of company/organization statistics. Journalists adore numbers: they are easy to read, easy to compare, work well in headlines and impress readers. Get a head start on potential questions involving numbers by composing such questions yourself. The result should be a file on statistics, a special page on the News Web site and/or a company profile that can answer questions about:

1. **Employee numbers.** These could be broken down by management/nonmanagement, union/nonunion, male/female, percentage increases in different universes, location/geography, ethnic growth

and distribution over the years, number laid off in the past year and the last five years. Member profiles follow a similar pattern.

2. **Facilities.** How many factories or office buildings or sales offices or service centers do you have? In what states? Countries? When was each facility built? What are their street addresses? How many facilities have you closed? Sold? Are you adding new ones? Where? When?

3. **Miscellaneous information.** What are the key dates in your organization's history? What are key dates of inventions? What is your best production/service record? Who is the founder of your organization?

4. **Executive information.** What are the biographical data on each of your organization's executives? What is the percentage of male/female, ethnic division, local/national/expatriate? What about your board members? Who are they and where are they from?

5. **Financial statistics.** Beside the earnings and other information available in an annual report, compile information on how much payroll your organization paid out in the last year. How much in federal/state/local taxes? How much to suppliers? How much to minority suppliers? How much to suppliers outside your country? How much did your organization contribute to community or service programs?

6. **Environmental statistics.** How much did your organization spend to meet environmental standards? How much did the company recycle in paper/trash/aluminum/plastic? How many employees were involved in some environmental clean-up campaign? How many campaigns did the organization sponsor?

Because you do not know until the phone rings or the e-mail beeps what might be on a reporter's mind, it is best to start gathering material now and to keep adding to it and updating it constantly. Convenient ways to store material are in your computer (with backup) or even in easily accessible, indexed binders to facilitate use by others when you're not around. Whichever method you select, remember the object is to have material at hand so that you can get to quickly and easily when a reporter asks you a question. A reporter will remember you if you are able to respond immediately without having to say, "I'll get back to you on that."

This is also a good time to begin compiling a list of subject-matter experts within your organization. When reporters call for an interview or general information, they do not begin by asking to speak specifically to "Mr. Jones, the manager of personnel statistics." Instead, the reporter is more likely to ask to interview someone who can talk about personnel statistics. The reporter does not know the people in your company—that is your job.

Start a list of subject-matter experts by thinking like a reporter and asking yourself: who is knowledgeable about pricing policies? Labor relations? Purchasing? Individual products? Transportation services? Food services? Financial statistics? Member services? Global markets? Quality? Environmental affairs? Government affairs? If you list the subjects alphabetically and then beside each entry list the subject-matter expert (with office, home, pager and cell phone numbers and e-mail address), you may find your job much easier the next time a reporter calls. Develop a subject matter expert list and distribute it to the media as well as posting it on your organization's News Web site.

## Introducing Yourself

Now that you have a media relations plan and a well-coordinated office, it is time to start letting the media know who you are. With your media relations plan in mind, you need to select the persons within the media whom you need to meet. Do not assume that you have to know all the editors and program directors at all the newspapers, magazines and television and radio stations in a 500-mile radius or around the world.

You should select only those media, and only those editors, who can help you meet your goals and objectives. Those are the people critical to your efforts. Once you have made that list, do not rush out and attempt to call on all persons at once or immediately call and invite each one to lunch. Instead, take the time to think about what you want to do and plan your activities accordingly. If none of the editors know you because you are new to the job and/or new to the area, then your primary reason for contact is just to get to know these people.

Select your list of people and begin calling to set up appointment times when you can drop by and introduce yourself. Make sure you call at the least busy times: after the newspaper has been put to bed, after the television crews have received their assignments and have gone on location, after the radio newscast, after the bureau chief has filed the latest report. In making these appointments, you should ask for just a brief amount of time. Do not try to crowd all your appointments into the same day because you also want to be on time for each appointment.

As you meet each editor, assignment director or program director, present him or her with some basic material about you and your organization: the information kits mentioned earlier, several of your business cards and Web addresses that will provide photos of the company executives, your company's logo and graphic standards, and, of course, the XYZ Company News Web site.

## Summary

Setting up your media relations plan and program requires research about your role, your organization's intentions for media relations and you, and a clear understanding by both parties of what can and cannot be achieved through effective media relations.

Setting up also requires attention to the practicalities of the job, from setting policy to developing a functioning office, from writing a plan to writing news briefs.

Sadly, too many novices believe that sending out a news release is all that's necessary to being a media relations specialist. Your efforts in developing an outstanding media relations program will separate you from them.

---

### Ten "Be" Attitudes for Successful Media Relations

1. **Be cooperative.** Recognize that newspeople face constraints and expectations that most of us never dream of, and that if you can say "yes" to a request for information or an interview, you are making their job much less of a hassle.

2. **Be accessible.** Don't even think about restricting your availability to the media to regular business hours. Give out your home phone, cell phone and pager numbers freely, and encourage reporters and editors to use them. If your organization is a 24-hour-a-day operation and someone else can handle routine inquiries after hours, it may be perfectly acceptable as a matter of policy to direct those routine media calls to that person. But if the reporter calls you first, don't ask him or her to jump through hoops by saying, "Why don't you call so-and-so"; give the answer yourself and suggest that the next time the reporter call the person on duty. Let the reporter know that you are always available if a question cannot be answered by someone else satisfactorily. Try to return all phone calls from the media within an hour.

3. **Be direct.** When you can't help a reporter, say so, and explain why. Don't be defensive, don't sound pained and overburdened and above all, don't display arrogance. You should be genuinely sorry that you can't help a reporter, because it is a missed opportunity for both of you.

4. **Be fair.** Don't give opportunities for in-demand interviews only to certain media outlets and not to others. If your chief executive officer is suddenly thrust into the spotlight, for example, and

agrees to just one block of time for an interview, don't offer that time only to the news organization screaming the loudest.

5. **Be a resource.** If you can't arrange an interview or answer a question for a reporter, whenever possible suggest someone else who can. It is always better to end a conversation with a reporter by giving him or her another direction to pursue instead of a dead end.

6. **Be an authority.** Learn all you can about your organization and its industry: history, financial condition, goals, future, mission. And learn everything you can about how newsrooms—both print and broadcast—operate. Your goal should be to inform newspeople of important trends as well as converse knowledgeably with them about their business.

7. **Be an educator.** You need to educate two very different constituencies—your co-workers and media representatives—about each other. Hold workshops, informal meetings and media training seminars if appropriate, to defuse distrust and misunderstanding.

8. **Be an advocate.** It's sometimes tricky to walk that tightrope between two sets of clients—those within your organization and those in the media. Although one of your primary responsibilities is to present your organization favorably to the media, it is just as important to reinforce the value of the media to your organization.

9. **Be a strategist.** This is where "proactive" media relations comes in. Don't make the mistake of thinking that if you're not out there pumping up the organization's agenda every time you have contact with a media person you're not doing your job. Be selective in what you promote about your organization.

10. **Be a team player.** This rule is really the internal version of Rule Number One. You'll find that becoming a team player is a great way to let your organization know how successfully you are practicing the preceding nine rules. Seek out information from key people throughout your organization so that you can stay informed about critical developments. Keep others in your department who don't work in media relations apprised of your activities. What does all this lead to? Building relationships and credibility—both inside and outside your organization.

—Debra Gelbart, Phoenix, AZ

# News

## What It Is and
## How It Gets to the Public

### That's News to Me

Times change. And along with them, definitions change. Trying to pin down what is "news" becomes an endless exercise, with as many definitions as there are public relations practitioners, journalists and academicians. Or even playwrights. George Bernard Shaw opined that the media are "unable, seemingly, to discriminate between a bicycle accident and the collapse of civilization."

Former U. S. Senator Alan Simpson, never a great fan of the press, declared that the media is about controversy, conflict and confusion—not clarity. Simpson further castigated the media for creating disengagement and disenfranchising the electorate.[1]

Simpson and Shaw both observed the number-one characteristic of news: Conflict. An objective news story will offer both sides of the conflict but it is the conflict itself that is of interest. Conflicts can be intellectual (evolution vs. creationism), moral (employee layoffs vs. CEO compensation package), economic (trade imbalance vs. free

25

trade), political (drill for oil vs. protect the environment) or legal/bio-ethical (right-to-die vs. life sustaining treatment).

David and Goliath conflicts can be of special interest (the big corporation vs. the well-intended whistle-blower) while conspiracies or conspiracy theories can be of even more public interest. Conflict is easy to create and often comes from disgruntled employees, competitors, special interest groups, proposed legislation or rumor.

Modern-day observers of the media are also bemoaning the obsession of networks, print media and Web sites with "infotainment," a hybrid of news and entertainment, designed to hold viewers longer. Is this the definition of news?

The original definition of "news" is thought to come from the four points on a compass: North, East, West, South. But that definition doesn't mean that all information from all points on the globe are newsworthy. For readers, viewers and listeners, "news" is what they personally are interested in. A long-ago rule-of-thumb definition stated that the importance of news varied inversely as the square of the distance from the reader. Example: "Two people killed in a local factory explosion in Cincinnati" gets more play than "100 people killed in a landslide in India." Readers are especially interested in those things that do or may affect the pocketbook, safety, employment, health or environment.

Sometimes, though, the simplest definitions are the best: "News" is whatever the editor—or the gatekeeper—says it is.

If information does not get past the final editor's desk, it does not get printed, it does not get read on radio, described on television or put online and, thus, it does not become reported news. Editorial processing of information is not unique to the news media. All of us make decisions each day—about which pieces of information we will keep to ourselves and which pieces we will share with peers, subordinates, superiors, families and friends. In our hands, this is a benign process; when in the hands of news media the process seems to be a show of power with a blatant disregard for the "real" truth.

## Media Relations and News

For the media relations professional, the task is not the delivery of news to an editor. A more accurate characterization is the delivery of properly prepared material that might be passed on by an editor to become news. What criteria do editors use in determining whether or not material will become news?

Michigan State University conducted a survey for the American Society of Newspaper Editors and the Newspaper Readership Project to answer that question. The journalists queried defined news as having the following characteristics:

1. **Consequence.** Educates and informs; is important to lifestyle or ability to cope; has a moral or social importance; is "should know" material

2. **Interest.** Is unusual, entertaining, has human interest, arouses emotions or would cause people to talk about it

3. **Timeliness.** Is current; is a new angle on events or a new trend

4. **Proximity.** Pertains to local issues, trends or events

5. **Prominence.** Concerns famous people, famous events; has received other media coverage.[2]

Other perspectives emphasize different factors. Some assert that news is information that is timely, interesting and significant. Others say it's new information that interests a large number of people. Still others claim that news is not what you want to tell other people but what other people want to know about you. Whichever definition you choose, remember this: news is a perishable commodity. Nothing dies more quickly than yesterday's news.

For the media relations practitioner who has been given the edict to "Get this news out right away," determining if that material has a chance of becoming news is not as intimidating as you think. Your information must be good enough to meet the ultimate definition of news: it's whatever the editor says it is. However, there are questions you can ask yourself about the material. These questions correlate well with what most journalists believe to be news criteria:

- Is the story local? Does it have a local "hook" to it, something that will interest readers or viewers in this area? For trade or specialty publications, is the material of interest to the targeted readership?

- Is this information unique or unusual? Is this the first, the latest, the last, the biggest of something?

- Is the material timely? Is this something happening now or that will happen in the near future? Does the material relate to another item that is currently being discussed publicly? Is this a new trend?

- Is it timeless? Is this a topic with a long shelf life, such as AIDS, the environment or terrorism?

- Does this information concern people? Our curiosity about the lives and events of others is evidenced by the strong sales of periodicals devoted just to people and by the growing number of "reality" shows and talk shows on television.

- Does this material create human interest? Pathos? Humor?
- Does this information have consequences that affect lives? Does it educate/inform? Is it of moral/social importance?
- Are the people involved famous or prominent?
- Does this story have strong local/regional/national/international interest?
- Is this news of the widest possible interest to all those who are within the scope of the medium's distribution (print or electronic)?

If the answer to any of these questions is yes, chances are your material will get an editor's attention and perhaps be placed in the newspaper or on the evening news or on a major news Web site.

## Hard versus Soft News

News generally falls into one of two categories. Hard news most often happens by itself. An explosion or category-5 hurricane is hard news. The results of a board meeting can be hard news. A strike at the factory is hard news. This is news that the public needs to know. Soft news, on the other hand, is news that the public does not need to know. Soft news is a story about a teenager who volunteers to help the elderly. It is the dedication of a war memorial. It is the story of a blind operator at a keyboard. Soft news also is called "evergreen" because it most often has a long shelf life and does not have to be used today. Hard news must be used immediately or it perishes.

Media relations practitioners probably will find, if they examine their placement activities, that they deal most often with soft news. Hard news items that must be planned for and placed each year are easily determined: annual meeting results, quarterly earnings, election of new officers, opening a new office, launching an online business, announcing a new product, global expansion, increase of services or merger/acquisition. These items constitute a small percentage of the practitioner's effort. The bulk of work likely deals with soft news placement—trying to interest the media in timeless material that can inform, educate or entertain readers or viewers.

Many practitioners fail to take advantage of soft news placement opportunities because of the preconceived notion that the media would not be interested in the story of a company-sponsored refurbishing project or the planning involved in setting up a major exhibition of agency services. To keep from falling into this trap, remember that what may be "old hat" to you because of familiarity may be con-

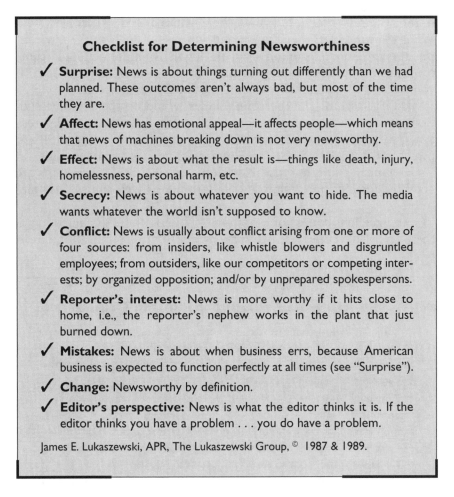

**Checklist for Determining Newsworthiness**

✓ **Surprise:** News is about things turning out differently than we had planned. These outcomes aren't always bad, but most of the time they are.

✓ **Affect:** News has emotional appeal—it affects people—which means that news of machines breaking down is not very newsworthy.

✓ **Effect:** News is about what the result is—things like death, injury, homelessness, personal harm, etc.

✓ **Secrecy:** News is about whatever you want to hide. The media wants whatever the world isn't supposed to know.

✓ **Conflict:** News is usually about conflict arising from one or more of four sources: from insiders, like whistle blowers and disgruntled employees; from outsiders, like our competitors or competing interests; by organized opposition; and/or by unprepared spokespersons.

✓ **Reporter's interest:** News is more worthy if it hits close to home, i.e., the reporter's nephew works in the plant that just burned down.

✓ **Mistakes:** News is about when business errs, because American business is expected to function perfectly at all times (see "Surprise").

✓ **Change:** Newsworthy by definition.

✓ **Editor's perspective:** News is what the editor thinks it is. If the editor thinks you have a problem . . . you do have a problem.

James E. Lukaszewski, APR, The Lukaszewski Group, © 1987 & 1989.

sidered news by an editor unfamiliar with your organization. If a story idea passes the ten-question test outlined previously, it could become news.

## Looking for News

Whether you practice media relations full-time, part-time or as a volunteer, the way to find news in your organization is to become a reporter. If you think as a reporter trained to ask questions, you will find that you are constantly coming across story ideas.

Do not just accept the existence of your company's training or engineering departments. Why are they there? What role do they play in the accomplishment of overall organizational goals and objectives? What relevance can they have to current issues such as the environment, education, loss of job security, downsizing, literacy, child care/ elder care? Why does the organization invest in these departments? If you look closely, you will find a mine of interesting stories.

Do not assume that personnel news would not be used. Promotions are newsworthy not just to the business, financial or trade press but also to the person's hometown papers, alumni magazines and professional society journals. Some of these items, depending on visual appeal, could interest television as well. All of these items are good fodder for your organization's intranet as well as its News site or blog.

An excellent source of story material about your organization is the internal newsletter or newspaper. Sending this publication out to

---

### Ways to Generate Media Interest in Your Organization

* Look for logical connections between your business and the goodwill services you may be able to offer your community at little or no additional expense. A manufacturing company with a large grounds-keeping staff launched a neighborhood tree-planting program.

* Consider launching a public information service aimed at educating consumers on issues you and others in your organization are experts on. A hospital uses nurses and doctors to talk about child care. A detergent company uses its technicians to discuss the best ways to care for furniture, clean stains and organize housework.

* Never miss the chance to develop a year-end wrap-up story on your organization's successes during the past 12 months. Also, consider doing a look ahead as each new year approaches.

* Spend some time developing local angles for your organization during national awareness weeks and days

* Always include freelance writers on your news-release distribution list. While this may not result in an immediate story, it will keep you and your organization in front of folks who frequently develop magazine and newspaper feature stories.

* Look for ways to promote a cleaner environment in your city. Donate materials (trash bags, trucks, refreshments and so on) to groups sponsoring litter clean-up programs.

*How to Get Results with Publicity* © 1992 by Communication Publications and Resources, Blackwood, NJ.

editors in your area—either via a printed copy or online—often can generate a flow of activity as the media seek to expand a story or get a different angle on it. Items covered in an internal publication that could interest journalists include:

1. **Suggestion award winners and entrepreneurs.** Rewarding an employee for ingenious thinking makes for a good story beyond the company gates, as does a story about an employee who acts as an internal entrepreneur.

2. **Company-sponsored blood drives.** Finding out who has donated the most blood for the most number of years can help an editor get a story idea. Perhaps there is an employee who has traced his/her donation to see who received it. Perhaps blood collected at your facility was sent to a disaster site.

3. **Unusual jobs.** Not all jobs are glamorous, nor are they dull and boring. There are, within most organizations, jobs that do not fit the normal mold. For example, who inspects the cables that haul up the elevators in the Twin Towers in Kuala Lumpur?

4. **Service projects** sponsored by the company. More and more companies are being judged by the external service they provide to the community. The stories still need to be unique in order to be considered news. Having a clothing drive is not unique but refurbishing computers to donate to nonprofit organizations is.

5. **Introduction of new technologies, equipment or software.** The information age brings with it an abundance of items about new, laborsaving, information-sharing, global-connecting devices and software. Depending on the function, there probably is a story. Technology stories work well in—and from—the media of developing countries.

6. **Seasonal events.** Special activities planned for major holidays should be brought to the media's attention as soon as possible. There are more organizations wanting to highlight their activities than there are media slots in which to place them. Look for what makes your activity different or unique. Humanize it.

7. **Production records.** Turning out the zillionth widget can be an item worth noting if your organization is the first to make a zillion widgets, or if you did so in record time. For the nonprofit area, there can be production records in terms of time, numbers of people served or other units of measurement.

8. **Construction news.** If your organization is building a new facility or renovating an existing one, information about the progress may be welcomed by the media as a possible visual story or, at

the very least, a reminder that a story will be coming when the work is completed.

9. **Visiting dignitaries.** If a home-office executive or your senator is visiting the local plant and can make appearances or be available for interviews, the media would like to know. The same holds true for national or international officers of civic or professional organizations.

10. **Organization milestones.** There are always anniversaries of one kind or another to commemorate; often, these dates will be relevant to the community or offer an opportunity to reflect on changes brought about by your company or service organization.

11. **Organization awards.** Vendors, government agencies, service groups and others often present awards to organizations for achievements in such areas as conservation, quality and community support. Both groups benefit from publicity on the award.

12. **CEO and executive profiles.** Business and other journals like to profile key leaders in the industry and/or town.

This list is far from complete, but it shows the possibilities for news that already exists within your organization.

Coming up with a list of story ideas that can be presented to editors is like preparing a menu: there will always be regular offerings for customers, and there should also be daily specials to entice customers to return. Do not be discouraged, however, if the editor decides he or she does not want anything from your offering today; tomorrow, that same editor may decide your fare is the best in town.

## Directing Your Story to the Right Medium

Too many media relations professionals forget that television shows, magazines, newspapers, Web sites and radio newscasts are businesses and not services. As a result of this initial misunderstanding, these professionals often try to market the wrong story to the wrong medium.

As a start, request media kits from each medium you're interested in. These kits, used by sales staff to attract advertisers, provide demographic data about that medium's desired audience. For example, the newspaper you think you want to target may have a demographic of female readers, age 50+, with a college education and disposable income. If you want to reach male readers, age 25–34, with college education and in middle management, look elsewhere.

Another way to help direct your stories to the best possible medium is to break that medium down into its component parts—or products. Understanding the selling features of a medium's product will help you more carefully place your story. Editors will appreciate your understanding of their marketing process and will doubly appreciate that you are not wasting their time. Starting with five main media categories, you can develop your own selection list for the particular media that you wish to attract.

## Newspapers

Whether published weekly or daily, newspapers are divided into sections: national/ international news, sports, business, entertainment, home living, technology, real estate and other sections.

Knowing who makes the decisions for each section, what the requirements are for that section, and the schedule for the section's production are prerequisites to deciding where you should attempt to place stories. It is possible that one story might have several angles and could be of interest to several section editors. For example, the business editor would want to know the financial impact of your company's new product announcement and how it relates to the local business community. If it were a consumer product, the home or leisure editor would be interested in knowing what the product does for the customer. The lifestyles editor might want to know of your organization's new services. Each editor serves a different constituency and is interested only in what each story means in terms of the interests of that constituency.

Newspapers also have columnists, local and/or syndicated, who specialize in areas that may support the sections or reflect the general editorial stance of the newspaper. Columnists can be strong selling features for newspapers, so getting to know them is important.

A columnist writing on economics is a good target for an in-depth explanation relating to new pricing policies for your industry's products or services. The columnist in the family section who provides household hints wants only "how-to" material and cannot use detailed or lengthy background information. The columnist catering to farmers and gardeners would be interested in your company's new herbicide. A medical columnist might welcome information about your organization's new counseling and referral services. And all of these columnists need almost-daily grist for their Web site versions.

When marketing a story that has several angles or possibilities, make sure each editor, columnist or writer knows you are talking to the others. You should never assume that internal communication on a newspaper is at peak efficiency. If your story appears twice in the same edition, you have lost your credibility.

## Newsletters

Newsletters, whether in print or on the computer screen, are a popular—and still growing—medium in a world crowded with publications. Their rise can be attributed in part to the format of the medium. Newsletters offer bite-sized chunks of information in a small publication, or e-pub, that can be easily stored—or just as easily tossed away or deleted. Because of their brevity, newsletters can concentrate on one specific topic within a broad area of interest or can be devoted to a particular broad issue. For example, you might find a newsletter written for investors in petroleum products only, another designed for all investors, still another for collectors of antique silver, and another for human resource professionals.

Newsletter staffs are small and generally appreciate your news releases and story offerings as long as the information is geared to their newsletter's audience. In serving newsletters, you should inquire whether they are interested in photographs or graphics.

Be sure to check publication schedules. A printed newsletter has a set publication date where an electronic one may vary in publication dates and/or updates.

## Magazines

The proliferation of specialized print and electronic magazines is making placement in this medium easier in terms of identification but more difficult in terms of quantity. The first step is to identify which magazines reach your particular audiences. You may have to compile several breakout lists if your media operation is extensive. For instance, you may find you need magazines that reach your customers (by level of decision making, by geography, by financial status), your industry (by specific area of technology, services, support) or the public at large (for business, leisure, product or consumer issues).

Like the newspapers, each magazine may then be divided into sections, such as marketing, finance, technology or people. However, because the magazine itself serves a special constituency, there will not be as much subdivision. The same rules of careful analysis that apply to newspapers also apply to magazines, with one added feature: magazines are candidates to run photographs and graphics supplied by you. Often, a photograph of a new product or one representing a new service may be run as a stand-alone piece if there is not room for the entire story. Check the magazine's requirements carefully, to avoid sending a product photograph to a magazine that never uses them.

Many magazines run special issues or annuals in conjunction with trade shows, fairs or seasonal events (back to school, fashion, city-wide events). You may decide to target these special issues instead of broadsiding the publication throughout the year.

## Radio

Radio is perhaps the least complex of the media and, very possibly, the most overlooked. It is also undergoing major changes in response to technology innovations that can make radio more accessible to more people in more ways and in a more profitable way.

Radio stations follow the trend of print by specializing and appealing to distinct, segmented audiences. This audio specialization produces a good product for the radio station but can frustrate the media relations professional who does not take the time to thoroughly investigate the medium.

The broadcast range of radio stations is an important factor for you to know. The stations with the widest, most powerful ranges are the ones you need if you have an emergency, such as an urgent call for blood at your hospital or the need to update the public on a chemical spill that may necessitate evacuation. You need these power stations no matter what kind of music they play! Your personal preference may not lean towards country, hard rock or classical music, but if you need powerful broadcasting strength, go to the source.

You need to determine the product line of each station to help you decide which stations to cater to at which times. There are all-news stations, all-classical stations, all-country stations and all easy-listening stations. The majority of stations are a mix of talk, music, commentary, news, sports, special programming, with each station trying to find its niche in a rapidly growing radio audience.

Many radio stations are changing from a format that includes disc jockeys, newsreaders and other on-air personalities, to subscriber-based radio that plays only specialized material, such as all-Elvis Presley, all-country or all-Beatles. Some subscriber stations are mimicking traditional radio with well-known personalities that will appeal to a specific listening audience.

Whether public or subscriber based, most radio stations manage with small news operations. They depend primarily on material that comes over the wire services, is delivered to the station or is called in to the news director. Many news radio stations, large and small, like to use "actualities" to liven up the newscast. An actuality is a live or taped comment from you or some other organization spokesperson. Being willing and available to provide an actuality will often enhance

### Radio

When television was created, pundits declared the death of radio as a mainstream medium. Little did they know. The number of radio stations vastly outnumbers the number of television outlets. The number of radio talk shows continues to increase. And, subscriber-based radio is doing to national radio what cable TV did to network television.

In short, more choices mean more opportunities. When considering using radio to get your message to your audience(s), keep these observations in mind:

- One in four Americans get some of their daily news from talk radio;

- Radio reaches 77% of people over the age of 12 every day and that group listens to radio more than three hours each day.*

- Radio is a mobile medium, traveling with you from room to room, in your car, at the office, in your headset.

- Radio stations are consolidating and using fewer staff.

- Subscriber-based satellite radio offers advertising-free, single-focus radio listening for a monthly fee.

- Podcasting gives you the opportunity to create and send unfiltered audio programming to key audiences, such as students, shareholders or bird clubs.

- Whether you use radio talk shows, advertising, actualities, podcasting or audio news releases, radio deserves a fresh look.

* "How effective is radio at getting my message out?", PR Week, September 27, 2004.

your position with the radio news director who makes the decision about your story offering.

Stations that offer call-in talk shows may be of interest to you if your organization is involved in a sensitive or volatile issue and you need to set the record straight or to respond to the public's concerns. Specialized radio programs offer opportunities where an in-house expert, such as someone who is knowledgeable about a particular consumer item, technological development or farm-related topic, can talk about the special topic in terms of the organization's product or services.

Talk with radio news directors and program directors to get detailed information on a station's opportunities. Then target your material carefully to a listening audience. For example, weekday early-morning and late-afternoons are reserved for talk shows, which

normally appeal to the large "driving audience" of automobile com-
muters, while Sunday mornings are largely reserved for public affairs
programming, because there are fewer listeners at this time.

## Television

Because television offers both sound and sight, because the
industry is fragmenting its audiences through cable television channels, and because television channels now double up with their own
Web sites, a media relations specialist must approach this medium
with a unique perspective.

Most people believe they get their news from television. However,
television news shows account for only a small percentage of the station's offerings. Supporting the newscasts are network shows, locally
produced variety/entertainment/talk shows, syndicated specials, doc-
umentaries, movies and network-produced, live coverage of events.
Even the news show itself is so fragmented that only 8–10 minutes of
a 30-minute show can be called "news."

Unless you are in charge of national media for your organization,
you should be concerned primarily with locally produced shows for
your story and news offerings. The local news shows are the prime
targets for your releases. Assignment editors at the television station
determine which stories will be covered for the noon, early- and late-
evening news. They make the determination based partially on the
real news value of the item and partially on its visual qualities. Television is a motion picture medium, which means that your news or
story idea should include suggestions about how the story can be
shown. A still shot of your company president may be visual, but it
gets dull after just a few seconds because it does not move. If your
item is short, then the visual may be all that is needed. Decide carefully if you can support your soft news story visually before offering it
to television news.

Local talk shows provide an excellent medium for your subject-
matter experts—if they are well trained—to talk about, demonstrate
and respond to issues. The show's producer can give you more
detailed information about the requirements for the program, time
needed for booking guests and capability for live demonstrations.

Cable television provides channels devoted to health, sports,
news, music, history, biographies, travel, religion, country music,
movies and many other interests. In some markets, there may be for-
eign-language channels. Working closely with a video production
team, you can provide certain cable channels with programs produced
by your organization to meet your target audiences.

Analyzing all the factors related to each medium will help determine where to send your message. One story idea may not appeal to all media, whether hard news or soft news. Quarterly sales results, for example, are considered hard news, but figures and percentages should be seen to be best understood. Newspapers and magazines may have the space to run this material, but a television assignment editor probably will decide the information does not warrant the effort it takes to create graphics well suited to television. Radio editors have no means of conveying visual information and may decide the material would require too much explanation in an already crowded newscast.

Conversely, a story idea about a picnic for disabled children may get excellent response from television because of its visual capabilities, no response from radio because of lack of imagery capabilities, and mild response from print media because of the amount of space needed to create empathy with the project through feature writing or still photography. The key, of course, is to carefully determine which medium should be connected with which piece of material.

And, not to be forgotten are the Web sites that accompany just about all media. Even a radio station's Web site might run more of a news release that it used during the noon newscast. Talk with each medium about their format, criteria, needs and uses of information for their Web sites.

## Directories and Mailing Lists

With the profusion of new media concepts comes the potential difficulty of tracking each medium, editor, writer, schedule and requirement. There are numerous directories available to a media relations practitioner. They cover print and electronic media from international to local levels. Determining which directory best suits your needs may take some time and study but will be well worth the effort.

Before rushing out to purchase an expensive directory or the latest CD-ROM, visit the public library to peruse the directories available there. In looking through the media directories, ask yourself these questions and any others you can think of that suit your specific situation:

- How often is the directory/CD-ROM printed? Updated?
- What geographic region(s) does it cover?
- Does it include trade publications? Specialty magazines? Ethnic publications?
- Does it list radio and television? Cable networks? Web sites? Blogs?

- Does it give the names of editors? Columnists? Webmasters?
- Are there editorial, graphic and photo guidelines?
- Is the circulation for the publication listed?
- Are the viewing audiences for television and the listening audiences for radio listed? Web site traffic? Blog traffic?
- Does the directory list television talk shows?
- Are scheduled print/air times listed?
- Does it give names of individual contacts?
- Are photo, video, audio, graphic criteria listed?

As a check on what you select from the directory, talk with your organization's marketing department. They can tell you which trade publications they think are important. You can then learn the names of editors and write or e-mail them for editorial and photo criteria if they are not listed in the publication. At the same time, you can get the latest editorial calendar.

Talk with your advertising department or agency. Your editorial media strategies should, at a minimum, coordinate with those of the advertising group. Preferably, the strategies should be integrated. Advertising must research publications to discover which ones reach a critical buying audience. From this you can easily learn which magazines target a key audience for your message.

Ultimately, you will want to create your own directory. In doing so, try to create the listing in a way that best reflects your media efforts. For example, if you deal almost exclusively with business news, you probably will not need a listing of sports editors. Your breakouts can be in various categories and even cross-referenced by geography, business publication or broadcast capabilities. One directory breakout could look like this:

I. Local
  A. Business publications
    1. Magazines (editor, columnists, criteria, phone/fax numbers, e-mail address)
    2. Newspapers (editors, writers, deadlines, phone/fax numbers, e-mail address)
    3. Newsletters (editor, deadlines, criteria, frequency, e-mail address)
  B. TV business broadcasts (assignment editor, lead time)
  C. Radio business broadcasts (deadlines, criteria)
  D. Wire services (editors, beats, deadlines)
  E. Syndicated columnists (topics, schedule)
  F. Web sites (topics, links)
  G. Blogs (topics)

## Chapter Three

II. National
    A. Business Publications
       1. Magazines
       2. Newspapers
       3. Newsletters
    B. TV business broadcasts
    C. Radio business broadcasts
    D. Wire services
    E. Syndicated columnists
    F. Web sites
    G. Blogs
III. Global
    A. Business publications
       1. Magazines
       2. Newspapers
       3. Newsletters
    B. Wire services
    C. Embassy press secretaries
    D. Web sites
    E. Blogs

Under each category should go all the information you can possibly get about each publication or electronic service. Perhaps the most important item is the name of the person with whom you will most often communicate. Remember, **you do not deal with newspapers, television, radio or Web sites: you deal with people**.

Some of the information you will need is

- Name of publication/station/show/service/Web site/blog
- Name of editor/reporter/columnist/Web-blog master
- Street address (for delivering packages)
- Mailing address (for ordinary correspondence)
- Telephone number(s) (including cell phone)
- Facsimile number(s)
- E-mail address
- Deadline(s)
- Photograph submission requirements
- Accepts case studies, by-lined articles/op-ed pieces
- Issues editorial calendar
- Use of actuality
- Circulation/Hits

- Broadcast range
- Times of pertinent broadcasts
- Special issues
- Accepts video or audio for Web or blog sites

Directories should be updated constantly. Keeping a directory on a computer is one way to make this chore easier, but there is nothing wrong with writing in the changes and updates by hand, as you get them in a printed directory. The important thing is to have available an easy-to-use and fully functional directory.

Clearly, determining what news is and where it should be directed involves more than just writing a release and sending it to every medium in your area. Careful analysis of the information itself and the media to which it should be directed will help you achieve your media goals.

# Tools of the Trade

## From ANRs to White Papers

In recent years, the tool kit for any media relations person has grown, become electronic, morphed into new dimensions. In this chapter, we review those tools, both old and new, that can be selected to do the best job of getting your message to your audience the right way through the right medium.

## Audio News Releases (ANRs)

An audio news release is exactly what it sounds like (pun intended): a news release prepared for the ear—for radio. This audio version of a news release used to be called an "actuality;" now, the "actuality" is a part of the ANR, often described as a sound bite. A typical 60-second ANR normally has an introduction, two-three succinctly written sound bites and then a closer or outtro.[1]

Just like a Video News Release (VNR), the ANR is produced and then distributed, generally through a vendor who has a good track record knowing the industry and selecting the right placements based on your targeted audiences.[2]

Keys to developing a successful ANR include using stories that can be told in 60 seconds, such as survey results or a subject matter experts' key points on a hot topic; knowing your target audience demographics in detail; selecting the right voice for the ANR; and accepting that ANRs are still difficult to measure.[3]

## Backgrounders, Briefings

Sometimes a topic may be too complex to handle in a single release or even a news conference. In this case, you may want to consider briefing key journalists and/or editors before an announcement. The briefing, or backgrounder, allows time for detailed explanations about a new economic plan, consolidation of services, proposed tax reforms or similar topics.

The briefing can take place in person, with a conference call or even in a videoconference setting. The purpose is to help the journalists better inform their audiences about the upcoming announcement.

## Blogs

A blog, or Web log, is essentially one person's journal or diary— posted on the Internet for all the world to see! The number of blogs increases exponentially each day; the range of topics covered in them is astronomical; and the jury is still out about the efficacy of blogs. However, they are a medium to be reckoned with.

Blogs are considered so powerful that most mainstream media have reporters or other staffers setting up blogs to "talk" with mainstream America. The intimacy of blogs, where electronic conversation among several people is instant and virtual, gives a reading, viewing, listening audience a different perspective on the topic. Many corporations and organizations are setting up blogs in order to talk directly to customers, investors or visitors.

In the case of blogs it isn't so much the medium that's important; it's what this medium represents: unintermediated access to information, opinions and perspectives. As a media relations practitioner, you need to (1) be on top of blogs that are posted about your company or organization—who's saying what and why and should you respond;

and (2) consider starting a sanctioned blog for your company or organization to make sure that anyone out in cyberspace can access correct information, have a point of contact or just get the latest information in an informal format.

## Editorial Board Visits

At least once a year, you and your CEO, a key subject-matter expert or some other company notable need to visit the editorial boards of the media you use most. These visits are not intended to result in stories (although that can happen). Rather, they are used to update the editorial board on the status of your organization, provide a general look at the plans for the year ahead or even give a heads-up on some upcoming challenge. Not all media have editorial boards but may respond to your request for a visit with the creation of one, just for that occasion.

The protocol is simple: your CEO, or subject-matter expert, gives a brief presentation and then sits back to answer questions. The result: a better relationship with the media and a better understanding of what makes your organization tick.

## FAQs

In preparing for any major announcement, or even a simple release, you can best be served by preparing frequently asked questions (FAQs) before issuing that release. These questions will most likely be asked by the media, or financial analysts, or shareholders, or neighbors, or community leaders, or political officials. Anticipating them—and getting agreed-upon answers—will make your postrelease life much easier.

## Feature Releases

An often overlooked tool is the news feature or feature release, a hybrid piece that combines the essence of news (remember: it is news if it meets the criteria used by the editor) and the style of feature writing. News features are pieces written about aspects of your business or organization that are interesting, informative and entertaining, but they are not necessarily "must have" news.

These features can describe jobs or behind-the-scenes "how to" operations or focus on one employee or volunteer. Smaller newspapers and magazines often are interested in these features because they seldom have adequate staff to research and write their own features. Also, weekly or monthly publications cannot compete with immediate, hard-hitting news, and features fill much of their editorial space with nontimely material.

Always confirm with the appropriate person at the publication that he/she wants feature releases. For television, you will need to research the story and provide visual content.

## Gimmicks and Gifts

The debate continues as to whether press packages or releases get more attention if they are accompanied by a gimmick or eye-catching element. Purists think that gimmicks, such as having confetti explode out of an envelope containing a release announcing a grand opening, are detrimental to the purpose of issuing a news release. Others believe that sometimes it's necessary to create some element of surprise in order to cut through the clutter.

Even a legitimate gift, such as a ballpoint pen, accompanying a release, may be going too far in trying to influence an editor to read a release. When in doubt: if the information in the release doesn't meet the criteria used by that media outlet for determining news value, then all the gimmicks, gifts and surprises won't matter.

## Interviews

The interview, whether individual or at a press conference, is a highly successful tool. However, its sophistication calls for serious study and preparation. Chapter 6, "Spokespersons: Training and Briefing Them for Their Role," provides the material you need to conduct a successful interview.

## Letters to the Editor

A letter to the editor should not be written every time a minor error, misquote or suspected bias appears in the publication. A letter to the editor to clarify a serious accuracy is welcome, for journalists are as concerned with accuracy and professionalism as you are. On the other hand, a letter written out of spite or over a minor error comes across as petulant and naive, and is treated accordingly. As with op-ed pieces, letters to the editor should be used judiciously.

These letters are generally in response to specific articles in the publication and can be used to clarify a point or refute one. Letters can also be used to try to create interest in a subject that has not been covered by the media. Your letter should state the situation, give the background and offer a solution to the problem or a change. Following certain guidelines will increase the odds of your letter being published. The letter should be short, directing its message to only one issue. It should never attack a reporter or editor, and it must be factual. Also check to see if the publication has additional criteria or guidelines.

Letters also must be signed before being considered for publication. To make sure the editor and the intended audience understand that the issue is of serious concern to your organization, have the letter signed by the CEO, if possible. This is a stamp of credibility an editor would find difficult to ignore.

There is no guarantee your letter will be used, nor is there a guarantee that the letter, if published, will appear in a timely manner. Finally, there is no conclusive way to provide—to yourself or your organization—evidence that the letter accomplished anything.

## News Conferences

Just as a release has "news" as its adjective, so should a conference. After all, why would you call reporters together if not to release hard news? Unfortunately, the news conference has been badly misused by publicity-seeking individuals or groups who offer little more than an orchestrated effort to gain attention. These publicity-based conferences have become more prevalent as the need for infotainment "news" has become more necessary.

A news conference should offer both the news and a forum for the exchange of information. Here are some guidelines:

- Make sure your proposed announcement is worth the time and effort needed to produce a news conference. Ask yourself some questions:
  1. Is this announcement something that will have significant impact on the reading/viewing audience? Examples: natural disaster updates, dramatic change in company leadership.

2. Is this a major product announcement? You can only *announce* a product once; after that, you promote and publicize the product.

3. Is this a complex issue that cannot be explained with a release? Does the issue demand a forum so that reporters can ask questions? Is the issue better discussed during a press briefing?

4. Does the occasion involve a new chief executive officer, football coach, celebrity or head of state from whom the media would want quotes?

- Always consider whether you can adequately give the information to the media via some other mechanism, such as a news release, telephone call, e-mail, briefing or editorial board meeting, before calling a news conference.

- If you decide to conduct a news conference, you need to bargain for all the time and support you can get. A major product announcement should come only when all the parties are ready to deal with the questions and demands that will result from the announcement, such as product orders, requests for information and product demonstrations.

The logistics of a news conference are critically important.

*Location.* A news conference does not have to be held in a hotel ballroom. Journalists will go to where the conference is, if the event is worthy of the time and effort. A product announcement could be held in the manufacturing facility, laboratory, warehouse or trade conference site.

Wherever you hold the conference, make sure it meets the needs of the journalists. There should be plenty of room for the cameras as well as chairs for the reporters. Make sure any power needs are met as well as any special lighting needs. Check the acoustics so that, if you have to, you can help set up microphones for better coverage.

*Online or e-conference.* A press conference online, via the Internet, can be easier on the pocketbook and easier on reporters' time. Instead of providing space in a facility, you create space on the Internet by setting up a special Web site just for the conference. Instead of giving directions to an in-person conference, you give out the URL for the Web site. Instead of providing B-roll, you incorporate streaming video on the site. Instead of making copies of releases and supporting material, you load the information onto the site for easy access and quick links.

Your online conference can be audio-only or include video and graphics. You can also archive the conference for future reference and follow-up.

*Timing.* With media now operating 24/7/365, the timing of a news conference no longer has to be dictated by time of day or day of week. Consideration still needs to be given to your primary media and their schedules but national or global conferences, especially if they are online or globally live, can occur at any time.

*Notification.* For an in-person or online news conference, notify the media several days in advance, and remind them once. Your notification should show the importance of the conference to their audience.

*Protocol.* For any news conference, greet reporters when they arrive or log in. For in-person conferences, show reporters and crews where to sit and/or set up equipment; for online conferences, have a preset list of procedures, agenda and links for information.

Start the news conference on time. Just as your speakers have other commitments, so do journalists. Stay within the specified amount of time for presentations and don't let the question-and-answer period linger beyond the point where questions become sparse.

Finally, thank all attendees for coming and participating. Don't assume they know how grateful you are for their appearance.

*Available material.* The material you give to the media before or after the conference is critically important. Press kit information should include only essential items such as the primary news release, supporting material (fact sheets, FAQs, time line, etc.). Include photographs only if they are essential to the news announcement, such as a product photo of mug shot of the *new* officer.

Online material can be extensive but don't overload the online attendee with too many hyperlinks, Web page references, attached photos or graphics or other materials.

There is no need to include B-roll if you can electronically send it to TV stations or put in on the Web site. There is no need to include an audiotaped actuality if you can electronically send it to the radio station(s) or place it on the Web site.

Create your news kit to fit the occasion; don't force fit the conference to the kit.

## News Releases

Of the many ways to get into the media, the most commonly known and the most often misused is the news release. The cries of editors seem to be heard only in the wilderness as practitioners repeat the same mistakes under the guise of, "But, *my* release is different."

Most releases are not different, according to those in the know: the editors. These oversurveyed guardians of the media repeatedly cite horror stories of grammatical and typographical mistakes, cutesy-poo press kits, out-of-date mailing lists, lack of local angle, missing information, an abundance of meaningless management commentary and releases that are out of date, or too long or contain corporate jargon that is indecipherable.

News releases are not designed to take the place of a reporter. Instead, a news release is a for-your-information memorandum to an editor. A release simply acquaints an editor or journalist with the basic facts of a potential story, just as a memo would. The editor will then decide if the proposed story warrants attention; if so, a reporter is assigned to gather more information and rewrite the material to fit the format of the print or Internet publication or radio or television broadcast.

The idea simply is to get editors to read the release—a difficult task when editors are bombarded with e-mails, faxes and pieces of paper thinly disguised as news. Just as a memorandum should be short and to the point, so too should a news release. Additionally, there are some prerequisites:

1. **Have some news to report!** Unfortunately, the definition of news is not always the one we want to hear: News is whatever the editor says it is. So, it's critical for you to know the audience you want to reach and attempt to reach them through the right medium. If you don't, the editor you approach will decide that your information isn't news.

2. **Pay attention to the Ws.** Which of these is most important: Who? What? When? Where? Why? How? And don't forget the sixth W: Who cares? Answering each of those will help you determine if you have real news and also the best way to position it.

3. **Leave the fluff at home.** A news release is not an advertisement, nor is it a marketing piece. "Too often, public relations writers load down releases with generalities and platitudes that do little to advance the story with editors."[4] Keep to the facts.

There also are basic components to a release:

1. **The name of the organization.** Whether the news release is on paper, in an e-mail or faxed, it is essential to use your company/organization letterhead. The name tells the recipient the source of the release and gives credibility to the information.

2. **Contact name and numbers.** At the top of the release should be the name of the person to call for more information. All pertinent numbers (office, cell, home, pager, fax) should be listed (do not

forget the area code or an "800" listing) as well as an e-mail address. The media do not operate in a uniform nine-to-five day; even if they did, they are not all in the same time zone or the same country, so they need all this contact information in order to reach you. Remember, also, that the pages of a news release sometimes are separated, so it is a good idea to have the contact name and numbers on the last sheet of a faxed or printed release as well.

3. **A headline or subject line.** This piece of information is not intended as a substitute for the publication's headline writer's efforts, Instead, it gives the editor a capsule phrase summing up the essence of the release. The headline tells the reader if this is something that needs to be attended to right away or if it can wait. For e-mail releases, you may want a subject line that pulls strong visual attention. Tina Koenig, writing for *The PR Network*, suggests following the Yahoo model: "When you have the choice between a ho-hum word and a hoo-haa word, go with the latter."[5]

4. **A release time.** This information, also at the top of the release, says when the information can be published or broadcast. It can read, "Release upon receipt" or "Release immediately" or "Release Friday, December 16, 20__." A word of caution, however. Do not embargo information unless it is required. Editors know that embargoes on stories about a company open house are coy attempts at making the information seem more important than it is. There are times when embargoes must be honored; editors know and respect those times.

5. **A date.** Put down the date on which you are issuing the release; repeat the date in the release instead of using "today."

6. **An ending.** Of course a release ends, but editors, copyreaders and reporters are accustomed to looking for a "–30–" or "###" mark to say that the release is ended. Otherwise, a release that comes close to the bottom of a page could be misconstrued as only part of a longer story.

Those are the components of a release—the building blocks, as it were. Of equal importance is what the release says and how it says it. Other suggestions for news releases are:

1. **Follow an accepted journalistic style of writing.** Get a copy of *The Associated Press Stylebook and Libel Manual* and use it! It's especially important to use this text as new media, new words and new uses are challenging even the best of writers.

2. **Go easy on the length.** There are no hard and fast rules about the length of a release; however, two typewritten pages, double-spaced, is considered the approved length. If your release is sev-

eral pages long, you may wish to consider either breaking it up into several releases, each dealing with a specific topic, or issuing a short release with a longer fact sheet accompanying it. E-mailed releases should follow the same guidelines.

3. **Avoid breaks.** It makes for easier reading if you do not split words at the end of a line or split a sentence at the bottom of a page. Write "more" at the bottom of page 1 of the release to indicate there is a second page. If you are printing on both sides of the paper, write "over" at the bottom. If you are sending releases electronically, make sure recipients can tell when the copy stops by using –30– or ###.

4. **Clear writing.** Writing a release in corporate jargon, legalese or some other alien language makes as much sense as preparing a release in Mandarin and sending it to people who speak only English. Why? As an AT&T executive once cautioned writers: "I have used lawyer-talk out of what seemed to me to be necessary care for accuracy and safety. And it comes out the other end as a credibility gap." Keep it simple, keep it factual, keep it error free.

5. **Remember the pyramid.** The inverted pyramid style of writing is not used just for news releases. The same style applies in writing personal letters, memos, briefs, white papers and other material. *The important information or the conclusion is given first*, with less important information following and, finally, the least important information at the end. Using the pyramid calls for a bit of taste, however. Although the lead paragraph of a release carries the most important information, it is not necessary to cram the answers to "Who? What? Where? Why? When? How?" into that first sentence or paragraph.

6. **Adjectives are dangerous.** Avoid the temptation to use superlatives in describing your organization's latest product, service or new executive. For one thing, such superlative claims may not be legally defensible; for another, use of adjectival claims hints that the writer had nothing of substance to say about the subject and threw in the adjectives for lack of anything else. An adjective can be used in a direct quote, however.

7. **Make it local.** One of the key criteria listed for what sells a release to an editor is the local angle or "hook" it has. For example, a national release announcing a new product can be localized by telling when the product will be available in your area, through what outlet and at what suggested retail price. Or, you may want to issue a release saying when a new medical treatment will be available at your hospital.

8. **Attribute the news to a person,** not a company or organization. Information is more credible if "John Doe, product manager of XYZ Co., today demonstrated the company's newest product" than if "XYZ Co. today announced it has a new widget."

9. **Indent the paragraphs.** This will make it easier for the editor to read your material.

10. **Select a good typeface.** This is true for hard copy and electronic versions of a release. You want the recipient to be able to read your material easily. For electronic versions, consider increasing the type size by 1 or 2 points and boldfacing the copy for easier reading.

11. **Think twice before using a CEO quote.** Your CEO doesn't talk the way you make him/her sound in that quote. If you can't create a quote that's reflective of the way your CEO talks and sounds, as well as a quote that actually says something, then don't use a quote.

## News Releases for Electronic Media

Isn't a release always a release? No. Not when one is for print and another is for electronic media. Both television and radio have special characteristics that require you to handle your release differently than if the release is going to print media. Primarily, the difference is that radio news is written for the ear; television news is written for the eye and the ear; print and electronic news are written for the eye only.

The best test for electronic news writing is to prepare the release as though it were going to be read directly from your computer screen. Then, read the release aloud to someone and ask him or her to retell the message. You may find a disparity between what you said and what was heard.

Radio and TV broadcast style is not difficult, however. A few easy-to-remember rules will help you through:

- Along with the release time, put down a "read time" such as ":15" for 15 seconds or ":30" for 30 seconds.

- Because the material is written to time and not space, everything must be spelled out. There can be no abbreviations, no numerals, and all names or unusual words should be spelled phonetically.

- Sentences are short, with descriptive words before rather than after nouns. For example, "the thirty-nine-year-old vice president" instead of "the vice president, 39."

- The inverted pyramid rule is not used in broadcast journalism. In print and on the computer screen, a reader can go back and reread a paragraph or a sentence; a radio listener cannot go back. Radio and television journalism is linear. In broadcast style, the release tells what the news is, then tells it again, and then tells it again. Here is an example:

  *The Smith and Jones Company will build a new manufacturing plant here in Anytown. The new facility will employ two thousand people to make the latest in electronic devices. Smith and Jones' newest operation will be ready in two years, cost five million dollars and add several thousand dollars a year to the local tax base.*

  The fact that there will be a new plant was repeated three times to the listener.

- For television, remember that the paramount consideration is visual interest. Your story about new ways to invest money for greater return sounds great and reads better but looks cluttered and confusing with its charts, graphs and a "talking head" expert. However, it's perfect for an electronic version, such as your company Web site, because you have the luxury of linking to, or showing, all the supporting material. In contrast, a story about a white-water rafting trip for children who have never been out of a city reads like many other stories, sounds like a bunch of squealing children against a backdrop of rushing water but looks exciting, enticing and dangerous.

- More and more, organizations are turning to video news releases (VNR) and audio news releases (ANR) or "electronic news releases" to reach television and radio stations. These are pre-packaged stories—news or feature—distributed either by satellite or on tape.

There are pros and cons about VNRs and ANRs you should consider before adding them to your program. On the plus side, both VNRs and ANRs can be beneficial to smaller TV and radio stations that do not have the capability to send camera crews or reporters to faraway locations to cover a story. Also, including the results of an annual report with either type of release can help boost coverage of an otherwise routine story.

Of growing importance is the value of VNRs to global operations. If having a multi-nation, live tele-press conference is not an option, then issuing VNRs via satellite to support your conference might be a good alternative. Add to this the benefit of being able to add voice-overs in different local languages, and you can begin to see the strength of VNRs.

Perhaps the biggest plus is that you control the message and the footage. This control doesn't give you *carte blanche* to offer an advertisement in the form of an ANR or VNR, but it does help assure your message will not be lost.

On the negative side is making sure your electronic news release meets the criteria of TV and radio news directors and assignment editors. The stations will only use an electronic news release that has been professionally produced. This means you need expert help in shooting, editing, scripting and taping releases; such help can be expensive.

TV stations also can't edit or rework a VNR as easily as they can video they've shot on their own. Because many VNRs exceed a recommended length, they seldom will be used "as is." Different technical standards can make it difficult to edit a U.S. tape in other countries, and the quality suffers as a result—assuming a TV or radio station will go to the trouble of editing a tape prepared elsewhere. Further, some stations feel that using a canned release diminishes their credibility.

Measurement also is a key concern. While there have been many advances in measuring usage electronically, there remains the difficulty of learning the context of the usage. It's the equivalent of counting print column inches without knowing if the article is positive, neutral or negative.

Before you decide to add VNRs and ANRs to your tool kit, you need to spend time understanding the time and expense involved as well as the payback. You also need to determine whether a VNR is more appropriate or if "B-roll" footage would serve the same or a better purpose for television, and if call-in actualities might work better than an ANR.

If you decide to issue VNRs and ANRs, make sure they are prepared professionally and are sent to the right person at the right station for the right reason at the right time and in the right format.

## Op-Ed Pieces

Named for its position in a newspaper or magazine—opposite the editorial page—the op-ed piece provides a place for your organization to offer an opinion on a subject or perhaps take a stand on a current issue.

Criteria for op-ed pieces may vary by publication but there are some general rules.

On average, op-ed pieces are run every day, from one article to two or three. The length appears most often to be about 750 words. Almost all editors agree that op-ed pieces must have two things:

## Publishing Your Op-Ed Piece

1. **Have something to say.** The best op-ed pieces are tough, straightforward, categorical.

2. **Be timely.** The best op-eds concern subjects triggered by breaking, front-page news.

3. **Be topical.** Topicality means that an op-ed is relevant to readers.

4. **Start with a grabber.** It's particularly important to "hit the ground running"—begin the op-ed with a straight-to-the-gut sentence.

5. **Have a point.** There's not enough space to make more than one point.

6. **Back it up with facts.** Op-eds must be loaded with evidence.

7. **End with a zinger.** Many people will remember the initial thing you said and few will remember the middle—most will remember the last.

Fraser P. Seitel, "The Op-Ed," *O'Dwyer's PR Daily*, February 5, 2002

timeliness and creativity. The best advice is to read the intended publication to see how other op-eds have been written, and to contact the publication for specifics on length of piece, submission criteria, etc.

Some editors like to discuss the idea for an op-ed piece ahead of time; others prefer to receive the op-ed with a cover letter.

Topics for op-ed pieces are many, ranging from opinions and analysis of public affairs, politics, education and law to journalism, health care, religion, the military, science and lifestyles. Topics can be of a local, national or international nature. They must, however, be relevant and timely to something that is happening now or is about to happen. Some editors prefer to avoid extremely controversial issues, feeling that adversary journalism is a never-ending ping-pong game. Others encourage publication of diverse opinions on sensitive issues.

Op-ed pieces are not to be used as a vendetta medium against some alleged injustice to your organization, nor are they the forum for challenging a reporter's techniques. The key word in considering op-ed pieces is *judicious*. Just define the issue you wish to discuss or state the problem as you see it, provide whatever background or history is needed and then suggest ways the situation can be changed or improved.

## Photographs

Digital photography, especially cell phone photography, has allowed anyone to become a news photographer. With a click on your cell phone and hitting the "send" button, you can provide any media outlet with the latest images of a disaster, a public event or a grand opening. Don't let the technology get in the way of good images, however. The media don't want to be bombarded with thousands of unusable photos. Before carrying along your own digital camera or hiring a photographer for your event, check with the media you intend to reach to find out what their criteria are for receiving digital images.

Stand-alone photos that tell a story are still useful to and desired by many media, especially those publications that must rely on outside photographers. Make sure your stand-alone is accompanied by all the correct information about the people in it, the event and the day/date/time. Photographs are also easily distributed through news wires with your news releases. Be judicious by only sending photographs when they truly enhance or improve the news release and add value for the reader or viewer.

A photo gallery on your company's News Web site can be extremely beneficial to reporters, editors and photo editors, allowing them to select the image that they feel is best suited to your story. Keep photographs of your key organization leaders in a separate mug-shot file, available for use by the media.

## Pitches

Having a good story or story idea is great. Getting it sold to a reporter or editor can be challenging. They receive hundreds of releases and pitches daily and haven't the time or energy to review every pitch e-mail, letter or telephone call. Key advice:

- Find out how the appropriate editor likes to receive story ideas (phone call, e-mail, fax);
- Be able to explain your basic story outcome in no more than two sentences and the story idea in one to two paragraphs;
- Don't overplay your idea by making it the "greatest story of the year"—leave the embellishments in your computer;
- Be able to set up interviews immediately;
- Contact the editor only in the way and at the time she/he wants to hear from you.

"[The media] expect a news pitch that is not mistaken for an ad or sales presentation. It should contain content that is different from the countless other pitches newsrooms receive. Your pitch should be Dynamic, Unique, New and Exciting."[6]

## Public Service Announcements

If you work for a nonprofit organization, you might be able to take advantage of free radio and television airtime for public service announcements (PSA). It is impossible for stations to use all the PSAs that come their way. To increase your chances of getting your PSA aired, follow some of these tips:

1. **Quality over quantity.** Because your PSA is competing with professional advertisements, you need to make sure your PSA matches that quality. It is better to have one well-done PSA that gets airtime than 10 PSAs that don't. This means having the PSA created professionally, which requires a budget.

2. **Focus, focus, focus.** Instead of assuming that you need to contact all radio and TV stations in your area, investigate to see which ones reach your intended audience.

3. **Stop, look and listen.** Spend time with the public affairs or community affairs directors at your stations. Let them tell you if public service time is available and in what format(s) they want your material.

4. **Don't get greedy.** All nonprofit organizations want to have 60-second PSAs aired; why not offer 10-, 15-, 30-, 45- and 60-second versions of your PSA and be grateful for what you get?

5. **One at a time.** Your PSA should have only one message such as "Give blood," "Immunize your child" or "Get an eye checkup."

6. **Redundancy.** When you send in an audio- or videotaped PSA, always include a script—just in case.

7. **Be nice.** Always thank the station for airing your PSA even if it was at 3:00 a.m. If you're courteous and provide quality PSAs, you might get your PSA moved to prime time.

8. **Keep it simple.** Using flashy images or hip-hop style can often overtake the message.

9. **Celebrity spokesperson?** Use caution when selecting a celebrity for your PSA. Make sure she/he truly endorses your cause and can withstand public scrutiny.

---

### How to Write for the Ear

- **Write short sentences.** Simple declarative sentences work best. Sentences cluttered with unneeded adjectives and adverbs may not be clear. Make them memorable: "You need room to negotiate." "Brand names will lose their appeal."

- **Use short words.** Think about why people remember proverbs such as "A bird in the hand is worth two in the bush" and "A stitch in time saves nine."

- **Avoid rows of sibilant sounds** such as "Some supervisors seem stifled." They're hard to say.

- **Try to end sentences with a one-syllable word.** It's like having punctuation written in. Listeners can't see periods.

- **Avoid words listeners might not understand.** Use "although," not "albeit'; "polite," not "affable"; "secret," not "arcane,"

Frank Seltzer, Dallas, TX, quoted in communication briefings, Blackwood, NJ, November 1993.

---

10. **Call to action.** Make sure you ask the viewing/listening audience to do something. Donate time, money, goods. And include a toll-free number or Web address to help them do so.

11. **Language matters.** If creating a PSA for a Hispanic or other non-English audience, create the PSA in that language, don't just translate the English version.

12. **Look for space.** Work with print media or Web sites for two-for-one advertising; you pay for one advertising space and the host medium donates space for the second. It's worth the money for getting multiple space.

13. **Timing.** Don't try to post PSAs during heavy advertising times, such as just prior to elections or major holidays.

## Satellite Media Tours

Satellite Media Tours (SMTs) have been around since the '80s but have changed from their original stiff, talking-head format to upbeat, intricate and highly successful interactive events. A SMT is a live, "rolling" interview with preset interview times, in which one spokesperson can accommodate 10–20 individual interviews with reporters anywhere in the world in just 1–2 hours, from either a studio or on location. Since interviews no longer have to be in a studio, as technology makes remote sites more accessible, you can be creative with the set and spokesperson or celebrity by having the individual engaged in some activity, conducting a brief tour or demonstrating a product. The key is to broadcast from an interesting place. Furthermore, SMTs have a great advantage over VNRs. In a SMT, reporters get to ask questions and be active participants. A VNR is a controlled tape with no opportunity for exchange of information. At first glance, SMTs seem expensive, but compared with the cost and time of sending a spokesperson to 20 cities in 20 days for 20 interviews, they're a bargain!

Some keys to success for SMTs include having a well-trained media spokesperson, celebrity or subject matter expert for your SMT; offer information your audience can use or act on; select the time of day/day of week carefully to match your audience's viewing preferences.

## Standby Statements and Qs and As

If you know of an event that could break into the news and cause a reporter to call, there are two pieces of written information you might want to prepare as quickly as possible. The first is a standby statement. This gives the basic facts of the situation and your organization's position. It is not a news release. Rather, it is a piece the spokesperson (the media relations person or whoever is speaking publicly on this issue for your organization) will issue to the media and/or use to answer reporters' questions.

The second piece, Qs and As, is a list of expected questions a reporter would ask you and the answers you will give if he/she does. Again, this is not material to be handed out to reporters or to be published in general employee information media. It is for use only to help you reply to questions from the reporters.

To be valuable tools, the standby statement and Qs and As should meet three basic criteria:

1. They should answer the five Ws that every reporter asks: who, what, where, when and why.

2. They should—as much as possible—be cleared in advance so that you are ready to move quickly to answer a reporter's questions. The media's business is news, and a reporter's time frame is usually today. To get your organization's position in a story, you must meet the reporter's deadline. And you are

almost always better off when your organization's view is included. In the absence of information, people "fill in"—often with the worst possible scenarios.

3. They should not be words that are cast in concrete. The spokesperson should talk from the material—not read it like a script.

## Subject-Matter Experts

Subject-matter experts (SMEs) can be a media relations person's best friend. It's one thing to announce a new service, product or discovery; it's another to have an expert who can answer all the questions about it. Reporters don't want to talk to the people who announce the Nobel Laureate in Economics, they want to talk to the recipient. You may need an internal list of SMEs whom you can readily contact to help you respond to media calls. Or, you may want to develop a media guide of SMEs from your organization and let the media call them directly. Or, a combination of the two.

The media guide of experts should list the topic areas on which they speak, their full name, title and contact information, what languages they speak, if they are available for print only or if they will appear on television or a radio talk show. It is also critical to note if they can be available on very short notice for immediate response. Example, an expert on volcanoes would be needed when the volcano erupts, not three days later.

SMEs also can make good authors for op-ed pieces, editorials and special reports, but you may have to work with them to convert their expertise language into language the average reader, viewer or listener can understand. Make sure your SMEs are well trained in how to work with all media. Depending on the subject matter, you may promote SMEs from local to global media outlets.

## Video News Release (VNR)

VNRs have dramatically gained in popularity over the past five years as the ability to create more news-like VNRs aids in getting television stations to run them. However, this realism has fueled a debate over whether viewers need to be told if the news item they are watching was prepared by an outside source. The Center for Media and Democracy votes "yes" while the Radio-Television News Directors Association says there is no need for regulation on VNRs.[7]

Regardless of the outcome of the debate, VNRs seem to have developed a key role for many media programs to reach targeted audiences with unfiltered—but newsworthy—material. VNRs also provide a benefit to slimmed down newsrooms across the country.

Some key guidelines for VNR production and use:

- Always use a professional firm to produce your VNR; this is not the time to try out your amateur videography;
- Make sure you have a solid news story, preferably in the venerable areas of health, safety, finance or education;
- Make sure all facts are correct;
- If using a subject matter expert, make sure she/he is well trained;
- Test your proposed story idea with local TV reporters to see if the topic is of interest;
- Double check the demographics of your intended audience to make sure the VNR will be attractive to them;
- Tie VNR distribution to national months, such as cancer awareness;
- Discuss the pros and cons of asking for "guaranteed placement" from your VNR vendor, as that may dramatically reduce the number of outlets;
- Accept that valid measures of VNR effectiveness aren't there yet.

## White Papers

Also known as "position papers," white papers explore in depth and in detail an issue facing your company or organization and offer proposed stances to those issues.

White papers can ". . . educate the media and provide a wide variety of stakeholders with detailed trustworthy information."[8]

White papers traditionally are comprised of four sections:

1. **Situation or background.** This section provides a context for whatever position will be proposed. Describing the situation or providing the background should be concise, factual and free of rhetoric.

2. **Possible solutions.** There is no limit to the number of possible solutions that might be cited in this section, although common sense dictates that too many choices make it difficult to make a clear decision. Each possible solution must be presented with pros and cons in order to assist the decision makers.

3. **Position.** From the possible solutions will come a simply stated, well-written, fact-based position. The position statement should

be supported with hard data, examples and other elements that will distinguish this recommended position from all the possible solutions that were presented earlier.

4. **Next steps.** The position statement needs action items to bring it to life. This most often involves media interviews on key television talk shows, some op-ed pieces in influential publications, speeches to the right audiences and a meeting with editorial boards.

White papers are especially useful in assisting a management team determine how, and if, to take a stand on a sensitive or explosive issue.

## Summary

The media relations tool kit is filled with items you can use every day and others that are needed just now and then. The trick is to become familiar with multiple tools and selecting the best to reach your targeted audience, as well as to understand the criteria for using each tool in real-word situations. Basically, you should know how to use each tool wisely and well.

### How Would You Use Your Tool Kit If . . .

* Your company introduces a new product that will not be available in your region for at least six months. How do you handle the public announcement? How can you position the company as a forward-thinking organization without raising expectations? Without over-hanging the market?

* A reporter calls and wants confirmation of financial data on your company. It is obvious the reporter has figures from a recently held upper-management meeting but has interpreted some of them incorrectly. What do you do?

* The *San Francisco Examiner* is on deadline and needs a statement on the status of a new service offering from your organization. It is 5:00 p.m. in California and 8:00 p.m. in New York. None of the eastern headquarters executives are at home. What do you do?

* There is a wildcat strike at a plant near Washington, D.C. The electronic media show up in force. How do you handle the situation?

* A reporter calls you to do an interview with someone in your area on the deteriorating quality of service in your hospital. From your initial conversation with the reporter, you are sure that the story

basically has been composed with preconceived, unfavorable opinions about the hospital pulled off the Internet. What do you do?

- The *Financial Times* of London calls to confirm rumors that your company is attempting to buy out a major European manufacturing concern. It is 11:00 a.m. in New York and 5:00 p.m. in London. Your executives are in meetings. What do you do?

- A reporter says a person who has been laid off by your company just e-mailed him. The reporter says the employee works at a company location that you know has identified the need for a workforce reduction but hasn't announced it yet. What do you do?

- You have a product announcement, with a major press conference, scheduled for Wednesday. On Monday afternoon the business editor of a leading daily calls you with details about your product, including its name. The story will run in Tuesday's edition, and the editor wants confirmation about the material. What do you do?

- There is a major national trade show in your area. How do you work with the exhibits, product promotion and marketing people to make this a media relations opportunity as well as a sales tool?

# 5

# Reporters

## Helping Them
## Meet Their Objectives

The emphasis in a media relations program should be on the *relations* aspect—working to build long-term relationships with the people who cover your organization. Good media contacts proliferate once they are established. As is true with many good relationships, they are built only gradually, based on a variety of contacts over time and strengthened by experiences that foster growing knowledge and respect. They require you to have a thorough understanding of how newspapers, magazines, TV and radio stations, as well as the Internet operate on a day-to-day basis. According to Larry Weber, founder of Weber Public Relations Worldwide, "In order to get your message out in today's cluttered and complicated world, the approach must be demonstrative, intuitive, experiential and technology-based."[1]

In the end, though, this is a people-to-people business. A media relations person deals with writers, editors, producers and photographers—not with newspapers, television stations, radio microphones and Web sites. Knowing how to assist a reporter and his/her supporting cast will make the difference in long-term relationships with the media—the only kind to have.

## Deadlines Are Critical

The first thing to appreciate is that a reporter's life is controlled by very short deadlines. As former *Time* publisher John A. Meyers put it: "Journalists are fond of the saying that they write the first draft of history."[2] CBS network's Lesley Stahl called it too often being a quick-sketch artist rather than a painter.[3]

In every publication there is a "news hole" that must be filled by a predetermined time when the printing presses start running. At a daily newspaper that process occurs every 24 hours. Today's news must appear in today's paper—and tonight's news in tomorrow morning's editions. The reporter's success will be determined by how often his or her stories appear in the paper, rather than being "killed" (newspaper jargon is "spiked") by the editor. And if the reporter writes a particularly interesting or difficult story, he or she will be rewarded with a byline—the reporter's name appears over the story as the writer.

There are equivalent (and usually, more stringent) deadlines for electronic journalism. With the public demand increasing for frequent up-to-the-minute reports, radio stations' past practice of carrying news only on the half-hour or hour and TV stations' traditional two newscasts an evening are obsolete. Numerous spot reports, lengthier regular newscasts, all-news programming on radio and increasing numbers of 24-hour news formats on television (a true legacy of Ted Turner's Cable News Network) have replaced them. Because of the transitory nature of the airwaves, radio stations in particular usually repeat news reports several times a day. The broadcast journalist thus must meet more numerous and tighter deadlines than his/her print colleagues. Similar to publication bylines, the television journalist's reward for an unusually fine reporting job will be an appearance on camera to report the story in person; for a radio reporter it will be an actuality where the interview is carried on the air, rather than having the anchorperson or announcer simply read the story.

## Internet Demands Even Shorter Deadlines

The Internet provides stiff competition for the traditional media because of its ability to transmit news virtually instantaneously. The media day has turned into the media hour and now into the media minute or even second. Internet magazines and business/newswire sites such as CBS Marketwatch cover the news, as do publications like the *Wall Street Journal's Smart Money*, which exists in print and also appears online with its own news team and unique content.

Internet technology has created access to and demand for immediate information and frequent updates. Decisions relating to the media now must be made in an accelerated time frame with little lag time between actions and reporting. Posting your news promptly on your organization's Web site is a must so that a communications channel you control is accurately reflecting your positions at all times.

Two fundamental desires are motivating the reporter: (1) to report the story well, that is, accurately and in an attention-getting way and (2) to write it quickly. To have the story used, the reporter must meet both requirements; to meet those demands *you* must meet the *same* criteria. A cogent statement or key fact is useless to the reporter today if it was needed as an integral part of yesterday's news story.

The first rule of good media relations, then, is to meet the reporter's deadline. This will usually demand that you respond the same day—frequently, within hours. That is easy to accept in theory. In practice, it often demands the time and authority to stop other work to devote your full attention to the reporter's needs until they are met. If clearances are necessary before you can release certain information, you also will need the influence to ask others to break into their routine to support you.

## Learn the Media's Deadlines

You should know the regular and late-breaking news deadlines of all the media that normally carry stories on your organization.

Some papers have editions going to different areas; if you are interested in a rural or suburban location, that edition may close a couple of hours earlier than the final or city edition. These deadline times will differ depending on the distance between the paper's publishing plant and its circulation boundaries and the time required to transport copies to the most distant subscriber or newsstand. As well, technology has helped shorten deadlines, as publications now travel via satellite rather than truck. Feature and Sunday sections close several hours, or even days, earlier. Weekly newspapers, which normally publish on Wednesdays or Thursdays, frequently have deadlines a few days before press day, except for major news stories.

The news desk of any publication or station will be happy to tell you its deadlines. You might want to phone those with whom you deal regularly and then make a list of the deadlines that you can keep handy when you are working with reporters.

In any case, it is a good habit to ask a reporter what his/her deadline is each time you get a request for information. This will ensure there are no misunderstandings between you and let the reporter know you appreciate the importance of media deadlines. Over time you will come to a position of mutual understanding regarding deadlines: the reporter will learn he/she can trust you to do everything possible to meet deadlines, even the extremely short-fuse ones. In return, you will expect him/her not to "cry wolf" by creating artificial deadlines—and to give you additional time when the story is of a softer nature not demanding "today" treatment or when the request is for a large amount of information not readily available. If you cannot get all the information promptly, it often is wise to call the reporter to give an update on progress in case the story is being held for your input.

You also will want to avoid phoning a reporter around deadline time with anything but critical information related to that day's news. He or she will be busy writing, talking with the editor, checking last-minute facts or working with the art department on the cutline for a photograph that will accompany the story—in short, getting the news out. There will be no time for chatting about a possible future feature story.

Attention to deadlines also is critical when you are issuing a news release or planning a news conference, because the hour you set as a release time almost inevitably favors some media over others. If you issue your news in the early morning, for example, noon and evening TV newscasts, as well as news Web sites, will be the first to carry the news. If you schedule the release in the late afternoon you are giving the opportunity for first coverage to the morning paper and making it difficult for the evening TV news to carry anything but a brief mention unless your news is worthy of live on-air coverage. As one TV reporter rebuked a reluctant spokesperson who asked if an on-camera interview could be delayed: "It's the six o'clock news, sir—not the six-forty. They'll be on the air with or without us."

## Announcement Timing Is Important

The media in your particular area—and your analysis of the importance of each publication or station to your organization—will determine the time you schedule news releases and news conferences. A good general rule of thumb is always to set news events and schedule release times to meet your weekly's deadline if it is the leading newspaper in your community or the key trade publication in your industry. The Internet, radio stations and all-news broadcasts report just about instantaneously, or at the minimum every 60 minutes, and repeat the news frequently. So the time you choose is not that critical to them.

To meet regulatory requirements relative to release of material information if your organization is a publicly held company, always issue your news releases via news wires. Also, make sure they are posted on your company's Web site immediately. In addition, if you work for a public company, you will want to coordinate timing closely with your colleagues in investor relations to be sure financial analysts covering your industry get prompt and personal distribution of your news, since reporters almost always contact them for comments on a major announcement. You can issue the same news release to the financial community, but change the contact information from the media relations professional to the person responsible for investor relations. If you are hosting a news conference, plan a separate but identical briefing for analysts immediately before or right after the news conference.

Remember that good relations with the media often begin—not end—with a news release. You must allow reporters enough time to contact others about your story, ask questions of you and them, gather visuals to illustrate it, and generally adapt or rewrite your release to meet the interests of their particular audience.

Saturday can be a good day for nonprofit organizations to issue news releases or to hold news events. They will be covered on that evening's television news and in the next day's papers. Reading the bulging Sunday paper has become a daylong activity in many American cities. Also, you are less likely to have to compete for space with news of business, the stock market, the economy, the government and other organizations that operate on Monday-to-Friday schedules.

## Take Advantage of Technology

Unless it is a timeless feature story, you should electronically transmit your news release. This will avoid the problem of your news arriving so late that it has lost its news value. It also will ensure that you get your news to all the media at about the same time, so you do not inadvertently help one reporter "scoop" another.

Address your release to a particular reporter or editor by name so it quickly gets to the right person—and perhaps also phone or e-mail those who cover your beat regularly to tell them a release is on the way if the news is major. Also, if you are sending more than one copy to the same news outlet—for example, one to the assignment editor and one to the reporter who recently wrote a story about your organization—it is a courtesy to add a brief note that says so. Be aware of any distribution idiosyncrasies at the publication or station. To cite an extreme example, if you fail to write "Personal and Confidential" above the addressee's name at the *Wall Street Journal,* the news release likely will be whisked away to the parent Dow Jones News Service for distribution over its wire service. Thus your reporter may not get the news at all, much less by deadline time.

Most reporters check the Web while writing their stories, especially broad-based pieces. Make sure your organization's Web site is updated regularly and can be easily accessed so that reporters who regularly cover your organization and industry come to consider it a current, useful and trusted source. You will know you have a useful site based on return visits, length of stay and degree of interactivity.

Work with the information technology specialists in your firm to be sure your Web site is registered on various key Web search engines. Reporters will not visit your site if they cannot get in and get out easily, especially when they are on deadline. Also put your news conferences and special media events on your Web site for reporters who cannot attend in person.

In fact, consultant and author Shel Holtz advises PR people to "make friends with IT [Information Technology]. Go to the technical staff for help, get them to solve problems, take them to lunch," he advises. "You should have a relationship with IT that's no different from your relationship with your printer, video producer or graphic designer."[4]

Your IT people can help ensure that your organization's Web site takes advantage of the technology. You need a design format and visual logic to help people move about the site quickly and easily. Too many Internet offerings mimic static print without reconstructing it to make it appropriate for the medium. Similarly, you will need to learn how to write for the Web. The opening chapter of *Wired* magazine's hardcover book, *Wired Style: Principles of English Usage in the Digital Era,* offers excellent advice, as does *The Web Writer's Guide,* by Darlene Maciuba-Koppel. And Shel Holtz's *Public Relations on the Net,* published by AMACOM, is another outstanding source.

## Plan Ahead for PSAs

There also are many times when the confusion of last-minute deadlines can be avoided altogether. If your organization has an annual fund-raising event or is planning a major celebration like a fiftieth anniversary, you should write a letter several months in advance to the public service people if you will be requesting help with public service announcements, and a week or two in advance to the news editor if you think there are opportunities for straight news coverage.

Even if you want to keep the nature of the news a secret until the event, a phone call or e-mail advising a reporter who you think might want advance notice to keep the calendar clear on a certain day is the kind of thoughtfulness that helps build long-term personal relationships. A follow-up e-mail the day before the news event is also a fine idea. Busy journalists are reminded of your event, and you can inquire if each journalist will be attending so you get an idea of how many people will be present. But do not overdo it by pestering them for a definite RSVP. Even if an editor has assigned a news team to your event, late-breaking news could result in a last-minute change in the team's assignment.

## Accessibility Is Paramount

On a pleasant fall day, the media relations staff at AT&T's New York City headquarters had a luncheon honoring one of their members who was celebrating his fifteenth service anniversary. As was their normal practice, one staff member stayed behind to cover the office over the lunch period in case a reporter called with a request for information that could not wait. Also as a matter of routine, they left the name and phone number of the restaurant. In the middle of the luncheon the person covering the office answered a call from a reporter in Chicago who was phoning to find out why the New York Stock Exchange had suspended trading in AT&T stock. One call to the restaurant and everyone returned to the office to learn that the Department of Justice was about to file a major antitrust suit against the company. Within two hours AT&T was hosting a news conference to respond to the charges and answer questions on what became one of the biggest and most publicized cases in antitrust history—resulting in the breakup of the Bell System.

AT&T would not have wished for such a vivid example to demonstrate the value of its media relations administrative systems. But the fact remains that when an emergency hits and you are making instant history, there is no substitute for routine procedures already in place to ensure the accessibility of key spokespersons. They are crucial whether you work for a large, multinational corporation or staff a two-person office for a trade association.

As much as is practical you should match your office hours to the hours of the key media that cover your organization. Certainly you need a responsible person available throughout the luncheon period. If you have more than one person on your media relations staff, you should consider staggered hours to broaden your office coverage. If you work alone, e-mail, cell phone, voice mail, Web site and fax machine are necessities.

In any case, you need to set up a message system that helps you quickly get word of reporters' phone calls so that you can promptly return them. Reporters checking late-breaking news or calling from different time zones should always be able to reach you.

Here's another tip that will demonstrate that you truly are accessible: answer your own phone.

## Update Your Home Files and Emergency Contact Lists

It also is extremely helpful to keep an up-to-date file of information about your company at your home. Your annual report, most recent financial results, latest organization chart, product catalogues and price lists—such information readily available at home will save you the embarrassment of appearing ignorant of basic facts about your organization. Make a regular practice of taking home every release you issue that day—plus backup information—in case someone calls you or e-mails you there after normal working hours.

Sometimes the topics will be too complex for you to feel comfortable handling without counsel from the person responsible for a specific area. Or sometimes a reporter will want to attribute the response to a high-level executive in your organization. Just as you want reporters to know how to get in touch with you after normal office hours, so you will want the residence, cell and vacation phone numbers of key executives or experts in your organization.

You also will want those executives to be able to call you day or night if an emergency arises that might result in media attention (for example, an injury to a worker in one of your facilities, a plane crash involving your employees, the death of a top executive or a bomb scare). If your organization does not have an emergency contact list, you may want to take the initiative to create one, distributing copies to all employees involved, and keeping it up to date. If you have a main office switchboard operator, make sure she/he has the list—and be certain all news media calls are referred to you or your staff first, day or night.

We frequently have been grateful that reporters have our home numbers—and we in turn have the numbers of other key company people around the country. A significant case-in-point occurred during a period when the recessionary economy was having a big impact on AT&T's equipment sales. The phone rang at home at 9:40 p.m. It was a reporter from *The Wall Street Journal*. He also was at home, and he was very apologetic. "I'm sorry to call so late," he said, "but some 'looney tune' just called the news desk in New York with a silly rumor that you are laying off 10,000 people and pulling out of the telephone manufacturing business. I know that's crazy, but they wanted me to check it out with you to see if there is any truth to it." As is the case with most crazy rumors, there was a grain of truth behind it. But this reporter knew our business well, so he immediately recognized that, at a minimum, the alleged news tip was highly exaggerated. Like the good reporter he was, he called to check.

We told him that indeed there was going to be a large layoff— 1,200 people, not 10,000—that the news would be told to employees beginning with the night shift in about an hour, and that the company would make a public announcement the next morning. We pointed out that the anonymous caller's statement that AT&T was pulling out of the telephone manufacturing business was not true, but unfortunately the declining demand for new home phones as a result of the current economic slowdown was causing layoffs. We gave him some more details and then asked the key question: Did he plan to write a story? He replied that he thought he would.

If you read *The Wall Street Journal* the next morning you might have seen a relatively small five- or six-inch story on the layoff. But what you did not know about was the flurry of behind-the-scenes activity—both late that night and early the next morning—that the story caused. First and most important were the calls that night to our local public relations manager. We had to alert him to the leak, to the fact that there would be a story in the next day's *Wall Street Journal*, and we had to coordinate answers to some more of the reporter's questions. Also we wanted to let the PR manager and his staff know they had to move up their planned announcement to their local media. So they came in early and got their news release out at 7:00 the next morning. After all, it would not do much for their media relations if the local reporters read about a local layoff in the national *Wall Street Journal* before they heard it from our media relations people there.

Also very important were our other major offices and plants around the country. We got a quick alert out to them very early the next morning, so they would be prepared to respond promptly and professionally to the inevitable calls they would get from reporters wanting to know the local situation. And we in New York got ready to handle the queries from other national publications, the wire services and the trade press that we knew the *Journal* story would (and did) cause. It was a busy time. But there was never any confusion or concern about what to do or how to contact the right people, even in the middle of the night. The advance planning for the layoff announcement was also vital to the calm manner with which we were able to react to the leak.

## Know the Newspeople and Their Media

Another important element in your relationship with the reporters who cover your organization should be your knowledge of their special interests—either because the publication or station has assigned them to the area or because they have a personal interest in the topic. Many times reading the bylined articles or columns of a print reporter, listening to or viewing the programs of a radio or TV commentator and visiting the Web sites of journalists will give you insight into subject on which they seem to enjoy working.

If you think you have an idea for a feature, try to interest a reporter or an editor in doing it, rather than writing it yourself. Similarly, if you have a good photo opportunity, call the local paper or TV station assignment editor in the hope you can get a photographer or camera crew to come out. As former *Time* publisher John Meyers put it, "Scratch a photojournalist and you will find a reporter who wields a camera instead of a typewriter."[5] Publications and stations are much more likely to use material they have spent their people's time developing. But never talk to two journalists on the same publication, station or online magazine about the same story idea or event—for example, to both the education and business reporters about a high school job fair—without telling each that you have done so.

The Internet is teaming with sites set up by individual entrepreneurs and by major media giants catering to every niche interest imaginable. With so many new and changing sites, it can be difficult to know how and who to contact to place your news.

Gerri Kelly, a senior media relations supervisor at Edelman Public Relations Worldwide's Chicago office, believes that "PR pros must study print magazines to identify who online is attracting the buzz. It's all about getting information on a case-by-case basis, and it is different for all our clients. You just have to build online contacts and get to know the tech and Internet reporters." She admits, though, that e-mail to the letters page of some of the Internet-only titles is sometimes the only way to get a response. "It's tough to get contact names. You need to read all the trade magazines that review Web sites and look for new opportunities." In addition, Kelly recommends the *American Journalism Review*'s site (*www.AJR.org*) as a place to seek specific sites of interest.[6]

Drew Kerr, founder of Four Corners Communications in New York City, says it can be "difficult to pitch story ideas to opinion-focused titles, full of individual commentary." But he says there are numerous sites with dedicated online staff who are interested in pitches, such as CNet's News.com, Wired.com and SmartMoney.com, all of which are technology- and business-oriented sites with significant editorial backup.[7]

## Don't Let Failure Get You Down

Don't be oversensitive to failure when you contact a reporter with a news or feature idea. We unsuccessfully tried to interest the Associated Press national photo editor in two pictures before scoring with a unique shot of AT&T's "computer on a chip" paired with a South American fire ant. That placement resulted in the company's high-technology message appearing in more than two hundred publications, with a circulation of more than 20 million in the United States and overseas. Twice at The Reader's Digest Association our news releases were picked up in Ann Landers' column, which is syndicated to 1,200 newspapers in the United States and Canada. One offered free reprints of a *Reader's Digest* article about a home eye test, resulting in 35,000 reprint requests within six weeks. The other offered consumers hints on how to detect sweepstakes fraud.

So keep trying and you'll find ways to succeed. A few strikeouts are worth it if you hit home runs like that every so often. Conversely, you will want to do at least a little research before you suggest story or photo ideas. It would be very embarrassing to recommend a program on controlling health care costs to a talk show host, only to be told they covered that topic last month.

As valuable as knowing the reporter's interests is understanding the role the publication, station or online magazine has set for itself. The *Los Angeles Times*, for example, defines itself as a national newspaper. In fact, when airline deregulation resulted in fewer transcontinental flights leaving Los Angeles, the *Times* moved deadlines for one edition up 30 minutes so the paper could make the plane to Washington. "We want our paper on the desks of the President and Congress before they get to work in the morning," now retired managing editor George Cotliar explained. "We want to have the same opportunity to influence discussion that the *New York Times* and the *Washington Post* have.[8] Knowing that strategy, you would probably decide to try to interest a *Los Angeles Times* editor in a subject related to a national issue like energy and take an idea geared to a smaller community audience to a suburban paper instead.

If a newspaper is part of a chain like Gannett or Copley, which has a news syndicate, or heads its own news service like the *Chicago Tribune* or the *New York Times*, this association will also have some effect on an editor. He/she is likely to be more interested stories affecting people or communities beyond the paper's own circulation boundaries. (Incidentally, reporters frequently are not told if their stories are picked up by the member papers when they have gone out over the news service or syndicate. Thus, you often can build some personal rapport with a reporter by forwarding copies of his/her stories that your clipping service picks up—especially if they are from out of state or out of the country.)

No matter how friendly and frequent your contacts with particular reporters, always remember that they have a job to do and their number-one priority is getting the story. As former White House spokesman Marlin Fitzwater put it, "Treat them like professionals and they will be your friends. But treat them like friends and they will betray you every time."[9]

## Use Internal Media as Tools

If they carry news of more than employees' bowling scores and the company picnic, internal publications can be effective, inexpensive tools to keep reporters informed about your organization and stimulate interest in feature stories, particularly in smaller communities.

Some organizations include local media people on their mailing list for each issue of the company's employee newspaper or magazine. Others prefer to send only selected issues, with a business card or a note drawing the reporter's attention to a particular feature they think would be of interest. In any case, it is useful to remember that what we take for granted because we deal with it every day can be perceived as news by the local media—particularly if there is a local or human-interest angle. Employees participating in blood drives and the American Cancer Society "smoke-out" days, features on carpools and other employee energy conservation ideas, suggestion program winners, tutoring activities with disadvantaged children, family nights at the plant, safety and handicraft fairs—all these are feature ideas we have placed with local media.

Also, it is important for your management to recognize that once an issue is covered in your organization's employee media it can very easily get out beyond the boundaries of your company. If a story appears internally, you should consider it externally released as well.

You also will want to have handy a standard package of materials about your organization to use as a backgrounder for reporters doing stories on your company for the first time. The annual report and a fact sheet with a list of your key products and services as well as vital statistics, such as number of employees, location and unique features of your office(s) are some of the basics. You can then add other information, depending on the thrust of the reporter's story. Fact sheets need not be fancy. The important thing is that they be brief (preferably no more than a page), current and carry the date on which it was prepared.

Of course the latest background pieces and fact sheet information also should be posted on your organization's Web site—and updated regularly. Be aware, though, that once on the Internet the information can be accessed by those other than journalists so don't, for example, provide your home number on the Web site unless you are willing to receive a multitude of calls from various stakeholders.

## Handling Requests for Information

If you have an active media relations program, you are likely to get calls from reporters almost every day. They may want more information on a news release you issued. They could be working on a feature story. Or they might want your organization's view on a major news event of the day. There are, of course, myriad ways in which you can respond to these queries. But one overall rule applies: If you or your organization initiated interest in the topic, you cannot duck or evade reporters' follow-up calls; if a reporter originated the contact, your response will be dictated by your company's objectives, policy and style.

As you are working with people in your organization to write and clear a news release, you will want to remind them that most publications, stations and online magazines will have their reporters call with additional questions rather than use the release as is. That is why you should include anticipated media questions and agreed-upon answers as a routine step in your advance planning and production of any news release (see chapter 4). You will want to ensure that your internal contacts are available on the day you issue the release—

and stay in your office yourself that day and probably also the following one. You should also brief whoever answers your phone on the
importance of the release and the proper and rapid way to handle the
calls it generates. Reporters' normal sense of urgency quickly turns to
panic as their deadline approaches. Believe it or not, public relations
people actually have issued news releases and then gone into all-day
meetings, leaving their secretaries alone to fend off frustrated reporters seeking additional information.

On occasion you also may be called by reporters seeking to get
your organization's reaction to significant external news events, such
as the announcement of a proposed change in international trade or
federal tax policy or a local rezoning application for a new industrial
park. Whether you are requested to comment on such general public
issues will probably depend on the prominence of your organization
within your community. Whether you choose to respond will often
depend to a great extent on the personal style and civic involvement
of your organization's top leaders. You should know or help establish
your organization's general policy for handling such broad requests
so that you can promptly deal with this type of media request. Follow
your local media's coverage of such key issues so you can anticipate
and plan responses for the types of calls you may get.

When a reporter asks for information, do not hesitate to ask
enough questions yourself so you have a full understanding of the
story on which the reporter is working. If you take a single, isolated
question, you may not be able to give your expert enough to go on to
offer a competent answer. Or the answer to the question, when
relayed to the reporter, may lead to another question and you will
have to go through the process all over again. Get a good grasp of
what the reporter wants. Try to visualize the whole while you are
talking about the parts. Anticipate follow-up questions. Be a
reporter's reporter.

What you want to avoid is being perceived as a person intent on
withholding information or, just as bad, a person who does not have
access to information. There still remains a certain skepticism—and
sometimes definite hostility—from journalists toward media relations people. The only way to overcome this is to prove yourself every
time you work with the media. If reporters continually call other
sources within your organization, it is because either they do not
know you or you are not meeting their information needs.

Never give away an "exclusive." If a newspaper, radio or TV station or an online magazine develops a feature article on its own and
comes to you for information, or is approaching a news story from a
unique angle, its rights to exclusive use of that story must be

respected. If two reporters seek the same information, however, tell each person that the other is working on the story. It will avoid subsequent conflict and help keep you from being caught in the middle.

## Test Your Knowledge, Involvement

There is no sin in admitting you do not know an answer; simply say you will check it out and get back to the reporter. But if that happens very often, you should ask yourself some soul-searching questions:

- Am I doing everything I can to keep current on company activities and industry trends? Should I expand my regular reading or use of the Internet or blogs? Make a point of keeping in touch with people in other departments? Be more active in trade associations or professional societies?

- Am I anticipating news and activities in this organization that would cause media interest and preparing to handle news queries in advance?

- Am I—or is my boss—included in planning meetings and in the decision-making process? Do I have the confidence of top management so that I am among the first to know what is happening within the organization? (If not, you cannot be considered a spokesperson; at best you may be a well-qualified reference point.)

Recently, a fellow media relations practitioner complained vociferously that he was left out of the planning and media announcement activities when his company was awarded a major government contract in a bid against a Japanese company. But even superficial questioning made it clear he had not kept up with the current highly sensitive government negotiations on lowering foreign import barriers. Nor was he aware of the various congressional committees conducting hearings on international trade at the time. And he was not a regular reader of the trade press or visitor to Web sites covering his industry. So he was never up to date on what his company's competitors were doing or how the industry viewed his company. Little wonder his boss—and perhaps his CEO—felt that he was not qualified to be the company's spokesperson on this critical subject.

George V. Grune, retired chairman and CEO of The Reader's Digest Association, told the public relations directors of its worldwide operations that one of management's key expectations of them was that they have a thorough knowledge of the business. "That means you need to understand our corporate strategy, our marketing plans, our products, our competition, our internal challenges and our future opportunities. Go out of your way to build working relationships with your operations colleagues," he advised. "They are your clients and excellent sources of information. Attend marketing meetings and ask the product mangers to brief you on their plans. Participate in brainstorming sessions, join task forces and become more proactive in the way you act on key business issues."[10]

## Master the Fundamentals

Equally important is that you master the basics of your craft. That means you need to be an outstanding writer and editor in all media—especially news releases and other media relations materials such as photographs and videos.

Watch to see what happens to your news releases. You will soon come to accept the fact that reporters will rewrite your carefully crafted sentences. If they do it too often, however, you might ask yourself why. Are you following the accepted rules of press style? (*The New York Times*, Associated Press or another widely accepted stylebook is a must to be kept handy as a constant reference source.) Or maybe the reporter's sentences are shorter and easier to understand than yours.

Another excellent feedback vehicle is a media audit—hiring an outside research firm to ask reporters covering your organization (and those who do not whom you would like to attract) how you are meeting their needs. If your question list is short and to the point, most journalists are willing to answer because upgrading your skills and services helps them as well as you. This also is a good opportunity to get their views on the usefulness of your Web site.

A reporter is a lot more likely to get your position right—or indeed, use your statement at all—if it is a "quotable quote." Similarly, the public is a lot more likely to agree with you if you speak in terms they can understand. It is critical that news releases and statements be written in plain English—not in "legalese," and not in corporate gobbledygook, defined as incomprehensible or pompous jargon of specialists. Unfortunately, our experience has not shown that to be the case. But if it is true, as an AT&T advertising campaign once told us, that to communicate is the beginning of understanding, surely it must also be true that we must all comprehend the terminology.

Organizations bring much of the public's misunderstanding and mistrust upon themselves when they issue news releases and statements full of highly technical jargon and industry lingo. You can get so lost as you read or listen to so-called information sources that you don't know if you have been eating magic mushrooms or wandering around Alice's Wonderland. "You're not more informed," says Tom Rosenstiel, a former *Los Angeles Times* media critic, "you're just numbed."[11]

## Handling Requests for Interviews

Many times reporters will call an organization asking to interview someone about a particular topic. The natural reaction is to try to find an appropriate person for the reporter to talk to—sometimes a time-consuming and unnecessary effort. Often, a better response is for the media relations spokesperson to be the primary source of information for the majority of requests, reserving the interview for occasions when another person is needed for his/her particular expertise or when the medium warrants an executive-level spokesperson. Having the media relations person be the primary spokesperson will probably mean your organization responds more promptly and more efficiently to reporter inquiries.

When you determine that an interview with someone else in your organization is the best approach, however, there are a number of steps to follow. This section will deal with your support of the reporter in an interview situation.

The first decision is whether the interview will take place on the phone, via the Internet, via video teleconference or in person. It is a good idea to ask the preference of the reporter. Radio or international reporters normally want a telephone, Internet or video teleconference interview because it is so much faster. Print or TV reporters' choices are usually determined by their deadlines and distance from your interviewee.

Equally important is your input into the decision, which should be based on your knowledge of the spokesperson's desires and abilities in different situations and your evaluation of the significance of this particular medium and story. If your spokesperson is just one of many sources to be interviewed for a broad survey article in a newspaper or magazine, for example, a phone conversation is probably most appropriate. Telephone interviews are usually shorter because there is less tendency to chitchat. If your organization is to be featured more prominently in the piece—be it in print or on TV—a face-to-face interview is probably best. Your spokesperson is more likely to come across as a personable human being rather than a faceless bureaucrat. But you will want to exert some control over the length of the interview to prevent it from dragging on unnecessarily.

## Brief the Reporter Ahead of Time

Regardless of which medium is chosen, you should provide the reporter with a biography immediately—and a photograph, if one is readily available—of your spokesperson. This also is the time to point out how the spokesperson prefers to be addressed, in person and in print; the correct spelling and pronunciation of the name; and the person's particular field of expertise vis-à-vis the story the reporter is writing. Provide this information, along with other appropriate background information on your organization and the subject of the proposed story, in advance of the interview—even if this requires having the material delivered by hand. The more you communicate with and provide background to reporters before the interview, the more they are likely to get the facts straight and not waste their and your spokesperson's time with basic "How does it work?" or "What does your company do?" questions.

## Tips for the Phone Interview

If you have agreed on a phone interview, let the reporter know you will initiate the call at the agreed-upon time. Elementary as this may sound, double-check the time if different time zones are involved—especially with an international reporter. Because many people object to speakerphones, feeling their words are being broadcast all over, it sometimes is best to set up a three-way conference call. After introducing the reporter to the spokesperson, let the reporter take control of the conversation.

You, meanwhile, should take extensive notes of the conversation—verbatim if you can write quickly enough. Neatness definitely does not count when it comes to these notes. The only person who needs to be able to read them is you, so that you can check a quote for the reporter if you are requested to do so or check the finished article for accuracy. If you are dealing with a particularly sensitive subject, however, you may want to write up your notes, including key questions and answers, for your files in case there are questions later about what was said or done. As you monitor the conversation, make notations to yourself if you feel points need clarifying or further data need to be gathered. Resist the urge to intrude on the conversation unless your spokesperson is stumbling and clearly needs you to help with an explanation, or is in danger of giving out proprietary or other sensitive information in response to the reporter's questioning or prodding.

## Tips for the In-Person Interview

If the interview is in person, arrange to meet with the reporter a few minutes in advance. Then you can get acquainted briefly if you do not already know the reporter and review plans before you go to your spokesperson's office. After making introductions you should again avoid getting involved very deeply in the conversation. Take notes and offer counsel and follow-up where necessary. You should also politely end the interview if the reporter's questions become repetitious or if the time has extended much longer than originally scheduled to a point you feel to be inappropriate. It is rare for an interview to be profitable to both parties if it lasts much longer than an hour.

If a still photographer is accompanying the reporter for shots of the interview, there should not be much extra coordination required on

---

### The Reporter Blew It!

In an article for members of an international organization of CEOs called TEC, business consultant Andrew Birol listed as one of his "Ten Signs Your Strategy Doesn't Work," the following warning sign: "After a newspaper reporter interviews you, he leaves unclear on what your company does. Tragically, when you open the paper, you can't tell for sure the reporter was even interviewing you or writing about your firm."

Professional communicators understand that no matter what the medium, when you are positioned as an expert in a news environment your credibility is greatly enhanced.

Rather than shift the blame for a bad story on to a reporter, review your own internal practices in preparing for interviews.

* Understand the medium. Is it print? Broadcast? Who is their audience? Who in that audience do you need/want to reach?

* What do you know about the reporter? Pre-interview them before the real interview begins. Have they covered your industry before? Do they have an agenda (a point of view)? Who have they interviewed already? Is there a certain angle they have in mind? Do they need some background first, about you and your company and industry?

* Once you've identified your priority audience targets, what is the overriding, persuasive message you need to communicate to them? Write it down in bullet form.

* What are the individual messages that support, validate and drive that overall persuasive message? Write them down in bullet form.

* Remember, you're the expert. The reporter needs your input—your quotes and detail—to help flesh out the story.

From Interviewing: The Growing Media Gulf. January 10, 2005, www.imakenews.com

your part beyond alerting your spokesperson. But if you know the photographer wants to tour your operation to take additional photographs, and you have the staff available, you should stay with the reporter and get someone else to work with the photographer and handle critical details like photo permissions and safety and security concerns.

If a TV station wants to send in a camera crew, you should make sure the room where the interview will take place does not have too many windows or a busy or strongly patterned background. Most TV people consider the video far more important than what is heard, so it is worth your while to think through ways to meet the crew's needs while also getting your key messages across in picture form whenever possible.

### After the Interview

After the interview, get the reporter's deadline for any additional data you agreed to provide and ask for a general idea when the story is expected to run. (No reporter can promise a publication or airdate. That prerogative is reserved for editors and producers.) Offer to check quotes or verify any additional information needed as the article or report is being written—a polite way of letting the reporter know you care about accuracy but understand you cannot see the copy in advance.

Once the story appears, if you feel it was a difficult subject handled well or written in a particularly interesting way, you should not hesitate to tell the reporter either in a phone call, note or e-mail or the next time you meet in person. Like all of us, reporters are interested in honest feedback and flattered by positive reactions.

If the story does not appear within the expected time frame, it is acceptable to phone the reporter to check the status—as long as you make clear your understanding that editors make these decisions, not reporters. If the story is "spiked"—a term newspaper reporters use when a story is written but never printed—you must not protest too strongly. It is fine to inquire as to the reason, because you may learn from it and thus improve your media relations in the future. Most stories do not appear for the simple reason that news is plentiful, space and/or time is limited and editors must make judgments on the value of each story.

## How to Handle Errors

The news media have neither the space nor the time to tell the "whole truth." Rather, they carry the part their reporters and editors think important. Under pressures of time and without detailed knowledge of your business, it is inevitable that errors will occasionally appear in news coverage of your organization. Your behavior in this situation will have a major effect on your long-term relationship with the reporter and the publication or station. A natural first reaction is to demand a correction or write a letter to the editor. More appropriately, that should be a last resort. The publication of a retraction, like a double-edged sword, cuts both ways. Errors read only once may be quickly forgotten; read twice, they may stick despite the attempt at correction.

Whether you are approaching the print or electronic media about an error, you will be dealing with a person who naturally can be expected to be defensive if she/he wrote or photographed the offending piece, or protective if she/he is the editor to whom the person under attack reports.

Here, in order of consideration and seriousness, is what you should do if there is an error in print coverage of your organization:

1. **Acknowledge the difference between what is incorrect and what you don't *like* about a story.** List the factual errors; chances are they will be few in number and not all that major. Next, list what you didn't like about the story: the headline; placement of the article in the publication; the three-second sound bite; position of your quotes; quotes from your competitors. Make sure you're considering asking for a correction of important factual errors.

2. **In most cases, be charitable and do nothing.** Most errors are insignificant in the context of the overall story. They probably will not be noticed by any but the most knowledgeable in the audience who would recognize that there was a mistake. Sometimes it is the headline that offends. Remember that it is written not by the reporter but by a copy editor under incredible space constraints to summarize the essence of the story in a few words. With such brevity can come obscurity or misplaced emphasis. You should not blame the reporter, who probably did not see the headline before the piece was published or aired.

3. **In some cases, contact the reporter to request the item be corrected for the record.** It often is a good idea to get the accurate information into the electronic files. Your purpose here is to politely alert the reporter to the error and ensure it is not repeated in future coverage of your organization. An example of a mistake warranting a correction in the file copy might be a misstatement about your product line, the size of your facility, a name misspelling or an incorrect title of one of your executives. A particularly

clever complaint letter was sent by AT&T media relations spokesperson Wink Swain to a reporter who got her companies mixed up: "Oops! As much as I enjoyed [name of reporter's] article on Westinghouse Broadcasting, I'm afraid there was a slight error in corporate genealogy. Western Electric is not the parent company of Group W, though the article was so well done that I almost wish we were," the letter said. "Western Electric is a wholly owned subsidiary of AT&T. The enclosed booklet will tell you all about us. We're certain that the error was innocent, and we don't want to make a big fuss over it. I hope that you and [name of reporter] will accept the friendly reminders that I've enclosed and use them to serve the people of [the town]." Along with a booklet describing the company, Swain sent two pens carrying the corporate logo. The record was corrected and a mistake was turned into a friendly media contact.

4. **In a few cases you will want to write a letter to the editor.** This can be done when you feel your position was not adequately stated—as compared to being incorrectly stated—and you want to use the forum of the Letters to the Editor column to expand exposure of your views. It might also be appropriate when you want to publicly and formally correct the record, as when your organization is involved in a legal or regulatory action.

5. **In rare cases you will be justified in asking the publication to print a correction.** This would occur, for example, if your earnings or other pertinent financial information affecting the price of your stock were misquoted. Sometimes a correction can be masked by the addition of updated information; for example, including the time and place of the funeral in a second article when the person's name was misspelled in the initial obituary.

6. **In no case should you contact the competing paper to tell them of the incident and to ask them to set the record straight.** Ethical journalists will not participate in vendettas against their colleagues. That applies to radio and TV as well. Do not call competing stations and ask them to carry the "true story."

7. **If the error is critical, post the correction on your organization's Web site.** Remember that two-edged sword, though; many people now will see something they may never have noticed before, so be sure it is worth it.

There are differences, however, when you are dealing with the broadcast media instead of print. If you call up a radio station to complain of an error in coverage, the station often will ask your permission to tape you over the phone then and there, giving your side of the story. They may use your comments live if the program is a talk show with a call-in format. Or they may save the tape for a later broadcast. Before you call you will want to be prepared with two or three key points written down to help you state your position coherently. A TV station could also ask you to appear on a guest editorial giving your position if the issue is controversial or of long-term significance to your community.

You, of course, must be even more swift in correcting any errors that go out in your materials to the print or broadcast media. No matter how careful you are, one day an error is going to slip through your checking and proofreading system. If it is clearly only a typographical error, there is no need to issue a correction and a second release—although you will want to redouble your proofing efforts because even small errors reflect on your professionalism and desire for accuracy. If it is a significant mistake—a name misspelled or a factual error—you must *immediately* get on the phone, send a fax or issue an e-mail alert to everyone you sent the release to, offer a quick apology, and give the correct information. Then you should also send out a revised news release to everyone on the original distribution list, with the words "corrected version" prominently written on the top of the first page.

## When to Say No

In spite of the fact that your major role for reporters is to facilitate access to data and people in your organization, there are legitimate reasons for you to refuse to divulge information. There is, however, no occasion we have ever run across when it is appropriate for you or any spokesperson for your organization to reply to a media query with a terse "No comment." That is a desperate response, almost guaranteed to make the reporter search for other sources for the facts.

Tell the reporter *why* you can't discuss an issue in much detail—because it involves proprietary information that will divulge too much to your competitors, because as a matter of policy the company does not discuss rumors in the marketplace that might have an effect on the price of your stock, because you are in the midst of sensitive labor negotiations and want to keep discussion going around the bargaining table rather than on the pages of the daily newspaper, because it is too soon after the accident to know what actually happened, because your lawyers have not yet received the court papers, or whatever is appropriate. The reporter then has a legitimate quote from you, and yet you have released no inappropriate information to the public. Both the media's and your organization's objectives have been met.

In an interview with *Fortune* magazine, Barnes & Noble CEO Leonard Riggio gave us a perfect example of how to say "no comment" without saying it—and to get a positive point across at the same time—when he refused to divulge his comeback strategy in his company's struggle with Amazon.com: "I have so much I'd like to say that I can't say. It's a very competitive marketplace. What I can tell you is that we have the resources to do many, many entrepreneurial things."[12]

When you are citing proprietary information as the reason for refusing to disclose information, you want to be sure it really is proprietary. One spokesperson refused to acknowledge the existence of a new manufacturing process, only to have the reporter pull out a company brochure with a photo of the alleged secret equipment. On another occasion a media relations person refused to divulge the salary of the CEO and president until caustically reminded by a reporter that the figures were carried in the company's legally required public filings with the Securities and Exchange Commission as well as the annual meeting mailing to shareowners.

On some occasions **you may decide to say no to a reporter's request because of the time it would take to gather the information** or because the information is not available in the form the reporter wishes. These types of requests often come from editors or reporters seeking to localize news of a regional or national company by breaking down sales or financial information at the local manufacturing or sales office level. In these cases, a simple statement that it would be too costly for your organization to keep statistics in every conceivable format, combined with an offer of the information in a somewhat different arrangement, is usually sufficient. Also, many companies do not release sales and profit information for local business units, subsidiaries or product lines for competitive reasons. Reporters will understand if you cite that rationale.

There also are situations **when reporters do not seem to know what they want.** When we come upon a writer whose questions and requests for information indicate a time-consuming fishing expedition rather than a story, we sometimes politely but firmly ask him/ her to determine the focus of the piece, at which time we will be pleased to help.

In extreme cases you might want to decline a guest appearance on a TV interview or radio talk show. For example, **if the host has a record of asking loaded questions** or espousing positions contrary to your organization, industry or issue, your appearance may provide only a target for complaints rather than a forum for discussion. If a fellow guest is a bitter ex-employee or vocal union leader complaining of working conditions, your appearance could tend to legitimize the complaint and hurt relationships with your current employees. If the theme of the coverage is not supportive of your objectives—the favorite recipes of a woman candidate for senator, for example—a polite no may also be the best response. Sometimes no publicity is better than frivolous publicity.

Another case where saying "no" is totally appropriate would be **requests to appear on scandal-driven programs** with hosts who care more for ratings than facts. In these situations both the format and the mood of the program are so unprofessional that your appearing would demean both your organization and yourself. Unfortunately, these types of programs are proliferating. As James Fallows wrote in a scathing and powerful piece in *Atlantic Monthly,* too often these days journalists ask questions "with a discourtesy and rancor that represent the public's views much less than they reflect the modern journalist's belief that being independent boils down to acting hostile."[13]

Even *60 Minutes,* always known for its hard-hitting style, has crossed the line into combative journalism, as it too has fallen victim to the blurring of hard news and tabloid journalism. In her autobiography *Reporting Live,* Lesley Stahl described how the change occurred:

> With the falloff in audience, we also began to introduce more conflict into our reports. Actually, the drift toward hostility journalism developed out of the best of intentions. When we realized that the new technology allowed us to squeeze three or four sound bites into one piece, we began to search for 'opposing views' to flesh out our reports. We thought of it as good journalism, but it had the unintended effect of exacerbating a public discourse of disputatiousness. Our bosses began asking for extreme views—a 'stable of arguers'—in the hope that the audience would like the dueling. Soon we were searching for the most polarized views so we could get a real battle going.[14]

In the end, your research into the program, host and other guests—combined with your gut instinct—will no doubt tell you whether to say yes or no.

Other legitimate times to say no may be those rare occasions **when you cannot confirm that a free-lance writer or photographer is actually on assignment** for a publication or station. If you are not familiar with a person who says he/she works for the media, it is a good practice to call the news desk or assignment editor of the appropriate medium to verify the assignment. The editor in charge will be happy to take your call; no publication or station wants unaffiliated people posing as their staff reporters or stringers (writers in smaller markets who occasionally are assigned news stories and features for a large publication).

There may be rare situations when you or your organization have dealt with a particular reporter on several occasions and believe **he/ she has such a bias or is so careless** that almost all the resultant stories have been negative or inaccurate. A businesslike but candid discussion with the reporter's editor—in person rather than on the phone—will usually result in the assignment of another person to cover your company if your complaint is deemed valid by the editor. This is a last-resort action that should be taken only in exceptional cases when your allegations are well documented. Editors tend to be defensive of their reporters and profession, especially when criticized by the subject of an article.

## Other Helpful Hints

Here are some miscellaneous hints to help you anticipate (and thus be prepared to respond promptly to) reporters' requests:

1. **Be wary of sending out news releases with embargo dates**. They can be counterproductive to your organization's relations with the news media and to your objective of getting wide coverage of your news if one medium breaks the release date and scoops the others. As *PR News* pointed out in a discussion of the practice, "Traditionally embargoes have been used to give reporters time to digest complex issues or lengthy tomes well in advance of the release date. They've also been used to provide fair access. But that was before the 'press' became the 'media,' with the advent of broadcasting."[15] Unless you have a very special circumstance, it is safer to plan a release time that is good for you and the most important media covering your organization and then release the news with no embargo.

2. **When you are issuing a news release on an executive speech, make copies of the full text to have handy in case a reporter asks for it.** The request may be caused by the reporter's desire to rewrite or to expand on your news release. Or, the reporter may want to file the talk for use as background or source material in future stories. In any case, your anticipating such requests will enable you to get the speaker's agreement in advance to release the full speech—which can be annotated, if necessary, with the phrase "as prepared" or "as delivered" if there are or could be changes to the typed text. It also is a good idea to have copies of the speaker's biography and photo posted on your Web news site for those publications that regularly use photos.

3. **Documents filed with a government regulatory agency such as the Securities and Exchange Commission or at a courthouse as part of a trial automatically become part of the public record.** You can save the reporter some trouble, buy your organization goodwill and help assure that your position is accurately carried in the story by copying an extra set of such filings if a reporter requests it or providing the URL for the information online.

4. **Set up a file of biographies and photographs of your organization's key officers, managers and board members.** Create a standard form to be filled out, or write up a one-page narrative including such information. Ask for each person's community newspapers if you live in a large metropolitan area; sometimes news of your managers appearing in their local paper or alumni magazine means more to the family than coverage in a big city newspaper. Update the biographical data whenever there is a job change or every two years. Photos should be black-and-white formal studio shots, with identification on the photo file and new ones taken every five years at a minimum. You may also want to include some candid photos of your top executives—and some color shots if you expect TV coverage. Digital photography has made it easier to supply media with exactly what photographs they want, when they want them and in what format.

## Remember Your Organization's Employees

Your desire to be responsive to reporters' information requests cannot supersede your responsibility to the employees of your organization. They are your best ambassadors or loudest critics, depending on how fast they get relevant information and the context in which it is received. With global wire services, CNN and BBC World News, there is no such thing as "local" news. A layoff in Milan can make news in Madrid; an environmental problem in London can be on drive-time radio in the United States. And negative quotes from uninformed or angry employees can quickly undo an otherwise positive news media effort.

When you are making an announcement to the external media, you will want to coordinate the release time with the person responsible for internal communications so your employees do not read news of your organization in the local paper or on the Internet or hear it on a newscast before they learn of it from management. When there is an external leak ahead of the planned announcement time, you should immediately alert the employee communications person so a decision to advance the internal release can be considered. (Your colleagues should be equally considerate of you and provide advance copies of all employee communications materials so you are aware of what is covered in case they get into reporters' hands.)

Similarly, set up a close relationship with your customer service people. Be sure they have copies of your news releases, standby statements, and questions and answers, so they are giving out the same information to your customers that you are to the news media. When you know media coverage affecting your organization is going to appear, you should also alert your internal communications person. If a positive piece is expected—for example, a feature on one of your workers or an interview with your CEO—your employees will appreciate knowing in advance, especially if it is on radio or television, so they do not miss it. If a negative piece is upcoming, you will want to ensure that employees have your organization's position on the topic in case they get questions from their family, friends and customers.

Set up a high-traffic area like the cafeteria to demonstrate your publicity efforts in cyberspace and on TV. If the media coverage is significant enough, you should also consider an advance alert via phone, broadcast fax, e-mail, Internet or letter to your organization's board of directors or trustees, key customers or contributors and perhaps also send them a clipping, transcript, audio- or videotape after the event.

## Helpful Hints from Journalists and Media Relations Pros

Here is some advice from journalists and media relations pros on how media relations people can do a better job of meeting the media's needs:

According to Public Relations Institute of Australia surveys of journalists, "newsworthy" stories need to contain one or more following characteristics:

Impact—size, money, consequence

Timeliness—is it happening now?

Proximity—is there a "local angle" (of particular relevance to local newspapers)?

Novelty—is it the first ever? Is it otherwise unusual?

Prominence—is there a famous name involved?

Human interest—how will events and issues affect people?

Currency—does it reflect on current social issues?

—Media Skills Guide for UTS Staff

http://www.uts.edu.au/new/experts/mediaskills/mediaskills3.html

November 29, 2004

To begin with, know your target newspapers. Read them. Learn what kinds of stories they run. Don't bombard them with press releases just so you can assure your client you've shot off a thousand releases that day. That's killing trees for nothing. Most self-respecting papers don't run news releases anyway. At best, they use them to trigger story ideas.

—Bernie Silver, Managing Editor
*Silicon Valley/San Jose Business Journal*
April 20, 2001

Think like a reporter, ask the right questions and get the facts right. Be substantive. Ask what are the facts and what is the truth. Do your homework. Don't talk to the press until you're ready.

—Former White House Press Secretary Ari Fleischer
PRSA National Capital Chapter 33rd Annual Thoth Awards
June 7, 2001
Quoted in *O'Dwyer's PR Daily*, June 13 2001

The key to a successful relationship, of course, is symbiosis rather than parasitism—or, even worse, delusional, stalker-like tenacity. Proving your knowledge and worth even before you ask anything of the journalist is the best way of getting the first pitch considered. Like any relationship, you can't expect a home run on the first date.

—Eleanor Trickett
"Building relationships with reporters"
*PR Week*, January 14, 2002, p. 22

Know what makes a good story. When evaluating a potential story, journalists are not simply looking for information. They are looking for stories that:

**Reflect conflict.** Can the story hold the audience's interest by describing competing groups or competing individuals?

**Demonstrate human drama.** Who are the characters? A young scientist who dazzles colleagues, an old scientist who still has the passion, or middle-aged scientist who is motivated by personal tragedy or triumph?

—Jason Socrates Bardi
News & Views—The Scripps Research Institute
Vol. 4 Issue 20/ June 21, 2004
*http:www.scripps.edu/newsandviews/e_20040621/*
*print-science.html*

Dealing with reporters, winning their trust and working with them to promote one's organization constitute the most fundamental of PR objectives. A number of principles are important—among them, knowing what "news" is, understanding the "rules" of journalistic engagement, thinking strategically and generally treating all reporters in a professional manner.

—Fraser P. Seitel
"Media Relations Don'ts"
*O'Dwyer's PR Daily*, December 4, 2001

It doesn't matter whether or not you like the ground rules. You have to play the game.

—Anonymous

The best type of PR person is the one who is receptive when we call—who is willing to tell the company side of the story in bad situations and good. If the company comes forward with whatever they can say about what's happening, then the news media will report that. We are looking for information. We want to know your side of any story. I think the fairest reporting will come when a PR person is helpful and informative when the news is bad as well as good.

—Jim Scott, Assignment Editor
WISH-TV, Indianapolis

Never lie. If you don't want to answer the question, just say so. If you say, "I can't give you that information right now," I can accept that. I might not be happy as a reporter or an editor, but it won't make me lose my trust. People appreciate realness. If you are accessible . . . if you are open and honest . . . if you say, "Here's what I think and here's why," people will respect you and your organization whether or not they agree with your position.

—Dan Warner, former Editor
*Eagle Tribune*, Lawrence, Massachusetts

# 6

# Spokespersons

## Training and Briefing Them for Their Role

In Joseph Heller's book *Good as Gold*, the hero is invited to go to Washington and be a "reliable source." If he is good at it, he is told, he will be promoted to being a spokesman.[1] It is true that performing effectively as a public spokesperson often brings accolades from within and outside the organization. But, as with all high-risk, high-reward situations, there can be pitfalls.

When you are dealing with the media, any mistake is liable to be a very public one. Visions of a terrible *faux pas* splashed across the pages of the local newspaper or appearing on television screens in countless living rooms throughout the community tend to make our stomachs churn. Indeed, *The Book of Lists* ranks fear of public speaking ahead of death, flying and loneliness[2]—and talking with a reporter for attribution has to be the most public of public-speaking opportunities. No wonder people in our organizations react with something approaching terror at the thought of a media interview, especially on a sensitive subject.

An anecdote cited in journalism circles tells of a city editor who called a reporter to the city desk to point out a mistake in a story.

"Well," he said, "you already have made two-hundred-eighty thousand mistakes today and it is only noon." That "two-hundred-eighty thousand" was the paper's circulation figure. The comment impressed the reporter, and it should impress a spokesperson.

Like so many other talents, the skills required to be an effective spokesperson can be practiced and perfected. That associate whom you admire for the apparently natural ability to speak with clarity and confidence undoubtedly is as nervous as you are. But training and experience have helped him/her to master fear—or at least mask it. The late John O'Toole, former chairman of the board of the Foote, Cone & Belding advertising agency, pointed out in his book, *The Trouble with Advertising . . . :* "No matter what you do in life, your success at it relies heavily on your ability to communicate and explain your point of view to others in a way that will convince them to share it, or at least consider sharing it. This is called persuasion, and every human being is engaged in it constantly."[3]

A vital part of your job in media relations is your ability to be proficient enough in interview techniques and knowledgeable enough of the organization's policies and products that you can help your spokespersons prepare for news media contacts. At best this interview techniques training should be part of an ongoing program. At a minimum it should be included as part of the routine briefing session you have with your spokesperson before any media interview.

## Choosing a Spokesperson

Before discussing the support of spokespersons, it is well to step back and talk about selecting the right one. The choice is not as obvious or as easy as many people think. Indeed, it is one of the critical elements that will determine the success of your media coverage.

First of all, the obvious and frequent choice—the chief executive officer of your company or organization—is not always the best one. CEOs deal with broad, general, policy matters. Rarely are they involved in the nitty-gritty of the organization enough to know the details of a specific project or issue. Unless your CEO has a personal desire to be the primary spokesperson, you are better off reserving access to him/her for reporters whose article requires comments on overall policy or strategic direction.

Nor is the head of the department involved in the topic always the right person. Promotions in organizations normally are based on outstanding technical or professional knowledge and performance. Department heads may have the ability to make a presentation at an

internal meeting or to the board of directors, but this is not quite the same as being able to meet with reporters.

As the media relations person, you should become familiar with the abilities of others in your organization so you can choose the best spokesperson for each media opportunity. Here are the characteristics you are looking for:

1. **Above all, knowledge of the topic to be discussed with the reporter.** Only with a firm grounding in the facts can anyone speak confidently and positively.

2. **An understanding of the organization's overall objectives and strategies.** There is no way every one of the reporter's questions can be anticipated. You want someone who can think quickly and walk gracefully the fine line between being responsive to the reporter's needs and "giving away the store."

3. **An ability to tell and sell what he/she knows—in everyday language and from the point of view of the reporter and the ultimate** *audience.*

4. **The confidence of top management.** This person will be representing your organization to the general public. You do not want to choose someone who is not well respected by those within the organization.

5. **A desire to do the interview.** If your proposed spokesperson demurs beyond what normal modesty and apprehension would explain, you probably should drop your request. People tend to be honest with themselves; you should take heed when people believe they are poor choices for the assignment. There is a world of difference between being named a spokesperson and serving as one.

6. **Overall presentation style.** It is important to select someone with presence and personality. Also, your spokesperson should reflect the personality of the organization. A person wearing a three-piece suit is out of place representing a progressive, young computer software company. Similarly, a woman who wears a low-cut blouse and short skirt does not match the persona of a Wall Street financial institution.

## Preparing Your Spokesperson

Once you have determined who will be your organization's spokesperson for a particular interview, there is a great deal the media relations person can do to support the one who has accepted

this sensitive and important assignment. The fact that many of the steps with your spokesperson parallel those you are taking with the reporter is no coincidence. Indeed, your role as the bridge between the media and your organization is amply tested in an interview situation. The quality of your work will be reflected both in the resultant media coverage and in the spokesperson's response to your future requests to talk with reporters.

Immediately after you have set the appointment and determined whether the interview will be on the phone, online or in person, you should talk with your spokesperson and provide the following information:

1. **Date, time, place and expected length of interview.** If this is a new experience for this person, state that you will attend to take notes and get any follow-up information needed by the reporter.

2. **Type of story the reporter is working on**—in-depth feature on your organization or survey piece on your industry, for example. Has the reporter's conversation already indicated a clear point of view for the story? Or is she/he doing an overview piece and searching for a local angle?

3. **What the reporter told you he/she wants from the interview**—quotes on corporate objectives, general sales plans for a new product line, the organization's opinion of a new community development plan or whatever.

4. **What you have provided the reporter.** Describe briefly what information you already have given the reporter. List the materials you provided the reporter as part of the background package and include them as attachments to the e-mail or memo or go over them in person. Your objective here is to let the spokesperson know what already has been said to the reporter so the spokesperson can expand on it rather than merely repeat it.

5. **Background on the reporter**—if this is the first time the spokesperson has dealt with this particular journalist. Does the reporter regularly write stories on your organization, or is this a first? Does she/he understand the business, or will the spokesperson have to be especially careful to explain the terminology? What has been your experience with the reporter in earlier contacts? Does she/he take notes or use a tape recorder? It is a good idea to include samples of the reporter's recent stories—or suggest that the spokesperson tune in to the appropriate program if it is a TV or radio interview and you have enough advance notice. This is particularly important for talk shows like ABC's *Good Morning America*, PBS's *The News Hour with Jim Lehrer* or their local equivalents, because

journalists' interviewing styles vary widely. In some cases, squabbling has replaced dialogue in the pressure to keep things lively.

6. **If photography is involved, any special arrangements you are making for the photographer or television crew.** Explain the set-up time required for TV production, especially if the interview is taking place in the spokesperson's office. Or arrange to move the interview to another office or location.

7. **Suggestions on the main message and one or two key points you think the spokesperson should stress in the interview.** Here is where you make your greatest contribution, not only as a media relations professional but also as a counselor to your organization.

8. **Advice on key interview techniques.** See the section, "Hints on Interview Techniques," for a full review of such advice. It is presented as a unit so that you easily can use all or part of the section when working with your spokesperson.

9. **Insist on the need to get together to review anticipated questions and possible answers before the actual interview.** This initial backgrounding is important. If the interview is two or three days hence, this preparation helps the spokesperson focus thoughts and prepare responses. If the interview is later that same day or early the next (as so frequently is the case) it provides a framework in which to operate. Your briefing session just before the interview is likely to be more concerned with content than logistics.

## Prior to the Interview

Media relations people should make it a routine practice to get together with the spokesperson for a briefing before the interview. Executives' calendars are crowded—but a half-hour meeting together before the reporter arrives is time well spent. It gives you both an opportunity to talk about your main message, review expected questions, constructively critique proposed answers, look at alternative ways to highlight key points, and discuss the thrust of this particular journalist and article.

It is a good idea to prepare for the worst-case scenario. Talk about the questions you most hope the reporter will *not* ask, and agree on your answers. Write them down and sharpen them until you are comfortable the spokesperson is presenting your organization's case in the best possible way without being defensive. Get others' input, including legal counsel, if the issues are sensitive.

You also can work out a plan to end the interview if the reporter appears to be getting long-winded or repetitive. You should remind

the spokesperson to tell the reporter that follow-up information will be channeled through you. For a phone interview you can alert the spokesperson not to be unnerved by a request to tape the conversation or by the keyboard sounds of a computer. Indeed, it is positive feedback that the reporter's questions are being well answered, since many journalists do not take notes until they hear a newsworthy comment.

If there will be photographs, it also can be helpful to remind your spokesperson to be tolerant of what may appear to be strange requests to move objects or rearrange poses. The photographer likely is looking for ways to get an interesting picture out of what is essentially a routine setting.

## During the Interview

Your role as media relations person during the interview is to make introductions and then let the reporter take over while you take notes, interjecting only if a statement needs clarifying, a number requires verifying or a promise of follow-up information should be made. If you are physically near the spokesperson during a phone interview, you might want to pass a note if you believe the person has missed an opportunity to make a key point or has made a statement that needs further explanation.

A decision to tape the interview—whether or not the reporter is doing so—should be made with care. Some reporters who consider it normal for a media relations person to take notes are offended if you ask to tape the session. On the other hand, if you are reluctant to honor a reporter's request not to tape because a reporter or program has a reputation for distortion, you may want to insist on taping as a condition for your spokesperson to be interviewed.

## Follow-up after the Interview

For the media relations person the job is not over after the interview. At the same time you are following up on your obligations to the reporter, you should devote similar attention to the interviewee.

Right after the interview you should call your spokesperson with feedback—giving both your impressions (helpful for the next time) and the reporter's (whose reaction right after the interview is a good indication of the probable tone of the story and thus should be shared with the spokesperson). If the reporter is critical, you will want to

think carefully about how much detail you pass along—and how you communicate it.

If you foresee a potential problem in the resultant coverage that you cannot resolve with the reporter, go ahead and mention it. Your spokesperson would rather be alerted in advance than blindsided when the story appears. If the spokesperson did a particularly bad job, either confusing the reporter with poorly stated points or blithely releasing proprietary information, you will probably need to find a different spokesperson in the future for that area of your operation.

As soon as the story appears, check the quotations and facts for accuracy. If it is print coverage, always get a copy of the article to the interviewee in advance of wider circulation within your organization. Offer your reaction—and get the spokesperson's.

If it is radio or TV coverage, purchase a transcript or a tape from those tracking firms that sell such services.

If it is on the News Web site, forward a link or the story to the spokesperson as quickly as possible.

## Hints on Interview Techniques

Most reporters are far too sophisticated to be impressed by style over substance. Conversely, a fine position can be misunderstood if it is not presented with clarity and confidence. Interviews are not conversations—they are highly structured situations.

Some of television's top news people support your becoming more skilled in interview techniques. "It makes perfect sense to me because people should have every opportunity to make the best case they can for themselves," Mike Wallace told the *Washington Journalism Review*.[4] The late John Chancellor, longtime news anchor at NBC TV, added, "It's okay to bone-up for an interview as long as it teaches one not to hide the facts."[5]

Formal media interview techniques training—especially with an outside expert—is well worth the investment, for you and for others who will be spokespersons for your organization. Make sure the firm you select can provide the individualized training your spokespersons need, from television appearances to telephone interviews, from in-person to online. Even if your spokespersons have a great deal of experience, they can make mistakes if they get overconfident or complacent.

Here are some interview techniques that should help you do a better job when you are interviewed by a reporter.

- **Remember your objective.** Is your purpose in doing the interview merely to *inform* the reporter's audience of some event or action? Or are you attempting to *persuade* people to adopt your point of view? *Inspire* them to change their behavior? *Motivate* them to take some particular action? Your ultimate objective will have a great impact on what you say and how you say it.

- **Prepare and practice.** Mark Twain once said it takes three weeks to prepare a good ad-lib speech. Have in mind one key message that you want to get across in the finished story. Ask yourself, "If I could edit the article that will come out of this interview, what one sentence would I most like to see?" Or, "If I could write the headline, what would it say?" Well in advance of the interview, write them out. Try to simplify and shorten them. Some people think if it is complicated it is clever. But Winston Churchill advised, "Short words are best and the old words when short are best of all."[6] Practice saying them out loud so they sound natural to the ear. Perfectly proper sentences in a written text are often too formal and cumbersome when spoken aloud. If it is a phone interview, keep your key points in front of you. Then at the earliest opportunity, try to capsulize your main points in answer to an interview question.

- **Simplify, simplify, simplify.** Communications consultant Ann Wylie says, "what we used to call information overload has gone way beyond that. Now we suffer from 'fact fog' and 'data smog'; we're drowning in an information deluge." She advises spokespersons to rethink the way they deliver information and "simplify, simplify, simplify."[7] That is your best chance to have your message break through the clutter of competing messages and options for your target audience's time and attention. It is impossible to tell everyone everything about your organization. So do not waste effort on unnecessary baggage or battles. Simplify the message and send it with consistency and clarity.

- **Place your most important points at the beginning of each response where they will be clear and isolated.** In 15 words or less, what is the essence of your message? In TV or radio interviews, this is especially important because broadcast journalists are looking for a very short "sound bite." Responses like "There are three reasons for that" invite poor editing. Rather say, "Price, performance and reliability are the key factors in our decision." Try to get your main message down to 9 or 10 seconds which, sadly, are too often all a spokesperson gets when the TV editing is complete.

- **It is not only what you say but also how you say it that communicates.** The effective speaker is not necessarily polished and

---

### Interviewing Hints and Tricks

- Don't let down your guard during an interview. You are most vulnerable when you let your mind wander. Stay focused, regardless of how long the interview might last.

- Whenever you hear "What if . . ." from a reporter, know that your answer, however speculative, will be open to wide interpretation by readers, viewers and listeners. It's best to refocus the question to a factual content and avoid all hypothetical situations.

- Respond to negatives with a positive. Aggressive reporters often use a negative line of questioning to put you or your CEO on edge. Deflating that stance takes patience, focus and a steady supply of positive, supportive data on your topic.

- "For example . . ." are the two words reporters most enjoy. They are not experts in your field so examples help bring focus to your information.

- Use "bridging" to help move the interview in a positive direction, such as "Let's look at this from the perspective of the customer . . ."

- Avoid: "As I said in my presentation . . .", "As stated in our annual report . . . ", "As you know . . ." The reporter may not have heard the presentation, read the annual report, and s/he doesn't know. That's why you're having the interview.

---

perfect. He/she is energetic, enthusiastic and direct. A forthright, enthusiastic response to a question portrays candor and confidence—in your organization, in your position, in the reporter, in yourself. Long pauses before you answer or a stiff, flat monotone indicate either a lack of conviction or a lack of interest. If the interview is being televised, this appearance of indecision and insincerity will be magnified.

- **You should not feel pressured to respond instantly to a difficult question on a complex subject.** Although we have just mentioned the possible negative effect of a pause before answering, it sometimes is appropriate to take a moment to organize your thoughts. When you are making instant history—or instant policy—you have the right to be comfortable with the way you articulate your organization's role. In a print interview you can verbalize the pause by saying something like, "I hadn't thought of it from that viewpoint before. . . ."

- **Think fast but talk slowly.** If the reporter is taking notes, it will help the accuracy. If you are being taped for broadcast—audio or video—it will help your audience's comprehension. For broadcast, however, you will want to speak a little bit faster because sound bites are getting shorter and shorter.

- **Never forget your ultimate audience.** You are talking to a reporter, but you are speaking to the people who read the publication or watch the program—your past, present and potential customers, employees, shareowners and suppliers. (If none of these audience segments is being reached by the reporter's medium, you can legitimately ask your media relations person and yourself why you are doing the interview.) Frame your answers from their point of view, not your organization's. For example, say, "Our customers now have three new colors to choose from," rather than "We have expanded our color selection." Or, "If this bill becomes law there will be significantly fewer parks where you can take your family," rather than "Our industry is opposing this legislation because. . . ."

- **Always include the "me factor."** The Zen masters have a good approach: "Tell me what window you are looking through and I will tell you what you see." It is crucial to appreciate your audience's viewpoint in order to understand how they will react to your message. The key word is *benefit*. If you can enunciate the benefit to each individual's life or family or career or wallet, you will turn a nod of agreement into a spark of interest—and, ultimately, action. People listen and respond in terms of their own lives. What are you telling them that will make their lives easier, more fun, richer or more rewarding?

- **Choose your pronouns carefully.** Don't call the company "it"; you, your staff and your spokesperson should think of your organization as "we" and "us," and your audience as "you." These pronouns convey a personal, interactive image of your organization. "We" demonstrates your synonymy with your organization and eliminates the egotistical ring of "I."

- **Humanize your responses by giving a little bit of your own personality as well as the organization's position.** Too often when we start to communicate a business message we freeze and start sounding more like a machine than a person. Your field is interesting to you. Make it equally interesting to the reporter. In addition to providing the reporter with a "quotable quote," you may help destroy the myth that all business people are stodgy and boring, particularly if you work for a large corporation. Retired Chrysler Corporation Chairman Lee A. Iacocca gave a notable and quotable response when asked, "What about mergers—any marriages yet?" "No," replied Iacocca, "but I think I've been kissed."[8]

- **Be sure your messages reinforce your organization's overall branding.** Each product or service has its own unique character and strengths that you need to articulate and build on to position it clearly with your target publics. Stay focused and pay attention to consistency. Whether communicating with reporters or financial analysts, employees or consumers, on the Internet or in traditional media, be sure your messages and key points always support the personality and performance of your brand. Learn from advertising, where repetition is a sacred tool. Repeat anything often enough—and simply enough—and it will be *remembered*. Base it on facts and back it up with performance and it will be *believed*.

- **Do not be embarrassed if a number or detail is not at hand, and do not guess.** Simply tell the reporter that your media relations person will get it. Also, don't feel obliged to accept a figure or fact the reporter cites. Say you are not familiar with it and offer to have it checked. Never—repeat, *never*—have other staff people in the room with you. Surrounded by too many advisers, you may appear to be an obedient Gulliver surrounded by Lilliputians. The reporter wants your views and comments, not facts and figures, from the interview. Your delegating such follow-up detail means your train of thought will not be interrupted and you will be perceived as an expert not concerned with minutia. As well, it explicitly reminds the reporter that the media relations person is and should continue to be the one entrance point to the organization.

- **Do not let a reporter put words in your mouth.** Whenever you hear the phrases, "Are you saying that . . .?" or "Do you mean . . .?" or "Isn't it really . . .?" alarm bells should ring in your head. Mishandling this type of question can result in your feeling your words were reflected back by a fun-house mirror when the final story appears. If you do not like the way a question is stated, do not repeat it in your response—even to deny it. The reporter's question will not appear in print. Your answer will. It is better to respond in a positive way, using your own words, not the reporter's. For example, if a reporter asks if one of your products is overpriced compared to the competition, don't say, "I wouldn't want to use the term 'overpriced.'" You just did! Instead, say what you would want to say: "We believe our products provide high value for the price. For example . . ." and go on to list the features. This is particularly important in a television interview, when time constraints will force severe editing. You want to be sure your main point is right up front in every answer, in case you are on the air with only one sentence. Look back at this example to see what a one-sentence edit would do to you.

- **Look for the hidden agenda in questions.** If a reporter is probing your recent hiring of salespeople proficient in certain skills, the resultant article may say that your company is in the midst of a marketing build-up to launch a new product line.

- **Never say you do not know an answer when in fact you do.** A good reporter will know—or find out—that you should have known the information and may be antagonized by your claiming ignorance. If a question that is not in the best interests of your organization is posed to you, explain why you won't answer it. And, as discussed previously, avoid "No comment."

- **Keep your cool.** More and more these days, interviewers deliberately frame their questions in emotional or accusatory tones, going for "attitude" or "edge" in their story. It is just a technique to get you to say something controversial. Do not let it work. It is okay to be angry; it is not okay to lose your cool.

- **Understand that the reporter may be starting out with negative opinions about you or your organization.** These opinions may stem from ongoing publicity about inflated executive salaries or by the fact that few journalists have training or experience in business or because they don't like your product. The interview is your opportunity to turn that opinion around.

- **Avoid tongue twisters.** We all have heard someone stumble on words like "specificity." Choose words with a minimum of S's so you do not sound like a hissing snake—an especially important hint for radio.

- **Avoid using jargon.** When a reporter interrupts with what seem to be basic clarifying questions—or, in the case of an interview with a foreign reporter, if the interpreter pauses and looks puzzled—it may be that you have unconsciously dropped into obscure professional or industry jargon. Look for ways to explain your point with simple illustrations or analogies from everyday life. In AT&T's highly technical business we had success with comparisons such as, "The first transistors looked like little top hats on stilts." Felix G. Rohatyn, the articulate investment banker from Lazard Freres & Company who helped lead New York City's perilous move from the edge of bankruptcy in the mid-1970s, even figured out how to describe that financial concept: "Bankruptcy is like someone stepping into a tepid bath and slashing his wrists—you might not feel yourself dying, but that's what would happen."[9]

- **Avoid "frankly," "to tell you the truth," and "to be honest."** These expressions serve no useful purpose. In fact, they may backfire on you by raising the question of how frank or truthful or honest you have been in all the rest of your interview if you suddenly say that you are going to be "frank" or "truthful" or "honest" with the reporter now.

- **Avoid negatives.** "No, we are not discriminating against women" is not as convincing as "We have a broad program to actively recruit more women managers." President Richard Nixon gave us an infamous example of what *not* to do when he said, "I am *not* a crook." Most people listen selectively and visualize while they listen. So more people pictured and remembered the word "crook" than caught the "not" in front of it.

- **Consider what your words will mean to others.** You don't want to be as parochial as Humpty Dumpty, who told Alice, "When I use a word it means just what I choose it to mean—neither more nor less." Frequently the same word can have different meanings to different audiences. A terminal in the computer business is a piece of equipment—but to many people it is a place where you catch a bus. William Safire offered another example: "To many a depression is what you take to a psychiatrist, not an economist."[10]And in the international arena there are classic stories of misunderstandings caused by a poor choice of words. If your organization actively sells its products or services globally, make sure your spokespersons and translators are very familiar with the language, including local idioms, of each country where you do business.

- **Look at each question from the public's point of view.** For example, if a reporter says, "You don't have many Hispanic supervisors, do you?" don't counter with "Our record is terrific. We're doing much better than most companies." That sounds defensive. Instead, be positive in your answers. You might say, "We still don't have enough Hispanic supervisors, although we are making progress. [Such and such] percent of our supervisors are Hispanic and we have these specific programs . . ."

- **Be realistic in your answers.** Veteran PR counselor Chester Burger reminds us that the best media relations campaign in the world "can't build trust while reality is destroying it."[11] And Arthur Page, an AT&T vice president who in essence founded the field of corporate PR as a strategic management function, taught that "while well-thought-out communications programs are vital to an organization's success, they must be based on the reality of its performance and not on Madison Avenue slogans." Page summed up his philosophy in a single sentence: "Public relations is 90 percent doing and 10 percent talking about it."[12]

- **Respond to a simple question with a simple answer.** Short, simple answers are better than long, complicated ones. A few sentences using everyday language give the interviewer less opportunity to misunderstand you. And on TV, where time is measured in dollars, this is especially important. In fact, in a TV interview you should be sure to make your key points in 10 or 20 seconds.

- **Never underestimate the intelligence of your audience—and never overestimate their knowledge.** We are not suggesting you adjust your prose to the words used by high school sophomores, but you must explain your terms, especially when you are covering a difficult subject. Two hours after a recent interview, a reporter phoned the media relations person to plead for a translation: "That interview reminded me of my college physics classes," she said. "I understood it while the professor was talking but when I got back to my room, I couldn't explain it."

- **Speak in the active voice.** Avoid the passive, which places the doer of the action at the end of the sentence or sometimes eliminates responsibility altogether. Say, "We will be moving our offices," not "Our offices will be moved." You want to portray your organization as a group of interesting, concerned people who decide and do things, rather than as a faceless, inanimate group. Similarly, don't duck responsibility for difficult actions. Say, "We reluctantly have decided that a layoff of some of our employees is required," not "The economy has forced a layoff." Companies don't make decisions or establish policies—people do.

- **Do not waste your brief time with a reporter by arguing against the other side.** You may want to refute their point of view but inadvertently end up giving valuable media exposure to their position. Instead, stay on *your* message. State your case positively, without mentioning your opponents by name. If you are forced to refer to your adversaries, avoid emotional labels such as "chauvinist" or "radical." Use "less experienced observers" or "the other side" instead.

- **Do not be offended by a reporter's questions about what you consider private or proprietary areas.** As Robert MacNeil, founder of PBS's *MacNeil/Lehrer Report*, explained in his autobiography, being a journalist is "a lifelong license to follow that most basic human trait, curiosity. . . . It is permission to probe and delve into whatever interests you as thoroughly or as superficially as you like. . . ."[13] True—but as a spokesperson it is your prerogative and responsibility to decide how much you want to say in your answer. If the questioning moves into proprietary or confidential areas, simply explain that providing such information would be too helpful to your competitors. When the questioning gets too personal, wit can be a good defense. Former President Ronald Reagan practiced this technique with the best of them: "Our family didn't exactly come from the wrong side of the tracks," he said of his beginnings, "but we were certainly always within the sound of the train whistles."[14] Broadening your response to divert attention from the narrow, personal nature of the question is a good tactic—particularly during a television interview. A female politician asked how she balances her duties to her husband, children and the public might reply: "That question clearly illustrates the problems faced by so many American women who are working mothers . . ."

- **Do not respond to a narrow question with an equally narrow answer.** Rather, take the opportunity to reiterate one of your key points. For example, if you are being interviewed on a downsizing and are asked how many people will be out of work, do not just say "about seven hundred." Instead, reply directly to the question and then immediately expand on it: "About seven hundred, and we are doing everything we can to help soften the blow. We will phase down operations gradually over the next six months. We have generous severance payments. And we are setting up an outplacement center to help our people look for other jobs."

- **Do not answer hypothetical questions.** Instead, particularize them with: "That's a hypothetical question so it is impossible to know what might happen. But let me tell you exactly what did happen in a similar case. . . ."

- **Never, absolutely never, lie to a reporter.** You may get away with it once or twice, but ultimately you will be found out. Then not only you but also your organization will have lost a priceless asset: credibility. As Winston Churchill put it: "To build may have to be the slow and laboring task of years. To destroy can be the thoughtless act of a single day."

- **Be yourself.** If you like to sit around a conference table when you are meeting with your staff, that is likely a fine place for the interview; you will feel comfortable and the reporter will have a surface on which to write and/or place a tape recorder. If you prefer to emphasize your points by drawing diagrams on an easel, do it. If you love sports, it is perfectly appropriate to use an analogy from the football field to illustrate your point. If your taste leans more to music, feel free to make a comparison using an orchestra as a metaphor. The reporter wants your perspective—not that of a well-trained but impersonal robot who gives the impression of speaking fluently but formally in a foreign language.

## Hints for Television Appearances

When you stare into the eye of a television camera and see that little red light go on, you are bluntly reminded that there is a huge audience out there who will see and hear whatever you say. Stage fright caused by the camera's relentless gaze and TV's wide exposure is natural, no matter how frequently you are videotaped. There are many things you can do in advance to prepare for the particular demands of television.

Appearances definitely *do* count on television. Its power in politics first became clear in the initial Kennedy–Nixon debate in the U.S. presidential race of 1960. Polls showed that those who heard the debate on radio thought Nixon had won, whereas those who watched the event on TV named Kennedy the winner. These days, executives appearing on C-SPAN while they are being grilled in Congress can appear evasive or "guilty as charged" if they forget the power of the TV camera.

**First of all is the choice of what to wear.** Blue is still the preferred choice for both men and women. But most other colors are equally good. **What you want to avoid are extremes**—either small, busy patterns or large, bold stripes on your tie, shirt, blouse or jacket. Solid colors are best, but you should leave pure white or solid black home in the closet.

Do not wear a large amount of jewelry, especially if it is bright, because it will cause the cameras to "flare," distracting viewers with a starburst of light. Men should wear calf-length socks in case they want to cross their legs on camera.

If you have a tan, do not get a haircut just before the interview in case your tan line is uncovered. Men with heavy "five o'clock shadow" should shave just before the crew arrives. Women should not wear too much make-up, especially eye shadow; the right amount for work is normally the right amount for television. Men should not refuse a little powder just before the cameras roll; if a TV technician makes the suggestion it means some perspiration is visible on the TV monitor's view of you—not surprising considering the bright lights and a normal amount of nervousness.

**All of the techniques you practiced to help present your position persuasively to print journalists apply to television—only**

**more so.** It is critically important that you speak in sound-bite headlines. **Make your points short and simple.** TV's formula is to use perhaps 100 words from the reporter and a "sound bite" of 10 to 20 words from the speaker.

Keep two facts in mind: First, television is a visual medium, so what the eye sees is more important than what the ear hears. And second, the camera magnifies whatever it sees. It sounds trite, but you should act naturally. Do not smile when it is not appropriate—you will look phony, not friendly. Do not gesture wildly or move suddenly—the camera may lose you altogether. Do not stare upward into space when you are thinking—you will look like you are praying for divine guidance.

If you are being videotaped in your office, you or your media relations person should suggest other attractive areas of your operation for shootings, or provide "already in the can" background footage. **Think visually.** Television is at its best when it can show something happening. A picture of nothing but a person—a "talking head"—is visually boring. Your chances for coverage will be immeasurably improved if you make it easy for the program's producer to illustrate what you are saying.

Take a look at existing props in your office that may appear on camera if the interview is taped there. Family photographs add a warm touch. But a plaque with two small gold axes presented as an award for an expense-reduction program can give the wrong impression if the interview is on layoffs or moving operations offshore.

Television is an intimate medium. You will be speaking not to the "general public" but rather to individual people—mom and dad in the family room, a tired worker dozing in the den, someone catching up with ironing while watching the news. Legendary journalist Eric Sevareid said he tried "to remember always that the public is only people, and people only persons, no two alike."

Normally the interview will be videotaped and then severely edited before being aired. Many times TV reporters will ask you the same question several times in different ways. They are giving their editors a variety of versions and lengths from which to choose. It may be disconcerting to have the reporter pay more attention to a stopwatch than to your words, and it may seem unnecessarily repetitive to be asked the same question. You should take the opportunity to sharpen your answer. **No matter how often you are asked, you should always include your main point in each answer—right up front—said in different ways, of course.** When the tape is edited, only one response will be left—and you and the reporter both want it to be a clear and concise statement.

**Do not be intimidated by a reporter with a microphone** during a fast-breaking "spot news" situation. An unnerving interview technique is to thrust the mike at you and then pull it back when the reporter has what he/she wants. You gain regain control of the interview with a smile and saying, "I haven't finished answering the last question yet," and go back to making your point.

**Assume you are on the air all the time when being interviewed on television.** And also remember: you are always *on* the record. Bright lights and a quiet room are no longer needed for an interview.

Sometimes attempts to be pleasant and polite can backfire. Try to avoid nodding as the reporter talks. It could be viewed on camera as acknowledgment of the premise behind the question. Similarly, be careful about saying, "That's a good point" after a negative question. Tight editing could wipe out the rest of your response.

## Hints for Radio

A radio interview has some different characteristics. Unless it is a major news story, the station will use only a very brief segment (10 to 20 seconds) of your interview—although it is likely to rebroadcast the item several times, perhaps using different sound bites each time. **So it is even more important that you make your main points succinctly.** Also, radio rarely uses the reporter's questions on the air. Before you answer you should pause a moment to be sure the questioner is finished and you are not "stepping on that person's line." You will ensure cleaner edits and warm thoughts from the audio engineer.

You are not seen by anyone, so **you can have your key points written out and handy where you can see and read them easily.**

**Practice out loud.** If you sound awkward or must gasp for breath, shorten your sentences and eliminate difficult phrases. You want to guard against sounding like you are reading a prepared response—on the air you will sound terribly stilted. You should speak in a conversational tone as you would with a friend on the phone.

During the interview **you should gesture as you would during a normal conversation;** it will help both your voice and your body to relax. As well, smile when you talk; it will make your voice sparkle and also help you to relax.

Be sure to **repeat your company or brand name several times during the interview.** People listening on the radio have no visuals to remind them who you are and what you are talking about. So your need to paint repeated word pictures for your messages to be remembered.

## Hints for News Conferences

When you are participating in a news conference, you have the obligation not only to answer reporters' questions but also to make a few opening remarks giving the purpose of the conference and formally announcing the news that caused it. Answering questions at a news conference is very similar to being interviewed except that you have more than one person asking questions and you are not in the comfortable surroundings of your own office. Making the opening remarks at a conference is much like giving a brief speech. As you look out over the crowd of cameras, lights, microphones, and people peering up at you expectantly, you may feel like a mother robin perched on the edge of her nest looking into the hungry, gaping mouths of her babies. Much like the mother bird, your obligation is to feed the media—that is, provide them with news in an interesting way in the shortest period of time. The same techniques you use for interviews and TV appearances will serve you well here.

**Before the news conference, come to the room to familiarize yourself with the set-up.** Work out signals with your media relations person as cues if you begin speaking too quickly or answering reporters' questions too abruptly. Then leave, and use the time to practice what you intend to say—and perhaps to go for a brisk walk to clear your mind.

**Do not show up again until immediately before the news conference is scheduled to start. Do not mingle with reporters ahead of time.** Whether you are introduced by your media relations person or open the news conference yourself is up to you. In any case, ignore the many microphones that are placed on the podium. *Do not ask if everyone can hear you*—it is the responsibility of the audio engineers and your media person to ensure all the mike levels are correct. Just begin your formal remarks, speaking slowly and clearly and following your text closely if it has been included in the press kit materials. Like any attentive participant, the TV camera will be focused on you. But if you become long-winded or the cameraperson's attention wanes, the camera may scan the listeners—particularly that station's reporter—for reaction shots. If things really get dull the little red light will go off as the technician turns the camera off altogether.

**After your introductory talk, open the session up to questions.** Use an open phrase like "Now I would be happy to answer your questions" or "What are your questions?" rather than the closed construction "Does anyone have any questions?" If you do not know them all, ask the journalists to give their names and publications or stations as they are called on. Do not pace around, or the microphones and TV cameras will have trouble following you.

If there are no questions right away, do not panic. The reporters probably are reviewing their notes on your opening remarks and framing questions that will appeal to their readers or viewers. Simply wait a few minutes (it will seem like hours) and then invite questions again. Or point to a reporter you know and say "Susan, you usually have a good question for me." If there still are none, thank the reporters for coming and say you are available for individual questions if they wish.

More likely, the questions will start popping several at a time. Once you select a reporter to ask a question, keep your eyes on her/him as much as possible while you answer. This will keep other reporters from interrupting and help the reporter's camera crew get both of you on tape if they so desire. Allow one follow-up question from that journalist—but then establish eye contact with another questioner so one person is not able to dominate.

Use the reporter's name in your answer whenever possible. Do not be unnerved if someone moves around with a hand-held camera or even crawls up to the podium on hands and knees to adjust a microphone or test the lighting with a light meter. You probably will be asked several similar questions by TV people, because broadcast editors generally like to show their own reporters on the screen asking questions. So don't hesitate to repeat your key point in answer to each question—again, only one version will appear on each channel—and be sure *not* to say, "As I said in response to an earlier question . . ."

**If very few journalists have shown up, you should proceed as planned.** But if the small turnout is obvious, you may wish to acknowledge it with a light comment such as "Ladies and gentlemen, it looks like you will have an exclusive by coming here today . . ." and conduct the session in a less formal manner.

Equally important is for your media relations person to be prepared with everything from extra chairs to additional press kits in case many more people than expected show up. But if they are non-media people, they should politely but firmly be kept out of the news conference room. Journalists do not appreciate an audience, which can create distractions and generate noises picked up by the sensitive TV and radio audio equipment. And you are likely to be nervous enough without having kibitzers present.

Twenty to 30 minutes is the normal length of a news conference. Nevertheless, if questions are still coming, you may decide to go a few minutes over the scheduled time. You can end the conference yourself or have your media relations person do so by announcing that you have time for one more question.

**Mingle afterwards with reporters** in case they want private interviews or individual on-camera shots of you talking with them. But remember that everything you say during these conversations is also on the record. Therefore, you should be no less careful with your comments than you were when you were at the podium.

## Interview No-Nos

Here are some topics to avoid when you are talking with reporters, since they inevitably cause misunderstandings.

* **Do not ask if you can review the story in advance.** Just as the reporter cannot expect to see your annual report or latest product plans until you are ready to make them public, so you cannot have advance access to their reporting of the news.

* **Do not mention how much your organization advertises in the reporter's medium.** No reputable publication or station permits its editorial judgment to be influenced by advertising, and you may unwittingly insult the reporter's personal and professional codes of behavior.

* **Do not tell broadcast reporters you think 30 or 60 seconds is too short a time to tell your story adequately.** They are no more satisfied with the time constraints they work under than you are. Only 21 or 22 minutes of a half-hour network television news program are devoted to news; the rest is commercials.

* **Do not tell a reporter you will provide written answers to questions if he/she will send them to you.** The media is not in the business of taking dictation. That type of exchange probably is too time-consuming to meet the news deadlines. In any case, it will make the reporters think you are hiding something because you will not talk face to face.

* **Do not ask a reporter to keep what you say "off the record."** Perhaps the public's perspective was permanently changed by so much talk of "deep background" in the Woodward/Bernstein chronicle, *All the President's Men.* Remember that the sole reason a reporter is interviewing you is literally *for* the record—that is, to write and produce a story for publication or airing. Editors are adamant that their reporters identify their sources in all but the most unusual cases. Presidents and secretaries of state may wish to continue demanding off-the-record status for their remarks, but it is a much safer practice for the rest of us to assume everything we

utter will be attributed. Thus, we should not say anything we would not want publicly associated with ourselves or our organization unless we have a long relationship and a special understanding with a particular reporter.

# 7

# Ethics

## What's Happened to the Golden Rule?

$A$t the height of the 2004 Presidential race, CBS News' *60 Minutes* program ran a story alleging that President George W. Bush had received preferential treatment as a young officer in the Texas Air National Guard.

In the weeks that followed, in spite of repeated reports from other media, bloggers and online commentators that the story was based on false information, CBS continued to hold its ground.

"What Dan Rather and the CBS News brass have done over the last two weeks is nothing less than classic corporate foot-dragging and stonewalling worthy of any Enron out there. Delay, deny, defend, justify, rationalize, mince words, and parse sentences," noted one observer.[1]

In January 2005, CBS fired one of its executives and asked three others to resign following the release of an independent report that cited "myopic zeal" as the culprit in the issuance of the flawed story.

The venerable *New York Times* took a major hit in 2003 when Jayson Blair, a *Times* reporter, resigned amidst charges that he committed "egregious plagiarism and fabrications" in a story about the family of an American solider serving in Iraq.[2]

A 25-member committee, headed by then assistant managing editor Allan Siegal, investigated the charges and, in doing so, found numerous problems regarding the *Times'* internal management system and policies. As a result, the newspaper appointed its first-ever ombudsperson, an independent reader representative. Also, two senior newspaper editors resigned.

These two highly publicized scandals within the hallowed halls of major U.S. media giants sent tremors across the country. If we can't trust journalists as the best of the best, who can we trust?

Although both CBS News and *The New York Times* could have acted in ways to prevent the incidents from ever happening and could have acted more quickly upon hearing the first vestiges of suspicion, they nonetheless have provided two case studies in ethics recovery.

In other words, any suspicion of wrongdoing requires independent investigations, full and open reporting on the results of the investigations, the firing and/or resignations of the key personnel involved in the deceit, and changed internal policies and management. In short: tell the truth, fix the problem. "Telling the truth," observes Kirk Hanson, executive director of the Markkula Center for Applied Ethics at Santa Clara University, "has been taking a beating from virtually every segment of our society." From politicians to company presidents, sport figures to judges, CEOs to the Catholic Church, the record is not very good.[3]

The appetite for uncovering business malpractice has reached unprecedented heights, primarily because of the advent of tabloid, Internet, and infotainment journalism, which seek—and find—the sensational in business, city government, the entertainment world, the small-town community, royal families and even grief-stricken families. "Freedom of the press" is redefined daily, with proponents seeing little reason not to monitor probes into lives and programs; opponents argue that "freedom" has become a legal way to pry unnecessarily, to peer into people's lives, bedrooms, boardrooms and institutions. Hanson notes that the communication environment in which we live can be held accountable for much of the zeal. More data is being collected about people and events. There are more news outlets competing for attention. We're living in a "gotcha" culture. And we're seeing an assault on privacy with very little in the way of "zones of privacy." The net result is that there are fewer secrets of any kind.[4] The question then becomes: where does ethical behavior begin and end?

Ethics is the hot topic of today with a proliferation of professional codes of ethics and numerous allegations of unethical practices. Ethics should be easy to recognize and define. But it is not, especially as the world becomes more homogenous and the ethics of one society are looked upon as ridiculous by another. Businesses in one region operate under different laws, mores and structures than businesses in another region.

Chester Burger, veteran PR counselor, suggests: "Ethics are nothing but standards of behavior."[5] Studies have shown that the general public readily understands what ethics are and that if ethics appear in the headlines, the story will tell about the lack of ethics.

Lou Williams, president of L. C. Williams & Associates in Chicago, has lamented:

> I must admit I'm constantly amazed at the continuing level of distrust between journalists and public relations folks. Is all of journalism an NBC report playing questionable tricks on GM trucks? Of course not. Is all PR a search for the big story placement? Of course not. There are good and bad reporters, just as there are good and bad publicists.[6]

## Lying or Spinning?

Caught in the suspicion of a lie, or actually caught in a lie, are the two situations in which companies most often continue to lie. However, hard evidence continues to show that the sooner the truth comes out, the sooner the story dies. A lie is a lie is a lie. No good comes of lying; particularly, no good comes from lying to the media. Eventually a lie will come out in print or on television.

Lanny J. Davis, former special counsel to President Bill Clinton, and George Stephanopoulos, former senior political advisor to Clinton and currently chief Washington correspondent for ABC News, describe in their respective books how the White House team routinely delayed getting information to the media or resorted to lying or misleading the media, rather than telling the truth quickly, expeditiously and thoroughly, actions which both men found to be counterproductive. While both also talk about "spin control," Davis elucidates: "Facts are facts—and no amount of spinning will alter those facts." He defines "good spin" as a way to minimize the damage—by surrounding bad facts with context, with good facts (if there are any) and, if possible, with credible, favorable (or less damaging) interpretation.[7]

"Lie once and you are a liar forever," according to Frank Swoboda, staff reporter for *The Washington Post*. He cited Mitsubishi Motor Manufacturing of America, saying the company lied and threatened reporters in an effort to prevent them from getting details about the

EEOC's sexual harassment suit against the company. "It just whetted our appetite," asserted Swoboda, who said the *Post* used the Internet to locate some of the women who said they had been harassed.[8]

Joseph Sullivan, writing in *Business and the Media,* reminds us "that both reporters and the public are sophisticated enough to recognize smokescreens, if not penetrate them. Honesty is the best policy."[9] Adds Judith Lederman, owner of JSL Publicity & Marketing, "Clients come and go, but the media is always there and they don't forget a liar."[10]

Lying to the public is no different from lying in the courtroom under oath. The sentence, however, can be tougher: loss of credibility, loss of respect, loss of customers, loss of trust by the community and by shareowners.

## To Comment or Not to Comment

Few words create more frustration for a reporter than "No comment." A key element in a reporter's job is the process wherein the reporter asks questions and the respondent answers. "No comment" throws a red cape in front of a very large and angry bull.

The problem stems from the connotations of the phrase "No comment." If you are the person saying "No comment," you believe this is a safeguard against putting your foot in your mouth. Saying "No comment" seems safer than saying "I don't know what you are talking about," or "I made a mistake," or "The company regrets that it made a decision 50 years ago that has adverse effects today," or "We prefer not to discuss that topic."

Reporters and the general public, on the other hand, have assumed that "No comment" really means, "I am guilty as hell but I won't admit it."

According to a survey conducted by New York-based Porter/ Novelli, when a company spokesperson declines to comment in a controversial situation, approximately 65 percent of Americans think the company is guilty of wrongdoing.[11] In support of that finding is one professional's look at the conflict between lawyers and public relations practitioners. He says, "Both professions have image problems. But the public's perception of both is actually the opposite of reality. Lawyers appear to want the truth to prevail. Public relations folks are seen as spinners of truth."[12] In actuality, the safest course to take is to answer the reporter's questions. If you do not know the answer, reply, "I don't know, but I'll get that information and get back to you." The more information you can provide, however, the less the reporter can speculate about your activities. Bill Harlow, former director of public affairs for the U.S. Central Intelligence Agency, said the CIA "almost never [says] 'no comment.' We'll find some way to say something in a positive way when we can't respond to a question."[13]

One way to gain control of a lazy reporter's "Would you care to comment?" question is to ask the reporter: "Could you be more specific about what you want to know?" Or, you could take the question away by saying: "Yes, I want to comment. I want you to know that our company has been making and selling these products for 37 years with no failures. I will show you the letters from happy customers . . ." You get the idea—take control and don't let a lazy reporter have control of you. Following is a list of sample situations with examples of ways to avoid "No comment":

1. **Rumors of an imminent layoff.** "When we have any such announcement, I will let you know at once. I am sure you understand that our procedure is to let the employees know first so they don't hear the news on the radio, television or Internet."

2. **Employee arrest for stealing, drugs, etc., on or affecting your organization's property.** Confirm the employment status of your employee. Then: "We are cooperating fully with the appropriate agencies [name them] in the investigation. Beyond that, it would be best for you to talk with the local police [or whomever] for further information."

3. **Employee activity (positive or negative) not affecting your organization.** Confirm employment and job title only. Then: "We do not give out any additional information about our employees."

4. **Sales projections, production plans and other proprietary information.** "I hope you can understand that answering that question would give our competitors valuable information about our sales plans [or manufacturing processes or marketing strategies or whatever]."

5. **Information from an employee.** "That's an individual's opinion. The company's position is . . ."

6. **Rumors of imminent dividend action, stock offering, debt issue, merger, etc.** "We have nothing to announce at this time. You are well aware that there are clear procedures [prior notification of the stock exchange on which a company's shares are traded, simultaneous release to the financial and business wire services, etc.] for any announcement that could affect our stock price or an investment decision." Or, "As a matter of policy, we never discuss or speculate on rumors in the marketplace."

7. **Frivolous charges.** Respond with "That's absurd," or even "That's hogwash!"

8. **Inappropriate questions.** "Our organization has no position on that issue one way or the other" is an appropriate answer to questions about political, social, religious or other issues on which a public position might unnecessarily alienate segments of the public. Also, "We are in the business of software development [or whatever], not religion."

9. **Leaks of settlement plans or other bargaining information.** "We are negotiating with the union in good faith to resolve the issues that separate us. Certainly we all want to avoid a strike. We shall confine any other remarks to the bargaining table, where we hope they will contribute to the negotiation process."

10. **Advance publicity prior to a new product announcement.** "The company has made no such announcement," or "We have read those reports with great interest," or "You know you are always among the first to know whenever we are ready to go public with new product plans."

11. **Question on a judicial or regulatory ruling.** "We will have to study the decision [or ruling or judgment] before we can discuss it in detail."

## When You Have to Say No

As a media relations spokesperson, do not confuse "No comment" with "No, I can't answer that question because . . ." There are legitimate times when information cannot be disclosed; reporters know and respect those times.

In an effort to make sure cases are tried in the courtroom and not in the media, many judges impose restrictions on the parties in the action, which prevents any discussion of the case with the media. Either party found guilty of ignoring this restriction often can be charged with contempt of court. Thus, if a reporter asks about a court case, it is perfectly understandable and permissible to reply: "I'm sorry but we're not allowed to discuss this case under terms agreed to in the court." You are neither commenting on the subject nor are you stonewalling; rather, you are explaining to the journalist why, in this instance, you cannot be of help.

Similarly, if you are asked about talks between your company and another, you can respond: "I'm sorry, but we have agreed to keep our business discussions private." This often will be the case as companies considering major agreements, alliances or acquisitions declare at the outset that no material will be issued to the media unless jointly agreed to by the parties.

Another instance of being able to say no without guilt is when the information sought is specifically proprietary. For example, if your company has been purchasing large quantities of aluminum for its products for more than a decade and then suddenly decreases its purchases of aluminum while increasing its supply of a different material, then the competition could assume one of many things: that your company is offering a new product line, that it has found a less expensive way to produce the same product or that it is having some difficulty as yet to be determined. Whatever the answer, it is the type of thing you would not want to have in the press because it is damaging to your company's welfare.

When it comes to employee privacy, more and more employees are seeking to disassociate themselves from their jobs. This separation of person and job can cause some gnashing of teeth when it comes to answering a journalist's legitimate inquiry and simultaneously respecting the employee's right to privacy. If there are no legal guidelines available, and no written policy on employee privacy, you should help create a policy.

A well-known, but not as well-used, procedure to protect all parties concerned during a photography session is the model release. This paper, when signed by an employee (or volunteer, student, visitor, etc.), allows your organization to use the individual's photograph in advertising, training or general publicity or for any other causes stated in the release.

Questions about a job function can be answered without concern for any one person who happens to hold the job. Questions about the job function as it relates to the person performing the job should be handled differently. For example, a reporter could ask about a specific piece of equipment. After being told that it is an advanced computer for the central communications room, the reporter asks, "How have your employees responded to this equipment?" If you reply, "Not well. The equipment seems to be too complex for them and we've had to put them through training many times," the reporter may ask to speak to one of the employees. This is an obvious dilemma. You have already given the impression that your employees are not capable of being trained on the equipment. To agree to an interview on behalf of the employees would be disastrous. In this case, it is best to ask the employees first, explaining carefully what the interview will be about so they can decide if they want to appear in public.

Obviously, a media spokesperson does not answer any question about employees that is beyond the realm of the spokesperson's responsibility. For instance, a question about an employee's financial status or personal habits must be referred to that employee. You should identify in advance those situations and circumstances in which you will have to say "no."

## Making Demands

In many organizations, some upper-level or executive management person reviews the material that is written for internal use, such as the employee newspaper, management newsletter, benefit pieces or internal magazine pieces. The annual report, an external vehicle, is also closely scrutinized by top management before being issued for public consumption, as are advertisements and other public documents. It is easy to understand, then, how executives might assume they have a right to review a reporter's copy. Sadly, this natural desire to make sure the material is accurate, fair and legally defensible often creates a totally different impression on a reporter.

Clearly, it is the responsibility of the media relations spokesperson to educate management about the differences between a reporter and an in-company staff writer, the different audiences being served by each and the rules under which each operates.

Andy Rooney of *60 Minutes* was once asked if he thought the manner in which the management of a large corporation dealt with him in imposing limitations on the questions to be asked damaged that company in any way. Rooney replied: "It made me suspect they had something to hide. To this extent it damaged them. And because it was difficult to get information from them, I got it from a dozen less sympathetic sources . . . former executives of the company, drivers, pilots and dissidents from within the company itself."[14]

Instead of making demands about an interview, you should make clear to your executive or subject-matter expert the purpose/topic of the interview, the time allowed for it and what the material will be used for. This is good common sense in establishing interviews, and both you and the reporter will be glad for the understanding. Also, while you should not ask to see a story before publication, you can suggest to the reporter that you are available to check quotes, facts and figures at the reporter's convenience.

## Off the Record

Although technically there is no such thing as "off the record" there is still controversy concerning the use of "off the record," evidenced by the definition of the term given to foreign journalists by the U.S. Foreign Press Center:

> The flat rule is that the material requested is not for publication, it is solely for the reporter's private knowledge. The off the record interview or briefing is most commonly used by officials to advise reporters of something that is going to happen so that they have the background or information necessary for planning purposes to cover the event when it does occur. For example, an official may explain that the Secretary of State is going to Asia on a given date and that he/she will be talking about specific topics. The reporter cannot print that news since it is off the record, but he or she can make plans to follow along on the same trip and to report on the speeches and press conferences that the Secretary of State may hold.[15]

Obviously, there are times when you must give background material to a reporter before he/she fully understands a subject. The same rules apply for background material as they do for current material: you do not give out proprietary information, legally restricted material or material that would jeopardize an employee's privacy. Everything left over, then, should be available for publication. In short, everything left over should be on the record.

Another argument about "off the record" contends that using this ploy will curry favors with reporters. Here's why it doesn't work:

- Being an effective media relations spokesperson depends on building trust and credibility, not building a "favors list."

- Telling a journalist information "off the record" cannot help but imply that there is still more information not yet released or perhaps being told to another reporter.

- Not all journalists will honor an "off the record" request. Many people know, from bitter experience, what the results of this can be.

- Giving "off the record" information allows a reporter to take that information to someone else in your organization and ask for confirmation of what you said. The reporter simply doesn't use your name but uses your information.

Supporting those points is a U.S. Justice Department official who has stated:

> Many Washington reporters today do not want on-the-record comments as much as they want to talk on some sort of background basis . . . I get the strong impression that reporters are being pushed by their editors, who must think that comments

made off the record are more truthful than those made on the record . . . All of the spokesmen for the Department of Justice have been told always to speak on the record and to have their names attached to comments they make. This policy makes them accountable for what they say, and it gives the readers assurance about what they are being told.[16]

If you are in doubt about which way to go, then use this guideline: **Never say anything to a reporter you are not willing to see in print or on a blog or a Web site, or to hear on the evening news.** This guideline should apply at all times, even in social settings, for reporters are creatures of habit and are seeking information from any available source. They are doing their job 24 hours a day, as should you.

## Advertising/Cash for Coverage

In recent years, there has been a substantial change in the gray area of advertorials, pay-for-play and other arrangements whereby money is exchanged for editorial space or coverage.

"There is nothing wrong with public relations persuading a reporter to run a story on its merits. That's our business. There is everything wrong with paying a reporter to advocate a cause. There is nothing wrong with providing a video to tell a story. There is everything wrong with concealing the source," says Thomas L. Harris,[17] former president of Golin/Harris International.

There also is something—if not wrong, certainly unseemly— about paying a "sponsorship fee" to appear on syndicated television shows such as Terry Bradshaw's *Winners Circle*, which appears on cable news channels, extolling the virtues of companies that display "forward thinking and consistent principles."[18] The companies "selected" for inclusion actually paid a $29,000 sponsorship fee each for placement on the show but no notice of that payment appeared on the program. Peter Himler, media consultant, flatly declares that this practice is "unethical."[19] Similarly, the increased use of video news releases (VNRs), many without disclosure of the originator of the VNR, is giving rise to concerns about pay-for-play material.

The International Public Relations Association (IRPA), in a survey on (un)ethical standards in media relations and journalism, reported the following as unethical:

- editors and journalists asking for inducements to publish news releases or feature items;

- company news releases appearing in exchange for paid advertising elsewhere in the publication;
- advertisements disguised as editorial;
- material appearing through influence or payment by a third party; and
- publications asking for payment not to publish certain stories.[20]

Conversely, companies are now beginning to insist—as part of an advertising contract—that media outlets notify their ad agency if "objectionable coverage" is planned. One company using this method of managing editorial coverage asked that it be "notified of the tone so that it can either move the ad or shift it to another issue."[21] Steve Ennen of American Business Media, an association of business-to-business publications, notes that one of the tenets of the organization's code of ethics is that editors do not allow advertisers to review articles before publication.[22]

Globally, however, bribery in the news media continues to create challenges for those companies that operate under a free press ethic. Authors of the International Index of Bribery for News Coverage note that "... many parties are adversely affected [by bribery in the news]—journalists, news sources, advertiser, government policy makers, and the consuming public." Further, they state, "Public relations professionals and journalists alike—as citizens who best understand the importance of media integrity—need to take leadership roles in eliminating this unethical practice."[23]

Paul Holmes succinctly sums up the dilemma and the solution: "There is a communications continuum with control at one end (paid ads) and credibility at the other (earned media). You can never increase your control over the message without weakening its credibility. And anything that blurs the line between paid and earned media undermines the credibility of journalistic messages."[24]

## Advice from the Pros

Recent scandals in the corporate world have made ethics a significant topic at recent Arthur W. Page Society conferences, where PR leaders have offered their advice on this key issue. Here is a sampling of thoughts from the society's Hall of Fame honorees from their acceptance speeches in 2002, 2003 and 2004.

> Certainly, truth can be hard to define. Some would say it is in the eyes—and/or pens—of its beholders: CEOs who are often iso-

lated and under-informed; corporations that are cultural defenders of the status quo; advocates who are masters of the anecdotal; and media who, almost by definition, are confined to the opposing view for headlines. So, the issue really is behavior—what we do—how and when and in whose interest we act. . . . The old caution that has stopped more than one of us in our tracks, "Don't overreact," may have been sound advice at one time. But today our publics are demanding that we *do* overreact. Contrary to the old adage, you can beat a dead horse, and sometimes it may be the perfect strategy. Advocacy is ours until we give it away—and then we all too often end up fighting even harder to get it back. To that point, our studies have taken a hard look at companies in trouble—big public trouble. It is quite clear that companies that behaved in the *public* interest came out of the problem better than companies that communicated in the *company's* interest. (April 2002)

—Kurt P. Stocker,
Associate Professor, Emeritus
Northwestern University
Evanston, Illinois

We can argue about whether good judgment can be taught, but I believe it can be acquired by paying close attention to the experiences we have throughout our careers, by distilling the lessons we learn through everyday experiences, and then developing an understanding of how to apply that cumulative experience to the situations that confront us. . . . We need to be sure that the balance in decision making on the tough issues always tips in favor of good instincts and good judgment, born of values and integrity and rooted in the truth. I use a very simple mantra or framework to organize my thinking when confronting tough situations: "What do we know? What do we believe? And what are we going to do?" (September 2003)

—W. D. (Bill) Nielson, Vice President,
Public Relations and Corporate Communications
Johnson & Johnson
New Brunswick, New Jersey

Community involvement was part of [McDonald's] culture from the very beginning. . . . I coined the term "Trust Bank" for all the community involvement, which helped them build "deposits" of goodwill in case they might need it for a "withdrawal" when a crisis or sensitive issue arose. . . . Today, more than ever, the concept of the Trust Bank should be central to every business out there. But you don't need to take my word for it. Our firm just completed a new study of corporate citizenship and American business. The two most important factors that emerged when evaluating the individual companies were: 1. ethical, honest, responsible business practices, including executive behavior; and 2. how a company treats its employees. These are essential to trust internally and externally—people want to do business with and work for a company they trust. (September 2004)

—Al Golin, Chairman
Golin/Harris International
Chicago, Illinois

# Media Events

## How to Make Them
## Work for You

Your organization may not always have dramatic new products, hundred-million-dollar new offices or a vital scientific breakthrough to attract reporters' attention. But the basic principles of announcements remain the same for all of us, and you too can hold an event to help your organization generate increased sales and positive media coverage.

In addition to new product or service announcements, a manufacturing plant opening, hiring a new CEO, an open house or market expansion all are fine reasons to host a celebration and news conference. These media events are staged occurrences, so you usually control the timing. They are held to promote good news, so you are on the offensive, not the defensive. They tend to have a more casual atmosphere to encourage person-to-person dialogue between the news media and your organization's executives.

Working on media events can be fun. The trick is to make it profitable for your organization in terms of increased sales, positive news media coverage, improved public opinion—and maybe also a jump in the stock price. There are two keys to getting the most effective media

131

relations results from these events. First, clearly enunciate your communications objective and then evaluate every idea by whether or not it helps meet that objective. Remember that when management asks what it is getting for its PR investment, it is asking for evidence that communications activities have supported business goals. Second, keep running lists that track progress and responsibility for all planned and possible activities. You must think constantly in generalities while at the same time living in detail. Michelangelo is said to have counseled a young artist, "Perfection is made up of details." It will be your ability to keep sight of the forest and every single tree that will make the event a success from a media viewpoint—and well worth the expense from your organization's perspective.

## Remember Your Target Audiences

Look at your event from the point of view of the reporters you will be inviting. They get invitations almost daily. So your event must be different in some way to attract their attention. It must be *unique*, to differentiate it from the competition. It must be *relevant*, to be considered newsworthy or worth being given attention. It must be *cost-effective*. And, above all, it needs to *sell*—because that is what we all are here for. As the late advertising legend David Ogilvy counseled his agency, "A good advertisement is one which sells the product without drawing attention to itself."[1]

If your company's stock is traded publicly, you also will want to coordinate with those colleagues responsible for investor relations. Reporters frequently call financial analysts and market experts for an outside, objective evaluation—and a quotable quote—to include in their story on a major corporate announcement. Thus it is to your advantage to keep financial analysts who follow your company and industry fully informed about your news, preferably on announcement day. You can have copies of the press kit sent or delivered to key financial analysts. Or you may want to arrange a separate restaging of the news conference for them. (It is normally not wise to invite journalists and financial analysts to the same announcement event. Their interests are different, and they deserve individual attention.)

Also, remember your employees. Broadcast the event live to employees via your internal video network or on a streaming video on your Web site.

## Announcing a New Facility

Announcing the purchase of property and the building of a new facility provides unparalleled opportunities for positive media and community relations. It also serves as a fine example of how to plan a media event. It will, however, tax your abilities if you find yourself operating in new territory without the benefit of established relationships with local reporters and editors (or even knowledge of the local geography) if the move is an expansion into a state or country in which your organization has not operated.

Integral to your planning should be the knowledge that your plans very likely are not going to be kept secret until announcement day. If the deal is a big one—in terms of size of the property, cost of construction, prestige of the company or number of potential jobs, for example—you should count on the fact that there will be a leak. Real estate agents showing property, local boards approached for zoning regulations, a hotel visited to evaluate conference facilities, a pilot hired for aerial photographs of the site—all these provide ample opportunities for the news to slip out no matter what precautions your organization takes.

You should have approved and ready for immediate use a standby statement in case a reporter calls seeking your comment on rumors. If your plans are so uncertain that you do not even have an announcement date tentatively set, you should probably say nothing more than your organization is looking at a number of potential sites for possible future expansion, but no plans are firm yet. If you have a timetable in mind, you might want to go further by adding that you will let the reporter know when a decision is made and an announcement is imminent.

You also will want to develop a solid relationship early on with others involved in the project. People from such disciplines as real estate, legal and finance, either on your organization's staff or retained for this job, will become critical resources as announcement time draws near. Your involvement in the planning stages helps build their confidence in you and in your contribution to the project's successful outcome. It also makes it more likely that you can get their early concurrence on an objective and working strategy—not to mention their personal involvement in the implementation of your information plan.

Once you know the announcement is a "go"—even before you have a firm date—you should immediately develop a checklist of all activities that need to be undertaken and write down any related issues that must be considered. This will be your overall master list.

It will also spawn a number of more detailed "to-do" lists for many of the entries.

For a major announcement, you will probably be working with other departments within your organization or even an outside agency hired to put on this event. It is critical that you and your colleagues know who is doing what and don't overlap your work. You are in charge of the media side of the event while someone else should handle the logistics of permits, food, parking, limo pickup and so forth. Included on your media list should be the following:

1. **Date/time of announcement.** Probability of bad weather? Other conflicting events such as a holiday or an election? Best time for the local news media? Availability of key participants?

2. **Site of announcement.** At your organization's headquarters or at location of new property? On-site or in a hotel or commercial establishment? Ease of accessibility for guests and news media?

3. **Main theme/primary message.** Expansion of your organization into new territory? New business? Move from older facility?

4. **Guests and media.** Federal, state and local government officials? Key community and business leaders? Local people helpful in site selection? News media—local? national? trade? Other VIPs? Employees? Spouses? Financial analysts?

5. **Speakers.** Only your organization's executives? Governor or top state or federal official? Mayor or local official?

6. **Type of occasion.** News conference alone? Low-key or big blast? With lunch or dinner? Reception?

7. **Media relations.** Press kit materials? Transportation to site? Satellite tour? One-on-one interviews?

8. **Invitations to media.** Reporters and editors? Editorial board members? Bloggers?

9. **Mementos.** Appropriate? Different ones for media?

10. **Collateral materials.** Exhibit? Printed program? "Who we are, what we do" brochure for guests? "Working news media only" sign outside news conference room?

It is a good idea to ask others who will be involved to review your list to see if you have left anything out or overlooked any local media customs. Next, you should establish an information objective and budget, assign responsibility for each of the activities, develop an overall timetable, and set specific due dates. Then you must oversee implementation of the media plans on virtually a day-to-day basis to ensure everything gets done on time.

## Guidelines for Media Events

### Planning before the Event

1. Make sure the objective and theme for your information effort is supportive of your organization's goals and your overall media relations plan and is agreed to by everyone involved. It should include both your key message and target audience. Before making any decision, evaluate it against that objective. For example, when we were discussing possible speakers for the official opening of AT&T's Network Software Center in Illinois, someone suggested we invite the vice president of the United States "to get publicity" since it was an election year. Our goal was not, however, publicity for the sake of publicity. If it were, we pointed out, we could do something bizarre, like have an employee stage a loud demonstration in the middle of the ceremony. Rather, our objective was to get media coverage on AT&T's software expertise and the contributions it would make to new information age services. Having the vice president speak—*particularly* because the ceremony would take place only a few months before a national election—could divert attention from our software message and focus it on politics. Thus, it might inhibit rather than support our information objectives. Better to invite the president of Bell Laboratories to join our CEO on stage so the speakers would personify the high-technology partnership that would deliver AT&T's products to the marketplace.

2. **It sometimes is good politics as well as good media relations to invite the governor of the state, or the mayor, or a high-ranking county official, to make a few brief remarks.** It is wise to restrict a politician to a five-minute official welcome rather than the keynote address; this way you control the length of the program and the main message the media take away from the event.

3. **Choose your spokespersons very carefully.** Then provide them with solid background information and help them practice.

4. **Do not let yourself be distracted by time-consuming tasks.** You don't need to worry about the menu—other staff will take care of that.

### Implementing the Event

5. **If a site or facility tour is part of your program, give the media a heads-up about the amount of time on the tour, what they will see, if photographs are allowed, etc.**

6. **Severely limit the number of officials introduced individually or allowed to speak as part of the news conference or ceremony.** "Obligatory" recognitions are terribly boring to the audience—and normally not required at all. They also distract from the main message your organization wants to deliver. Better to have your emcee or the organization's top speaker use one general statement to thank "all the local people who made us feel so welcome" or commend "the employees whose dedication and talent made this event possible."

7. **Document each stage of a new facility**—from architect's drawings through construction and official opening. Such a photographic history will be invaluable not only to meet the needs of the news media but also for your annual report, year-end video program or other external and internal information materials. Make plans early; you don't want to implement the plan only to find construction nearly completed.

8. **Review and update your checklists often.** The ball takes some funny bounces on occasion, and the only way to track it is to keep it perpetually in sight. Conduct frequent meetings where everyone involved shares progress reports. Occasionally send brief media reports to your organization's top executives.

---

### Helpful Hints from Journalists

At the 14th annual spring seminar of the Arthur Page Society in New York in April 1999, two panels of journalists offered tips on how reporters and media relations professionals can best work together. Here are some hints relating to major announcements and media events, from print, broadcast and Internet journalists:

> Have video available. You have a major merger or some big news, and we ["Nightly Business Report"] have to go scrambling for video. Our job is, "We want this on the air." So the best thing you can do is have a lot of in-house video and have it broadcast-ready on either beta or 3/4 inch that we can use. That's really important. Another thing is that on the day of an announcement sometimes what happens is that you just want to talk to the print media, and you want to do broadcast another day. We don't really like that, but if you are going to do that, at least talk to us so that we can hit the road running the next day.
>
> —Susie Gharib

Every time I pitch a story, every time I talk to our executive producers at CNBC [CNBC Business News] about something that I want to report on, the main question they ask me is, "What's the value-added for shareholders, for investors? What are they going to get out of this?" In order to achieve that goal together, we need to be able to bring them the most up-to-date information. . . . We are there to help you communicate your messages in order to provide shareholders with the information that they need. We're constantly being tested in new ways, trying to keep those lines of communications open. But all of the media outlets are 24-hour-a-day operations now.

—Martha McCallum

The suggestion I have for all of you is, with this 24-hour news cycle that we increasingly are facing, don't worry if you miss the first stop. Get on the train. If you don't get the first deadline, get on another one because things really have a way of feeding on themselves. Stories that we do [at *The Wall Street Journal*] are picked up by CNBC, with whom we have a joint venture, and on our Internet edition. Then it can really snowball. I think even on a daily basis, if you miss our first deadline for a comment or a perspective, give us a shout. Let us know because we are more than happy to change the cast of the story late in the evening if we get some perspective that's going to matter. Because to me the process, if it clicks, means everybody wins.

—Michael Siconolfi

There's one company, a very aggressive PR company, and whenever a press release goes out on the wires, the person there will always call my voice mail and say, "Hey, just a heads-up. We're sending this out." While we [CNN Financial News] monitor wires all day long, there are hundreds of press releases from companies. It's very helpful when I get a call like that.

—Rhonda Schaffler

All of our [*TheStreet.com*] stories, all of the bylines are hyperlinked to the reporter's e-mail. So if you read a story about a company that's in your industry, you can just instantly e-mail the reporters and introduce yourself. And that can be a good way of getting a relationship going.

—Jamie Heller

9. **If you decide to give a memento to the media, personalize it with your logo so that recipients are reminded of your organization when they use it.** Pens carrying your logo are useful, and they can be inserted into the press kit if you want to give them only to reporters. Tote bags or briefcases are especially good giveaways because they are carried and become moving billboards for your brand.

10. **Arrange for photography**—still and video—of the news conference and announcement ceremony.

11. **You can have a first-class press kit folder and also save money by carrying a photograph or drawing of the new facility along with your organization's name on the cover—but** *not* including the date of the event. That way you can arrange for production of the folders before a final date is set to avoid rush-job printing charges, keep your last-minute duties to a minimum and avoid wasted paper if the date changes at the last minute. You also can use the folders for other occasions such as open houses or background information packages for the media as construction proceeds or new reporters request materials.

12. **Target your press kits** so that each reporter has the right information for his or her audience—hometown angle for the plant site's local paper, long-term growth for the business and financial media, relationship to industry trends for the trade press, etc.

13. **Just before the event, write out a final detailed list of the media expected to attend the event.** Give copies to everyone involved so they will know to welcome the media and be able to recognize them in the news conference.

14. **Supervise all aspects of the news conference personally,** from the opening statement to the contents of the press kit. Anything affecting the information effort is your business, regardless of who is responsible. You may be the only person with the complete picture.

15. **If there will be a meal after the news conference, put "Reserved for press" cards on tables nearest the podium or head table.** Do not assume reporters will stay for the meal just because they are coming to the news conference. Ask them to RSVP to the news conference and luncheon or reception separately.

16. **If possible, arrange for a separate room for private interviews between your CEO and selected reporters after the news conference.** Allow time in your schedule for such interviews between the news conference and the meal, perhaps by

scheduling a reception between the two. Schedule Internet online chats for the next day.

17. **Try to have a separate "working room."** This is ideal for storage of press kits, mementos and other office materials such as computers and blank news release paper in case you have to revise the release at the last minute. If your event is taking place at a commercial establishment, get permission from the manager to ship as much of your material as possible to arrive early.

18. **Have plenty of copies of your business card to give to the media.** Try to find time to chat with any reporters you have not met before. The relationships you begin to develop at the announcement ceremony will serve your organization well as construction proceeds—especially if you face unfortunate events like an accident or a union problem—and if communication will be primarily by telephone because your office is not near the new facility.

19. **Understand that the primary focus of local reporters' questions will be on the economic advantages to the community** in terms of jobs, taxes and related support services. Anticipate their needs by being prepared to give out general figures and a probable timetable. Be careful not to lock yourself into a potential problem of appearing to renege on a promise a few years hence by being overly specific at announcement time. Use round numbers: "We expect to hire about a thousand people over the next few years" is better than "We plan to hire 1,083 people by next December." Also, for local taxation purposes be careful about placing a value on your project until your design and construction plans are firm and you have consulted with a tax expert.

20. **Make sure the head table and news conference setup photograph well** so that you get maximum exposure for your organization's message. The lectern should carry your logo, not the hotel's. If the drapes behind the announcement area have a busy pattern or inappropriate color, put up portable curtains or an attractive sign with your theme or organization's name behind the speakers. All visuals should be simple, with copies included in the press kit. View the staging through a camera's eye—literally if necessary.

21. **Set up a separate table staffed by a person who will help you handle the news media.** This includes press kit distribution, requests for private interviews or any other courtesies that should be extended to working journalists.

22. **Prepare a separate package of materials for your key executives involved in the program.** Include the press kit and a detailed agenda—and also private background and Qs and As that could come up, key officials and reporters deserving personal attention (with nicknames and phonetic spelling if their names are difficult to pronounce), potential local concerns such as environmental issues or union problems, and the executives' individualized itinerary and schedule—with a reminder of the times they should be available for separate media interviews. Give a copy of this package to each executive's assistant or chief staff person—and keep a few extra copies with you in case they are misplaced.

23. **Coordinate the agenda and schedule closely with the press secretary or chief aide of government officials and celebrities who are participating in the program.** Get on their calendars early because their schedules often are set well in advance.

24. **Arrange for setup time and personally inspect all the facilities the night before and the day of the event.** Test the sound and lighting arrangements for broadcast needs.

25. **Arrange for separate distribution of the press kit to reporters not attending the event, and put it on your Web site.** Distribution should take place at the time of or just after your news conference. Only in rare cases should you allow advance distribution, or you will hurt chances of the media's covering the event in person.

### Following Up and Evaluating the Event

26. **Monitor that evening's television news programs.** Arrange for electronic pickup of television, radio and Internet coverage. Get copies of the daily papers. Within 24 or 48 hours provide your organization's top executives with samples of initial news coverage of the event, plus a videotape of the full news conference and ceremony if you made one. Consider a separate, shorter version for showings to your employees and the board.

27. **Promptly after the event write thank-you letters to the media for the CEO's signature.** These should be sent to the media who came and/or covered the event.

28. **Set up a system to handle the inevitable queries generated by the news coverage of your announcement.** You will receive queries from real estate agents, relocation people, job applicants, banks and other prospective product and service suppliers. Make sure those responsible are prepared to handle them.

29. **A month or so after the event, when all the news coverage has been gathered, put together a summary that includes objectives and a brief analysis of how they were met.** This can be done in print or electronically, may include selected samples of news media coverage, and should be distributed to your organization's officers and board and to all others involved in the event.

30. **Consider putting together a formal scrapbook and video program to commemorate the event.** After circulation and presentation to your executives and board, copies could be given to the new plant manager and included in your organization's official archives.

31. **Put together a complete file including everything connected with the occasion, from your private memos and checklists to the press kits, official announcement speech and overall evaluation.** It will be invaluable not only as a record of an historic event but also as a model for planning future announcements.

## When Your Event Is for an International Market

Chapter 9, "Going Global: How to Manage International Media Relations," contains advice on operating beyond our borders that should be helpful when you find yourself working in an unfamiliar country. In addition, here are some tips specifically related to meeting and event planning outside your home country:

1. **Consider hiring a destination management company (DMC) or international public relations agency.** They can be very helpful in introducing you to local hotels and caterers, arranging visas, setting up tours, handling local transportation and selecting appropriate off-site festivities. Before choosing a DMC or agency, check references and determine their billing methodology—per person? flat fee? cost plus?

2. **While one site inspection may suffice here at home, you likely will need more in unfamiliar markets.** A first-class hotel in the United States is different from one in Europe or Asia. Also, organizers must plan for differences in audiovisual formats and electrical voltage, expectations of meeting rooms and news conference sites, even the size of tables and chairs.

3. **Exchange rates will have a great effect on your budget and decision making.** Be flexible as currencies fluctuate during the planning phase. And talk with your Finance Department colleagues about the pros and cons of hedging your foreign exchange risk.

4. **Understand the VAT rules.** Value-added taxes range from 3 to 25 percent, so they can have a great effect on your budget. Fortunately, many countries have a system in place to allow at least some of your VAT charges to be refunded. Get local advice on the rules and how you can determine your organization's eligibility.

5. **Transportation is a critical factor.** Most journalists do not have time for lengthy travel, so you need to consider a site's accessibility to airports as well as providing an online direct feed into the press conference.

6. **Check the U.S. State Department list before settling on a venue.** This security and alert list lets you know what countries and geographic areas it is better to avoid at any given time.

7. **Use only well-known, experienced shipping companies**—preferably those with whom your organization has a long-standing business relationship. You may need a freight forwarder who is also a licensed customs broker. Check references. There is no second chance when you ship materials to a trade show or special event and they disappear en route.

## Case Studies and Success Stories

### Contemporary Arts Center (Cincinnati)

When the Richard & Lois Rosenthal Center for Contemporary Art (CCA) moved into its new building, it was certain to draw global attention because of its unique design and the exhibits on display. But the museum wanted to do more than focus on its new home during the opening days; it needed to draw visitors, raise funds and increase membership. The director's guiding statement was: "Cincinnati is often seen as conservative. The message is that this is a forward-looking city that does investigate the new and embrace diversity."

Objectives for the opening included celebrating famed architect Zaha Hadid's design, positioning the building as an expression of the CCA's programs, showcasing the CCA as a local cultural and economic leader, and emphasizing its importance in the international arts community. The firm hired to assist with the opening, Resnicow Schroeder Associates (RSA), felt they needed to get not just opening coverage but to break through media perceptions and provide ongoing coverage of Cincinnati's cultural life.

The project overview was presented to more than 700 U.S. and international media outlets, especially those that focused on art, design, architecture, travel, business and lifestyle, using the "Firsts" theme: CCA—first institution in the region to present works by major international artists; first U.S. art museum designed by a woman; and first U.S. commission for Hadid. Media events were coordinated throughout the fall and winter in preparation for the late spring grand opening some months later.

*Results:* The grand-opening preview in May drew more than 11,000 visitors. The CCA gained more than 4,000 new members, exceeded its fund-raising goal by $9 million and raised its endowment to $6 million.[2]

## Nobel Prize Winner

While there is no way to know in advance if someone on your faculty will receive a Nobel Memorial Prize, there are ways to prepare besides wishful thinking.

The media staff at the W. P. Carey School of Business at Arizona State University had good reason to believe that Dr. Edward C. Prescott, professor of economics, might receive the coveted 2004 Nobel Prize in Economic Sciences. But because winners are notified directly by telephone from Oslo before the media or public are notified, there is little formal preparation that can be done.

Weeks before the announcement date (October 11, 2004), tentative plans were made, a time line was developed and fingers were crossed. Staffing would be needed for the media calls; the Web site would have to be updated; a press conference that morning was a must; plans for live television and radio interviews—from around the globe—were developed; notifications internally and externally had to be set up; news releases needed to be prepared and approved. With the help of KAET-TV, the Public Broadcast Station run by ASU, Dr. Prescott was given a trial run on how to handle in-studio remote television interviews. Tentative staffing plans for the announcement date were set up. Press releases, the updated Web site, e-mail announcements, press conference arrangements, congratulatory ads and a celebration event were all ready and in place to implement on a moment's notice.

Because the call would come in to Dr. Prescott at approximately 3 or 4 a.m. (Arizona time), all activities would be kicked off starting at that time.

*Results:* The call came amidst a number of through-the-night Web watchers who got the news at almost the same time that Dr. Prescott received the call at his home. Staff began taking media calls immediately from home and then transferred them to the office. The new Web material was launched on all Carey School and ASU sites and received more than 6,000 hits in the first 30 minutes.

Hundreds of media calls were pouring in and being arranged for return calls in a complex code that included order of importance, time zone, print/TV/radio/columnist/Web site, relationship with Dr. Prescott, and specific area of discussion. And, because Dr. Prescott was also a senior monetary advisor at the Federal Reserve Bank of Minneapolis, a similar scene was in place in that city, with a duplicate set of staff.

Dr. Prescott settled into a routine of simply making one return media call after another, while simultaneously trying to reach his friend, colleague and co-winner of the prize, Finn E. Hydland of Carnegie-Mellon University, who was in Europe and accepting in-person congratulations from university leaders and colleagues.

While Dr. Prescott was on the phone, wire service photographers were allowed in for first-run photos, an impromptu press conference was gathering outside the building, staff was sending out notices of the official press conference, television business and news shows from around the U.S. and Europe were jockeying for airtime, and a dedicated staff of two were constantly updating and rearranging the requests for interviews. This scenario continued well into the evening with one final live, BBC radio interview taking place from Sky Harbor Airport just before Dr. Prescott was leaving for Minneapolis. The staff in Minnesota picked up the momentum the next day and kept it going for the rest of the week.

Well-planned events seldom run as efficiently as this tentative, hoped-for event did. With few exceptions, all reporters and columnists had their time with the Nobel winner; the press conference was well attended and covered in print, on air and on the Web.

This event happened just two days before ASU was hosting the final 2004 U.S. Presidential Debate with an expected media force of more than 2,000. A quick rerun of the Prescott release was added to the media kit being made available for the Debate media and received additional attention as economics was expected to be a part of the debate topics.[3]

### Primerino—A Shear Success

Primerino, a small and unknown pastoral company in Australia, produced a bale of high quality, superfine wool and wanted to sell that bale for above-market value to an international buyer in order to attract attention from potential long-term superfine wool buyers to purchase Primerino wool.

Fighting a depressed wool market, few positive wool industry stories in the Australian media, and a three-week window of opportunity, The Phillips Group, hired by Primerino to accomplish the miracle, set up an innovative media plan with two goals: (1) create an environment in which a wool bale would attract international attention and sell at auction for a record price and (2) leverage international wool buyer interest in Primerino to help secure new supply contracts within six months.

Their strategies included: position Primerino's 11.9 micron bale as a world first; target the Australian media as the catalyst to rapidly gain notoriety; leverage initial interest to build appeal throughout Australian media; work with international wire services such as Reuters to send the story into the international sphere; create newsworthy media hooks to attract international editorial coverage; and maintain continual coverage in key target countries, such as France, Italy and China, to ensure active buyer participation and competitiveness at auction.

Their key messages: Primerino is the softest and finest wool in the world; at only 11.9 microns, this wool is destined for high fashion; and this bale is a world first and a world record.

Creative tactics helped kick this effort over the top. Examples include placing the wool bale in a bank vault with armed security guards; comparing the 11.9 micron width with that of a human hair (50 microns); showing wool from pampered "elite" sheep; seeing sheep housed in the "Wooldorf Astoria"; displaying designer jackets to protect the valuable fleece; and transporting the wool bale in a presidential-style motorcade for appearance on the *Today* program.

*Results:* The bale of wool sold for 577 times more than the market value, creating a world record; the price was $7,500/kilogram at a time when the world market price for superfine wool was $12–$13/kilogram. Contracts for the company's wool, other than superfine, increased in the weeks following the sale, and one of the Italian fashion buyers negotiated a supply contract for superfine wool.[4]

## Ingredients for Press Kit at a Special News Event

Even with our dependence on the Internet, there still are many reporters who find printed press kits useful. Here are the basic pieces that should be included in the package of special materials you give the news media, both in the press kit and on your organization's Web site:

- Main news release

- Other related feature or "sidebar" stories

- A disc of photographs or graphics, with cutlines, and a DVD of network-quality film to TV stations as background footage if you have it

- List of names, titles and affiliations of all people on the stage, at the head table or otherwise participating in the event
- Disc of photos and biographies of keynote speakers
- Basic fact sheet on your organization
- Annual report, brochure and other information on your organization
- Name and numbers (day and night) of person to contact for additional information

It also is critical that each of the pieces in the press kit be dated, since they undoubtedly will be separated and probably will be filed in the publication or station's morgue for future use by any reporter writing a story on your organization.

## The High Price of News Leaks

Frequently, employees are a major cause of news leaks. Sometimes they are salespeople hoping to impress customers by offering advance information about a new product, forgetting that they may be flirting with an antitrust violation by preannouncing a product. Or they are staff managers carelessly chattering about their work. Indeed, *Business Week* explained how a major article on personal computers came to be written by quoting a reporter as saying, "I heard intimations at a lunch, at a cocktail party, and again from a research expert while I was in a grocery store about a major product announcement coming." Said publisher James R. Pierce candidly: "Using these bits of information as a wedge, [we] got interviews with [the company's] executives."[5]

There is a very basic reason to keep a tight lid on new product information until the announcement day: You likely cannot afford to alienate the news media and lose the free—and probably positive—publicity they will give you. Except in rare cases, journalists will not cover the announcement of a new product as a major news event if the story has leaked out in dribs and drabs. They understand the necessity for a trial location or two. But any more widespread knowledge and reporters tend to say too many of their readers or viewers already know the story to make it news, and they send you off to the very expensive advertising section. As the old saying goes, "Loose lips sink ships," or make it very expensive to float them again.

Editors also frequently refuse to carry a story on a new product on their news pages or programs if your company has a paid ad running. Their feeling is that if your company had time to produce and place an advertisement, the product is no longer "hard news" to their readers and viewers and the publication is being used to provide free advertising. It is thus an important part of the media relations person's responsibility to ensure your news conference precedes any advertising by at least a day or two.

---

### Integrated Marketing Communications: Powerful Tool for Product Publicity and Brand Enhancement

The poster ads for the new Volkswagen Beetle will go down in advertising history: "Less flower, more power," and "If you sold your soul in the '80s, here's your chance to buy it back." But it was not advertising that launched the new Love Bug. Rather, it was public relations, according to *PR Week*.

The Beetle was introduced at the North American Auto Show in January 1999 with a satellite media tour. Volkswagen and Ruder Finn generated more than 900 national and local television segments about the Beetle in the first week alone. The publicity kept rolling in when the new Beetle was delivered. It made news by stopping traffic whenever it appeared, and customers responded by heading for their car dealers to buy. Said Rudder Finn creative director Michael Schubert, "We arranged it so that the car was seen in high-profile, high-traffic situations like Times Square in New York and Rodeo Drive in L.A."

By the time the advertising started in April, there was 65 percent awareness among the general public. And when a wiring problem caused VW to recall all 10,000 Beetles it had sold, owners who took their cars in for repairs got a loaner or a free taxi, a car wash, a tank of gas and a bouquet of flowers for their trouble—"Nice PR touches that embellished the Beetle's image and defused a potential crisis," as *PR Week* put it. The launch of the Beetle is just the latest in the growing line of companies and brands where PR has become central to the marketing program."[6] In fact, in an editorial titled, "Packaged PR Is Key to Branding," *PR Week* opined: "The success of strongly branded operations like Starbucks, Amazon.com, Virgin, and The Body Shop [is] predicated on public relations and not advertising."[7]

The softening of the traditional boundaries between marketing, advertising and PR is a natural response to the economic and competitive imperatives facing companies and clients. Organizational silos are out and teamwork is in. CEOs have little interest in what function traditionally had responsibility for a given task. Rather, they want the brightest and most creative minds addressing business challenges no matter where they reside in the organizational chart. Communicating priority messages cost-effectively to journalists, customers, shareholders, employees and other target publics is necessary to an organization's survival. Integrated marketing communications is an effective way to do that.

Said Thomas L. Harris, author of *The Marketers Guide to Public Relations*, "It is this need to get more bang for their bucks that has driven the growth of marketing public relations and the move to integrated marketing. The leave-it-all-to-advertising mindset is giving way to more targeted, more diverse ways to sell goods and services, maintain customer confidence and build brand equity."[8]

To create an effective integrated marketing communications program and avoid a cheerleading approach to promotions, get all the key functions together to decide on your priority messages and key selling points. Step back and look at the new product or service as a journalist would. Forget ego. Ask, what really is *news*? What is *new* or *unique*? What aspect of the product or service would have the most interest for the media's readers, viewers or listeners? Look for a human side as well as a business side to the story. Your role as a strategist and counselor means thinking through and guiding the entire publicity program, not just writing a news release.

In fact, Harris sees a long list of ways PR adds value to integrated marketing communications programs, including reinforcing brand position, building marketplace excitement before advertising breaks, making advertising news where there is no product news, reviving brand excitement, and building personal relationships with customers. "The opportunity is there if the talent is there to make it happen," in Harris' view.[9]

## Sophisticated Sequencing Maximizes Results

Too often great effort is expended on what will be said, with little attention paid as to when. Yet, sophisticated sequencing is crucial to maximizing your results. Experienced CEOs and CFOs plan asset sales and expansion activities to keep earnings rising smoothly and consistently. Similarly, all departments involved in marketing communications should plan so that there is a consistent stream of good news coming out of the company during the year, rather than a large number of new product and service announcements bunched together. Announcement dates should be set for those strategic moments in time when they will generate the most attention—for example, before a major financial analysts meeting or at an important trade show—rather than at the whim of one person or department. Get all involved parties together and agree upon an announcement calendar for the next year or two that benefits both the individual product managers and business units involved, as well as the overall organization.

Here is a planning model and time line for major new product or service announcements. It can be a tool to help you and your colleagues in your planning, especially for significant announcements of interest to a wide number of your priority audiences. Of course, all these activities are not appropriate for all products and services, and the one you choose will depend on your organization, its culture, the marketplace and the nature of the product or service being announced.

### *Announcement Day Minus Six Months*

- Interdepartmental planning committee formed, chaired by marketing or product manager responsible for the new product or service (consider including representatives from all sales and marketing functions involved, engineering, manufacturing, R&D, distribution channels, training, PR, advertising, promotions, investor relations, legal and customer service)
- Roles and responsibilities for all committee members defined, tentative meetings schedule and announcement timetable agreed to
- Research, product and marketing plans shared with committee members

### *Announcement Day Minus Five to Two Months*

- Beta tests with key customers as appropriate to get operational feedback (signed written confidentiality and nondisclosure agreements required)
- Agreement on priority messages, target audiences, key selling/positioning/copy points (consistent with overall brand strategies)
- Agreement on overall theme and visuals for all media and marketing communications materials as well as advertising, and new logo if any (consistent with overall corporate identification program)
- Announcement date agreed to, cleared on everyone's calendars
- Site selected and agreed to, hotel and travel reservations made if necessary
- Technical arrangements made for live Internet or video hookup for those who cannot attend
- Master to-do list agreed to, with responsibilities for each item and issue

- Standby statements and Qs and As distributed to PR and sales staff as well as customer service reps to respond to rumors and prevent preannouncement leaks
- Shelter magazines, quarterlies and/or other long lead-time publications given photos and general information if appropriate (signed written confidentiality agreement required)

*Announcement Day Minus One Month*

- Draft announcement materials (including scripts and background-only Qs and As), circulated for comments, clearance and buy-in
- Demonstration products loaned to two or three key reporters (signed, written confidentiality agreement required)
- Final timetable and responsibilities reviewed and agreed to
- Board of directors, senior management alerted to plans and schedule on confidential basis
- Spokesperson training for speakers at news conference, analyst briefing, customer seminars, etc.

*Announcement Day Minus One Week to One Day*

- Journalists invited to news conference, analysts invited to briefing, customers/distributors invited to reception relating to "important new product/service" (no specifics)
- Rehearsals for news conference and analyst briefing, at announcement site whenever possible
- Announcement materials on disks or printed, "ready to go" at key staging areas
- Advance copies distributed to board of directors and senior management

*Announcement Day*

- Stock market alerted if publicly traded company and new product/service is material
- Wire services notified, news conference held, press kits distributed, materials put on your organization's Web site
- Financial analyst briefing
- Announcement materials distributed to all employees, with news conference available via Intranet or video
- Notification of key customers via phone, e-mail, letter, reception, other special events
- Notification of legislators, community leaders, suppliers, other VIPs as appropriate

*Announcement Day Plus One Day to One Week*

- Advertising begins
- Customer/dealer/distributor seminars and executive briefings as appropriate
- Sampling of news media coverage circulated to board of directors, employees as appropriate

*Announcement Day Plus First Few Months*

- Messages and materials adapted based on monitoring media and customer feedback
- Products, announcement theme and visuals appear in trade show exhibits, product fairs, plant and factory tours, open houses—plus related handouts and decorations (banners, balloons, etc.)
- Announcement theme and visuals appear on all collateral sales materials including brochures, direct mail, Internet sites, point-of-purchase materials, billboards, giveaways and product training materials
- Customer testimonials distributed as news release to business, consumer and/or trade press and posted on Web site
- Customer testimonials, sampling of positive news media coverage and announcement advertising distributed to distributors, key customer prospects, financial analysts and employees
- Internet opportunities such as blogs, online chats, bulletin boards
- Audio or video satellite media tours to save spokespersons' travel time
- Speeches at appropriate forums such as trade shows, industry groups, chambers of commerce, Rotary, etc., with reprints distributed as appropriate
- Employee media features on customer reaction, sales results and staff who "made the product and sales happen."
- Product placements with media personalities (local celebrities can be as powerful as Oprah)
- Product contributions to selected charity events as appropriate

*Announcement Day Plus One Year*

- Seasonal publicity pushes at Christmas, Mother's Day, Father's Day, summer vacation time, etc., as appropriate
- First anniversary update to news media, analysts, board of directors, employees, key customers

# 9

# Going Global

## How to Manage
## International Media Relations

$A$t the beginning of the age of exploration, there was a warning on early maps that guided navigators heading off to new worlds. Unknown portions of the oceans were marked, "Here there be monsters." Such "monsters" provided opportunities for learning, adventure and heroes. That certainly is true today for media relations specialists whose companies or clients are expanding around the world. The opportunities are great, but so too is the risk of failure. There can be trouble if you are not sensitive to local conditions, willing to ask advice and eager to learn. As Robert L. Wakefield, an expert on cross-cultural issues, warned: "PR agencies frequently convert inexperienced managers into global executives simply because they handled a domestic account that now is going global. Beyond this, too often we in the U.S. look at our borders and see mirrors instead of windows."[1]

It takes savvy and sensitivity to succeed. Yet many firms—not only giant corporations but also smaller businesses—are adapting to become global enterprises because of the huge opportunities for

153

increased sales and profits in new markets and the cost-savings inherent in sharing resources worldwide. If your company or client is going global, you have expanded opportunities to make unique contributions on a larger scale than ever before. Media relations professionals can be vital resources in efforts to enter new markets; establish corporate reputation and brand identity; launch new products; and attract the respect of journalists, customers, investors, potential employees, suppliers and other opinion leaders. Key to being successful in each new market is finding the right balance between universal interests and local customs, taking advantage of global scale while also adapting to local conditions. "One size fits all" does not work.

Even the much heralded European Community did not result in one homogenized market. Nor did the introduction of the euro automatically eliminate cultural differences. Europeans have sharply contrasting outlooks, tastes and resources. More than 450 million people in 25 countries—yes, they have common interests but they also have distinct individual identities. The Dutch will remain Dutch. The French will remain French. And the Germans will remain German.

## Being Sensitive to Other Cultures

In fact, as trade barriers come down sometimes sensitivities go up. Witness ongoing conflict relating to the North American Free Trade Agreement about which countries are losing or gaining jobs. That's what makes going global so interesting—and doing business in international markets so dangerous if you do not keep your cross-cultural wits about you. In his book *7 Secrets of Marketing in a Multi-Cultural World*, G. Clotaire Rapaille says the key to marketing globally is understanding how cultures live and function. Every culture views the world from its own unique perspective. Every culture is sure that its view is the true one. But, in reality, cultures are neither right nor wrong. They are simply different.[2]

Even little things can mean a great deal. For example, entertaining effectively often is very important to doing business successfully. In China, there is no such thing as "fashionably late." In all of Asia especially and also in other countries, protocol must be observed at banquets because rank and status are serious matters. Seating arrangements and who is at or near the head table can be major issues. Huge partnerships have gone bad because North American executives who did not understand local customs and courtesies committed seemingly small *faux pas* that cost their companies millions of dollars in lost deals and opportunities. And what about Euro Disney refusing to serve wine in the new park outside Paris until customer animosity and staff defections forced them to "do it the French way"?

It is not a superficial shift. It is not business as usual. It is a major strategic refocus. As a result, media relations professionals have new opportunities to broaden our perspectives and learn a great deal about cultures and traditions other than our own. With the technological advantages of the Internet, e-mail, faxes, voice mail, satellite hookups and global networks, you can brainstorm magazine publicity strategy in Sydney and organize a news conference in Stockholm while still keeping up with the work in your home office.

## Cyberspace Lessens Importance of Geography

In fact, *Marketing High Technology* author William Davidow believes that in the information age, with citizens who live increasingly in cyberspace, "geography loses much of its importance as a defining element of history. Distance and physical barriers are spanned by the transfer of data over networks, not by the movement of people and goods over roads and bridges. Intangible assets such as intellectual property become more important than physical assets."[3]

These trends have massive implications for media relations professionals. If your company is going global, you should be at the forefront of its efforts to position itself in the worldwide marketplace. Organizations with a global business strategy also need a global media relations strategy—with agreement on objectives, priority messages, target publics and product promotion plans from New York to New Zealand, from Asia to Africa.

Each country's media relations activities should not only support local operations but also reinforce the corporation's global plan. The media relations strategy must align with the business strategy. The balance between global and local media relations programs depends on your company's or client's business strategy and organizational structure. For example, take the difference between a multinational and a global company:

- It may be appropriate for *multinational companies* with autonomous subsidiaries and independent strategies in each market to concentrate their communications on local plans, products, people, customers and competitors—for example, featuring local executives as the visible spokespersons and leaders while downplaying the connection to the corporate parent. Even so, consistency is a virtue. Johnson & Johnson is an example of a heavily decentralized organization that has worked hard to make sure they are speaking with one voice. A major element in making this happen is the public affairs advisory group, which includes key managers in the company and is headed by J&J's corporate vice president of public relations.[4]

- *Global companies,* on the other hand, operate as one business—an integrated system in which headquarters and all the subsidiary entities are interdependent in terms of strategies and operations. Every decision—from where it is most cost-effective to manufacture each product and purchase supplies to pricing policies and profit goals—takes into account the worldwide system. The sum of the parts is a whole lot more valuable to the bottom line than the pieces themselves. The Reader's Digest Association, for example, employs staff worldwide in

---

### Taking Advantage of Technology

Regardless of the country, the language or the politics, media will always be interested in the latest technology. So, too, are customers who want to be the first to learn of technologies yet to come. AT&T Bell Laboratories took this premise to its full conclusion by sponsoring in South Korea a one-day seminar for customers on "Technology Trends Toward 2010." To help ensure local support, AT&T partnered with Korea Telecom, DACOM, the Korea Institute of Science and Technology, and the Engineering and Technical Research Institute for cosponsorship.

A group of five AT&T scientists presented state-of-the-art technologies in photonics, global networking, speech image processing and managed data network services. Additionally, the customers were given a communications and computing overview of the latest technology and predictions into the next century.

The local AT&T public relations team combined the visit of the AT&T scientists with numerous interviews given to Korean daily and business press; Korean television and radio; computer, electronic and data trade publications; and regional trade publications. The number of total impressions generated by print and broadcast media was estimated at approximately 15 million.

Unassociated with the seminar but clearly influenced by it, a Korean TV crew visited AT&T Bell Labs in the United States and the resulting show on KBS-TV (Korea) featured AT&T's speech recognition system for 17 minutes in "Science 2001," a prime-viewing program.

The results from this initial program were overwhelmingly successful, enough so that AT&T conducted similar additional seminars in Korea.

more than 50 locations. Each of the international companies prepares a media relations plan as part of its annual business plan. The individual PR plans are based on local issues, local markets and local products—but collectively they all bear a remarkable similarity to each other because they also are based on the company's global communications strategy.

## Alert to Issues in All Markets

Such a role requires more than cleverly crafting messages. You also must be alert to emerging issues in all the markets where your company does business, not just in your home country.

Professionals headquartered in the United States and Canada need to remember that major issues do not always surface in North America. Although most would probably agree consumer activism began in the United States, the consumerist movement today could well be considered more proactive, for example, in Europe, particularly with economic boundaries falling and harmonization from European Community laws. Environmentalists in the United States often are not as politically involved as the "green" movement is in other parts of the world. For example, in Australia and Germany, conservationists have been elected and are making their mark on national policy and lawmaking. In England, environmentally conscious investors can check how "green" their investments are through a society that grades companies against certain criteria. Your antennae must be up whenever your organization does business.

When you *plan* on a global basis, you also need to *think* on a global basis. All the *"we"*s and *"they"*s need to disappear from your vocabulary, with each decision based on what's best for the total organization—and your *customers*. Ideas need to be given equal consideration whether they come from corporate headquarters or a field office, from San Francisco or Singapore. Wisdom flows in all directions.

## Think Global—Act Local

Key to being successful in the global marketplace is to find the right balance between local customs and universal interests and practices. The Bates advertising agency's theme sums it up well: "Think global. Act local."

In mounting media relations programs in other countries, it is essential to understand and respect others' cultures. Some differences should be noted in order not to offend or not to position your company in a negative situation. For example: Do not give clocks as gifts in China as they are seen as symbols of bad luck. Avoid bringing food and gifts in the Middle East lest you imply your host cannot afford them. Handle graphics carefully because symbolic abstractions in one country can be hex signs in another.

These are useful guidelines, but as we travel around the world, we find more similarities than differences. Thus, many media relations techniques that are successful in North America will also achieve your objectives in other countries around the world, with modifications.

## Practical Hints for Global Media Relations

A basic rule of thumb for the media relations professional entering the global arena might be: Stop, look and listen. The practice of public relations and all its related fields including media relations differs throughout the world. Before you develop a media plan to introduce a new product in a different country, take the following steps:

1. **STOP and read a bit about the country itself.** Get past the travel brochures and read material that gives an overview of the history, religion, culture, government and business of the country. This basic knowledge will help prevent you from asking questions that should have been researched before that important planning meeting.

2. **LOOK at the material already prepared by the marketing people.** They have probably taken advantage of extensive studies, white papers, research and on-site visits before coming up with their business and marketing plans. Reviewing that material will give you an understanding of the differences between doing business in North America and elsewhere.

3. **Always, LISTEN to what the marketing people and others with in-country experience tell you about operating in the selected country.** Sometimes there is a tendency to discount advice and information given by a person who has lived or worked in other countries. This no doubt is a natural outgrowth of the too-typical North American feeling of, "The whole world should operate as we do back home." This attitude disappears once you get to a country and conduct business there; however, valuable time can be lost by not believing words of wisdom from those who have been there before.

### Additional Tips for Media Relations
### in International Markets

**Don't start thinking about communication issues until you have studied and understood the local business issues in each market.** Take the European Community, for example. Just as U.S. or Canadian federal law has great impact on your business even if you operate in only a few states or provinces, so does EC law affect you even if you do business in only a few European countries.

As various directives are being discussed by the European Parliament, it is crucial that your business gets its views across to the decision makers *before* new laws are enacted. Yet in many European countries corporate lobbying is not accepted. Governments want to hear from trade associations rather than individual corporations. The prevailing view seems to be, "Do your lobbying within your association and then come to us with a composite industry view."

**Do your homework—twice.** Business and marketing plans are essential background to a media relations person's helping to introduce a product, service or operation in another country. These plans will highlight government relations, trade concerns, technology transfer issues, key competitors in the locale and other items that will be very helpful as you develop a media plan.

If you have no contacts in the new market, go on the Internet to find up-to-date information. Or, try the *World Press Encyclopedia*, a two-volume reference work that discusses history, press laws, editorial policy and readership of more than 170 countries. Other sources include professional organizations such as the International Public Relations Association (*www.ipra.org*) or the International Association of Business Communicators (*www.iabc.com*), each of which may be able to give you names of contacts in your countries. Additionally, in-country public relations agencies will be able to pinpoint for you the contacts and media you need.

**Get local advice.** As international PR pioneer John M. Reed put it succinctly, "The first rule of international PR is to get local help. No matter how fluent we become in other languages, no matter how deeply we understand other cultures, there is no way we can attain a native's instinct for his own place."[5]

Seek out an in-country public relations firm or agency that has done work in an area similar to your present needs. The best agencies we have found are those with strong North American or British ties and a combination of local and expatriate public relations pros on staff. That way you get a good balance—the professionalism you are expecting combined with local knowledge and contacts. An important caution: Make sure that the agency specializes in media relations, not advertising or political affairs. Many political has-beens are out of work or freelancing. Be careful. Unless it really is a public affairs expert that you need, insist on media relations skills and experience.

It is well worth the money to get an in-depth briefing from these local experts on how media relations—especially media relations vis-à-vis marketing—works in that locale. You'll also want local expertise to help you adapt to each market's customs while maintaining your corporate and personal ethical standards and, not incidentally, obeying your own country's and local laws. For example, "pay for press" is a common practice among many non-U.S. media operations. In one form, this means paying the publication a "publishing fee" to have your release printed. In another, it can involve picking up the costs for a journalist to travel to news conferences or come to the United States for tours and interviews. These are not bribes. They can be an economic fact of life in many countries where local media budgets are sparse.

In some countries the journalist you deal with may be a lawyer or engineer first and a journalist second. This often means the difference between a general information interview and an in-depth, detailed interview. Here again, listen to what these people say and do not scoff at a public relations practice that would not work in North America but is essential somewhere else.

**Study a globe.** Whenever you are heading to a new country, look at a globe. A globe is better than a map because it overcomes what we call the "Mercator effect"—the fact that North Americans were raised with school maps using the Mercator projection, which makes North America look bigger and more important than it is in the worldwide scheme of things.

Had companies expanding into former Soviet Union-dominated countries taken a moment to look at a globe, they might understand, for example, why people in the Czech Republic resent being called Eastern Europeans. Czechs think of themselves as Central Europeans, and if you make that mistake while you are there someone might point out that Prague is farther west than Vienna.

**Read some history.** It also is useful to read up on the history of each market that is new to you. That sounds obvious—but it is surprising how rarely it is done. A little history can help avoid offending local hosts. For example, in Warsaw a prominent U.S.-based company was criticized for running an ad produced in New York announcing they were "expanding into the emerging Polish market." The offended Pole was a professor at the Jagiellonian University in Krakow which, at the end of the fifteenth century, already was famous for mathematics, astronomy and graduates like Copernicus.

Similarly, Westerners view the People's Republic of China as an emerging market. From a Western marketing perspective it is. Yet the Chinese were making glorious silk in 1750 B.C. and their ancient paintings and sculpture are among the most beautiful in the world.

So sensitivity to local nuances and a keen respect for the richness of other people's heritage are essential to starting off on the right foot in a new market. You do not need dull history textbooks to get that knowledge. It is available on the Internet, in travel guides, biographies, newspapers and magazines, popular fiction and movies.

**Meet the people.** Imagine a visitor to North America believing he or she understood our values and culture after traveling only to New York, Washington, D.C. or Toronto. When you travel to a country new to you, take time to get out of the cities. John le Carre said, "A desk is a dangerous place from whence to watch the world."[6] Cities can be as well. Ride the trains and buses to see how regular folks live.

Talk with people in the countryside and smaller towns. Your local colleagues should be able to arrange such dialogues. Community leaders, school teachers and students frequently are willing to answer questions and give you their opinions over lunch or a few drinks because it is a great way for them to practice their English and learn about North America in return.

**Learn the language.** There is an old joke going around international circles that says someone who speaks three languages is trilingual, someone who speaks two languages is bilingual and someone who speaks one language is an American. At the minimum, you will want to learn a few basic phrases of the country's language before you visit. You truly will set yourself and your organization apart if you take the time to learn another language or two in some detail. Language skills are essential to climbing the executive ladder at European and Asian companies, and the lack of them is a key reason why so few Americans head companies based outside of North America.[7]

**Learn about your targets.** Whether your intended media targets are newspapers, trade publications or newly issued newsletters, become familiar with them. Read them (in translation, if necessary) as you would a new publication in your home market to find out the slant of the publication, key writers and columnists, use of photographs and type of advertising. Do not get hung up on the circulation of a publication as a key indicator of its importance. A publication with what would be a small circulation for North American practitioners could be the most significant publication in another country or region.

Check with local offices of international business or trade publications. They can save you frustrating attempts to get copies of in-country publications. Also, both the editorial and advertising offices can provide excellent overviews of national, regional or global media and their audiences.

Read international papers regularly. Many, like *The Independent,* the *International Herald Tribune* and *The Economist,* are accessible on the Internet. *BBC World News* also is available online, on Public Radio International and on PBS TV.

**Electronic media require extra study.** Electronic media in other countries may not be as prolific or as sophisticated as in North America but they often can be of enormous assistance to a media relations and marketing campaign. Learn the differing styles of government-owned or directed television and also keep in mind their similarity—a need to fill airtime. There are programs about educational, business and government issues that can greatly benefit your media relations program. Often they are pleased to receive background video footage—sometimes even complete programs about your company.

*Two important technical notes affecting worldwide video usage*: First, there are three standard video formats in the world—NTSC, PAL and Secam. Unless a tri-standard monitor and a VCR that plays all three formats are available, you will have to provide your video in the right format for the local market. Second, when creating a video for worldwide distribution to the news media, provide a timed script and put the English-language sound track on a track separate from the music and natural sound. Then the countries that need to translate the message can replace the English by recording the narration in the local language.

**Don't overlook the North American community "over there."** In most countries there are embassies and chambers of commerce with staffs willing and able to help you get started. Not only can they provide a platform for introducing your company and its products or services but also the staff can offer excellent advice for the novice coming in.

**Remember the "foreign" press corps in other countries.** Just as in Washington, D.C., there is a huge group of international reporters from Jakarta to Johannesburg and from Montevideo to Mexico City, so too are there U.S. and Canadian stringers or journalists from television and radio networks, major magazines and leading newspapers in many international capitals and other big cities around the world. Make sure they get special treatment such as private interviews if you want coverage of your news in your home country as well as the new market.

**Local press clubs are invaluable resources** for both learning about the country and making key media contacts. Membership often is broad enough to include public relations agencies and corporate professionals.

**Work those trade shows.** Trade shows offer one of the best ways to get to know the news media from another country or several countries. If your company is exhibiting at a trade show, make sure local and visiting journalists know you are there by issuing personal invitations for a visit to your exhibit booth. Host a reception for trade journalists to meet the key company officers.

Also, get away from your exhibit and visit all the trade publications' booths. Although you might meet only members of the advertising staff, at the minimum you can get copies of key publications, leave your business card to be passed along to the editorial staff and—most important—start building relationships. Business cards vary in size from the format used in the United States to larger, 3" x 5" cards. Most include business and home addresses and telephone numbers, as well as e-mail and fax numbers. In some markets, especially in Asia, information will be in the local language on one side of the card and English on the other.

**Attend international conferences.** In a global economy, international conferences have become a great way for North American companies to make the right international business connections and also leverage the local and regional media to drive brand awareness in new markets. It probably is well worth the money to invest in hiring a local PR firm to help your organization take full advantage of the opportunity—and not make small but embarrassing mistakes like formatting Word documents for U.S.-sized paper that then won't print properly when you use different-standard paper in other countries. Also, you may need help to make sure that any communications technology you will be using at the conference is proven to work in that country.[8]

**Serve as a "warning bell" to your marketing counterparts.** Just as you are trying to learn new ways of conducting media relations in other countries, so are your marketing people trying to cope with methods new to them. Sometimes you both may forget that you are not operating under North American rules. When that happens and your marketing colleagues come up with a "great publicity idea" that just won't work outside the United States, explain why the idea is still great, it's just the wrong country for implementation. In return, perhaps they will be just as tolerant of your "great marketing idea."

**Know your place.** After reading business and marketing plans, you may find that a media relations campaign isn't needed, at least in the early stages. Perhaps the public or government affairs department should be the key player with a behind-the-scenes strategy that does not involve the news media. If that occurs, be mature enough to step out of the picture temporarily and turn leadership over to someone else.

**Watch your language.** It is amazing how often words can trip you up when you least expect it. At The Reader's Digest Association, after half a century of *international* growth, we made a major strategic shift to become a *global* organization. In our U.S. offices we went so far as to avoid words like "domestic," "foreign," "overseas," "off-shore" and "abroad." It is more than semantics. It can be an unintentional sign of arrogance that it is best not to send. It also can be confusing to your listeners or readers, who must do geographical gymnastics in their minds to follow your meaning. After all, what is "foreign" here is "domestic" there. A journalist in Paris being briefed by a U.S. executive who uses the term "domestic sales" is likely to think the numbers relate to French sales when the speaker might have meant U.S. sales. Or a South African hearing about an "overseas expansion" is likely to think about the United Kingdom while a North American listening to the same briefing would think Europe or Asia.

Similarly, when you are preparing materials about activities around the world, be careful not to write from a U.S. perspective. When you are compiling a worldwide list, for example, do not always start with the United States. Rather, alphabetize the list, thus placing the U.S. information at or near the end, or name the countries in random order. At a Ragan Communications conference in Chicago that focused on communicating in the global economy, conferees agreed that a major impediment to American companies' success in international markets is communications being U.S.-centric and the tendency to use American models to deal with international situations.[9]

Also, allow extra time for the translations and all the extra checking that is required to get them right. At the Swiss Federal Institute of Technology in Zurich, for example, where Swiss German is most commonly spoken, each corporate news release issued needs to be translated into three languages—German, Italian and French. For science news, they translate the text into German and English. Imagine the impact of tinkering with the phrasing of words in the draft versions of these news releases![10]

**Announcement dates and times should be selected with the same care as in North America—but not necessarily with the same criteria.** In North America you would likely avoid breaking news on Fridays lest it be buried in least-read Saturday papers or reporters think you are hiding something. Yet Fridays may be great days for announcements in other countries. Holidays are different so that July 4 is perfectly acceptable in the Middle East but the days of Ramadan are not. Be alert to numerous religious observance days as well as local celebrations that might detract from your announcement.

Also, remember the time zones when setting global announcement times. U.S. publicly owned companies must release all material news before the stock market opens or after it closes. It often is best for global companies to set announcement times in the very early morning, before the market opens, so the fewest possible journalists, financial analysts, staff and other key members of your global audiences are asleep when the news first comes out. Seven a.m. Eastern Time works well for U.S. companies because when it is 7 a.m. in New York it is 8 p.m. in Hong Kong and 10 p.m. in Sydney. Take advantage of international electronic news distribution services like Business Wire Global (e-mail: *global@bizwire.com*), which has a satellite reach of 100 countries around the world.

**Translate your materials.** While many international journalists speak English well, they often prefer written material to be in their local language. This is important to remember when sending out media kits or preparing for international trade shows.

Berlitz Translation Service has made available general guidelines to writers working on projects for translation. They advise you to scan the copy for ambiguous word clusters of the type "modifier + noun + noun" (e.g., "plastic widgets and fasteners"). These are commonplace for English but for languages like Spanish and French, where modifiers must follow their nouns, it is critical that the translator know whether "plastic" refers to both the widgets and the fasteners or only to the widgets. Also, when you send photo captions for translation include the photo itself. Without seeing the visual, a translator does not know whether "widget assembly" means "widget unit" or "widget being assembled." In Spanish, for example, widget would be translated as *conjunto* in the first case but *ensamblaje* in the second.

Also, remember that most translations "grow." The translated version may take anywhere from 125 to 150 percent of the space of an English version. Indonesian can take as much as 200 percent. Chinese, on the other hand, with a writing system in which nearly every character represents a complete word, will frequently be shorter than the English version.

**Watch those words!** There are classic examples of embarrassing mistakes and product names that just didn't make it when translated into another language. There's the story that when Chevrolet marketed its Nova car in Latin America, it didn't sell. In English, *nova* is associated with the Latin word for new but in Spanish, *no va* means "it doesn't go." Another time Pepsi tried to use its slogan "Come alive" in Taiwan, which translated literally means "makes your ancestors rise from the dead."[11]

Check, recheck and then check a third time before introducing a name into a country. These multiple checks can save embarrassment—not to mention lost sales and wasted advertising and promotion efforts.

**Be respectful of the local culture and observant of local customs.** This is good business as well as good manners. Business customs differ worldwide. North Americans tend to be impatient to get down to business, while other cultures—notably Asian—prefer to get to know you first. It is mainly only in big cities like New York that "power breakfasts" are an accepted fact of life. When "early birds" phone Mexico, Spain or Portugal, for example, in the early morning or early afternoon and find only empty offices, they need to remember that the locals will make up for the late start and long lunch by working well into the evening.

Author Mia Doucet in the book *China in Motion* offers useful cultural tips in communicating with Asians who are not fluent in spoken English: "Use an interpreter from the start, even when it appears that your Asian counterparts speak and understand English. To avoid offending their pride, point the responsibility back at you. Say, 'Please allow me to have an interpreter here to assist me in making sure I understand your needs.' Also, when speaking through an interpreter, it is important to speak to the individual you are communicating with and not the interpreter." Another hint: "It is human nature to direct our conversation to the person who has the best English-language skills. This is an error because the person who speaks the best English may not necessarily be the most important or highest ranking person in the room. You could undercut the person's authority and cause loss of face."[12]

**Retrain your speakers.** While you probably already have put your key spokespersons through good public speaking and media interview training, they will need special training for interviews in non-English-speaking countries. For many reporters, English will be a second language. That means that the easy-going banter of North American news conferences probably will not come off elsewhere. Also, if your spokesperson is answering questions at a news conference with a simultaneous translator, it is essential to speak in short sentences or phrases and then wait for the translator to catch up.

Industry or technical jargon, business or government acronyms and non-English English ("actualizing your parameters" probably won't translate anywhere!) also can cause great confusion.

One of the easiest ways to retrain a spokesperson is to set up a mock interview with a "reporter" who does not speak English and must use an interpreter. The interpreter, only school-trained in

English, will interrupt constantly to ask the spokesperson to explain jargon or the meaning of such words as "reprioritization." It's a disconcerting experience for a spokesperson—and also a dramatic way to learn to state your case simply and clearly.

**Check for local taboos before coming up with giveaway items for trade shows, news conferences or other events.** A small digital clock might be perfect in the United Kingdom but received with dismay in Asia. Colors could have religious connotations in several countries. Key chains are of little use in lesser-developed countries. Two good resources for advice are in-country public relations agencies and protocol officers at your embassy.

**Leverage online technologies to overcome time zones and keep in constant touch with your worldwide team.** Intranets— typically affordable to firms of all sizes—are one of the easiest and most economical ways to foster communication between international locations. Intranets provide online portals that staffers can access to obtain client files, progress reports and other data related to specific media relations initiatives. Team members are able to revise drafts of news releases, strategic client documents, business pitches and other materials at their convenience—and to attach notes that comment on specific passages and explain why changes were made. Resources like case studies and teaching aids also can be made available through the intranet.[13]

---

### Test Yourself:
### How Would You Handle These Situations?

Following are two scenarios presented by the author (Carole Howard) for breakout groups at a communications lecture to public relations graduate students at San Diego State University on April 24, 2003, called "Global PR in the Real World: Strategies You Should Know Before You Get on the Plane."

**Scenario #1**

You are the media relations director in the corporate offices of a giant U.S.-based multinational company that is composed of highly autonomous business units. They are supposed to coordinate with your office any major announcement that will generate international public attention or media coverage—and, of course, expansion into new markets falls under that umbrella. The problem is that the definition of "coordinate" is rather vague and your corporate culture strongly supports divisional autonomy, with little interference from headquarters as long as sales and profit goals are achieved.

You and Gary, the investor relations director, have been talking about concerns you both have relating to your company's alliance and new market announcements. You usually hear the plans at the last minute, with little chance for input relating to timing or positioning of the announcement, and lots of scurrying is required to get the message out on time. Also, lack of coordination between business units results in two or three announcements coming from the company some months, followed by a long dry spell of five or six months with no significant public news. On one occasion, an Asian new market announcement requiring the CEO's attendance had been scheduled in Hong Kong for the same day as the company's annual meeting in Chicago until you caught the conflict and got it fixed.

You and Gary both believe that the individual business units as well as the overall corporation would greatly benefit from a more coordinated and systematized new market announcement planning process. How do you proceed?

**Scenario #2**

You are attending an interdepartmental update, which the international group president holds quarterly for all senior managers in his organization. You notice the agenda includes an item, "New product announcement," being given by Julie, one of the company's most highly regarded managers. As her presentation progresses, you realize that the planning is very far along. In fact, a joint venture partner already has been selected, and some of the advertising placements have been booked by your New York agency in media in the U.K., France, Germany, Scandinavia, Hungary and Italy.

You are surprised, since you are the PR director for the division, and furthermore you thought you had a pretty good working relationship with Julie. Yet here she is, giving details of a highly confidential (and newsworthy) expansion of her product line into major European markets to a room full of 60 of your colleagues. You also note that the only consumer research she sites was done in Atlanta, New York, Chicago, Denver and Washington, D.C.

Towards the end of her talk, Julie turns to you and says in front of the whole group, "And John, we are counting on you to get us lots of positive media coverage not only in Europe but also worldwide." You are upset because the date she mentioned is right in the middle of a long-planned vacation to the Caribbean with your wife. Furthermore, you know, on a confidential basis, that there is a good chance that a highly restrictive European Community directive, relating to her product line, will come down about a month before Julie's planned announcement date. What do you do . . . now at the meeting? Later?

## A Case Study from Russia, and Eastern and Central Europe

During the 1990s, The Reader's Digest Association established new companies and launched local editions of *Reader's Digest* in Russia, Hungary, the Czech Republic and Poland while the communist empire was disintegrating and capitalism was beginning to flourish.

We learned many lessons as we planned and implemented our media relations and publicity for these launches. These lessons provide useful hints for others moving into the Eastern and Central European marketplace:

1. **A "back to basics" approach is essential to success.** Don't be misled by the visibility of McDonald's restaurants and Pizza Huts around the world. Most North American companies and products are nowhere near as well known. In fact, journalists and consumers may have little or no knowledge of your brand—or your company. Take time up front to work with your operations colleagues to develop detailed business, marketing and communications plans. Do market research early so you have time to recover from surprises.

   You cannot assume your target audience knows what your company stands for and what you are trying to sell. In Eastern Europe, for example, consumers thought the Energizer Bunny commercials were selling little pink toy bunnies for children. A shampoo company drew blank stares and weak sales from ads for two-for-one shampoo. In North America the ads would have sold on emotions—like having sexier hair. In new markets the pitch must be more basic and factual—in this case, explaining that having the conditioner in the shampoo results in fluffier hair.

2. **Study the competition and others' perceptions of you.** As companies do business around the world, it can be useful to communications and marketing strategies to understand how your organization is perceived relative to your competitors in each country. It also is helpful to know how your home country is perceived in new markets. Anti-American sentiment, for example, can have a profound effect on your company. *New York Times* editor and Pulitzer Prize winner Leslie H. Gelb warned in 2004: "What we've seen in the last three years or so is anti-Americanism across the board. That is . . . not liking our policies, not liking our culture, not liking our power, not liking us." He predicts that business is facing a long-term problem where anti-Americanism will be "part of the landscape in which you'll have to do business."[14] Harris

Interactive and its London subsidiary HI Europe regularly conduct research on how other countries' citizens see the United States. It is available on their Web site: *www.harrisinteractive.com.*[15]

3. **Make sure your positioning is right.** Basic positioning questions that are key to success in home markets are even more crucial when you start communicating in new markets. First, is your product or service clearly defined? Second, is it differentiated from the competition? Third, does its performance match the promise? And fourth, can you play up the emotional benefits? The world's greatest marketers sell on emotions. Disney sells magic, not theme parks or movies. And Nike sells performance, not sneakers.

   Think through your positioning carefully. Then pick one or two simple messages and repeat them over and over again. Ours was *"Reader's Digest Válogatás*: World's most widely read magazine now on sale in Hungary" (and the same in Russia, the Czech Republic and Poland, with the local magazine's name). You saw the brand name and this phrase in everything we produced—news media materials, advertisements, promotional and point-of-sale pieces, VIP mailings, billboards—everywhere. Media coverage adopted the same emphasis.

   Never miss an opportunity to picture your product and your logo. Frequency, focus and consistency are key to making them familiar to your potential customers.

4. **Even more than you do in your home country, pay relentless attention to details.** Take a leadership role in planning the timing, location, key messages and spokespersons for major announcements. You can expect complications because you are operating somewhere other than on familiar ground—and frequently in a language other than English.

   You will need to make sure the translations of your news releases, media kits, speeches and other materials are impeccably accurate. Choose translators or interpreters with experience—and an understanding of the local idiom. Hire several if they will be working long hours—tired people may overlook possible misinterpretations that can cause embarrassment and inaccuracies. Provide them with copies of your presenters' speeches in advance so they can familiarize themselves with the content, then warn speakers not to ad lib.

   Be aware that some *translators* translate literally, which can result in crazy wording. *Interpreters,* on the other hand, work to put your key message in appropriate language or symbols so that it will be received the way you intend it to be. Make sure you know which

skill you're buying. We've had the greatest success hiring interpreters with experience in high-level government events where
nuances matter a great deal. Surprisingly, refugees returning home
after living many years outside their home countries may not be
the best translators if they are out of date on some of the current
usage and phraseology.

Hold your news conferences at business centers with experience
in and equipment for simultaneous translations. Make sure your
video plays in the host country's technical format. Print captions
in both English and the local language at the bottom or on the
back of your press photographs.

Watch for misunderstandings if you are not used to working in the
metric system. Get advice from local experts on the correct protocol for invitations, seating and toasts at banquets. Pay even more
attention to money and bills than usual. To protect yourself from
inflation and currency devaluations, negotiate so your bills are
paid in local currency. In some cases we have found it cost-effi-
cient to prepay local agencies the amount of their budget so they
can buy space and purchase other services as the dollar fluctuates.

---

### What Is an "Official" Copy of a Speech?

Media relations professionals learn early in their international
careers that providing journalists with copies of key speeches translated into the local language helps ensure accuracy—not to mention
control of the message. But that did not work in China for U.S. Vice
President Dick Cheney. He delivered an important speech at Shanghai's
Fudan University in 2004 after extracting solemn agreements from
China's leaders that the speech would be broadcast live, directly and
without censorship, to the Chinese people. In fact it was aired only to a
limited audience, unannounced, and with no prime-time repeats.
Worse, when Chinese officials sent a self-described "official full-text
transcript" in Chinese to the *People's Daily* and the government's official
news agency Xinhua, the vice president's words were so censored and
twisted that much of the meaning was totally changed. A lesson to us
all: Censorship has always been a vital part of Chinese government policy, so making statements in that country about topics like freedom and
democracy, Taiwan, security and economic cooperation is bound to
get you in trouble.

"Ch---y in China," *The Wall Street Journal*, April 27, 2004, p. A18.

Check the local country's laws if there is a value added tax (VAT); ordering and paying your bills through your local subsidiary can result in large savings. Don't be surprised if there is an ulterior motive to generate hard currency when some of your suppliers or partners make recommendations.

5. **Most media relations techniques that work at home will also work well in other countries as their business practices become more universal—and more Western.** You may be asked to advertise or get involved in a business venture by journalists. In some countries there is no clear separation between business and editorial, and it is common to pay a "publishing fee" to get your news release printed. But most professional news media relations techniques work around the world—when they are based on real news announcements and practiced with respect for journalists' needs as well as your own organization's objectives. In fact, in Mexico the local Reader's Digest media relations director helped get the "pay for press" practice stopped by refusing to participate. Her office supplied real news and got it treated like real news.

6. **Even universal media tools often require local touches to be successful.** We hosted news conferences for all the *Reader's Digest* magazine launches. The Eastern and Central European events followed our Western format fairly closely. In Moscow, however, presentations are expected to be significantly longer—40 to 60 minutes rather than our more normal 20 to 30—and if you can incorporate an historical perspective about your company and product, so much the better. In Poland they like numerical research from a reputable outside firm to support product and consumer claims. Most reporters ask their best questions at the news conference, not waiting to do so in private after the general Q and A session, as is true in North America. On the contrary, as soon as the news conference is over, everyone rushes to the food—traditionally a full meal consumed at record speed. Russian journalists have learned from experience that if they do not get to the meal quickly, it will be gone. Food also can be a major enticement to attend a news conference in other Eastern and Central European countries. To make your meals memorable, ask the locals what are the most desirable dishes for a party and try to serve at least one of them.

Giveaways are eagerly received and it is worth your while to make them special. Knowing the long lines that Russian citizens have endured, we gave each journalist a very large tote with a shoulder strap—featuring our new magazine's logo in English and Russian. Inside was a "traveling office" with a wide variety of office supplies in a leather case, also featuring our logo—just the items that were so hard to get in Moscow. In Hungary our giveaways also matched the market: another tote, with our logo in Hungarian and English—plus a business card holder, again featuring our bilingual logo. We were told executives were getting and giving business cards for the first time and had nowhere to keep them. These giveaways were popular because they were so useful. The totes became very visible "moving billboards" for our brand long after the news conferences were over.

Our bilingual invitations to the news conference were also special. We engraved them, pictured both countries' flags and individually wrote in the reporter's name in fancy script. We were told these touches made our event stand out in journalists' minds.

To attract media and consumer attention, we used large hot-air balloons and billboards. The balloons drew a crowd and the one in Moscow made the front page of *Advertising Age*. Our Moscow billboards were unusual enough that Tom Brokaw mentioned them on the *NBC Nightly News*. He'd seen them on his way from the airport into Moscow while covering the Bush-Gorbachev summit the week after our launch. It was great timing and gave us a second round of media coverage.

Direct mail also can be effective if you can purchase accurate lists. But in formerly communist countries, you might initially face suspicion and concern. Privacy is a major issue in countries like Poland. "Where did you get my name?" consumers want to know. After all, for years they lived in a police state where anonymity was the best way to survive.

7. **Always remember your objective and your primary audience.** In Moscow we got great pressure from suppliers to invite government officials and other so-called VIPs (mostly politicians) to the news conference. We refused, saying the news conference was strictly for working journalists and its objective was solely to generate media coverage about the launch of our new magazine and local Russian company. In most markets you lose focus when you begin to mix messages and target audiences. The one hundred-plus journalists who attended seemed to appreciate our concentrating on them alone—and the extensive positive coverage around the world about the new magazine and our local company reinforced our belief that we'd made the right decision. In fact, media coverage was so extensive and our magazine so popular in the republics of Russia, Ukraine and Belarus that we sold out within days. So we scaled back plans for significant additional pro-

motions, relying primarily on mailings of each issue of the maga-zine to key journalists every month.

In Asia, however, the situation is different. There they expect many local dignitaries to be on the stage with your company's pre-senters. The more VIPs in attendance, the more important your organization must be.

8. **Choose your speakers based on your business and marketing strategies.** As discussed previously, the balance between global and local speakers and content should depend on your organiza-tion's business strategy and organizational structure. Multina-tional companies with autonomous subsidiaries and independent strategies in each market likely would want to feature local execu-tives as spokespersons. Global companies, on the other hand, probably want to showcase both global and local spokespersons at news conferences and other announcement events. You also could provide a copy of your corporate annual report to journalists even if it is in English, while augmenting it with fact sheets in the local language showing the number of in-country employees, facilities, products, contributions to the local economy, etc.

9. **Allow much more time to accomplish each activity than you would at home—and be realistic in your expectations.** For generations people in the former Soviet bloc countries were denied access to the rest of the world, penalized for showing ini-tiative or making a profit and taught that capitalism and private ownership were evil. Indifference replaced initiative because that was the best way to survive.

You will experience problems with bureaucratic inefficiency, cor-ruption, shortage of high-tech equipment, manual systems and lack of experience. Cultural obstacles—legacies of the communist rule—will work against you. For years people waited for orders and responded to the demands of a grandiose central plan. There were no choices—Moscow did the thinking for everyone. Over-coming that numbness and encouraging individual initiative may take generations, as will attention to deadlines, the ability to be flexible and adaptable and the desire to work around obstacles that come up in any major project as a matter of course.

Even in 2005, more than 15 years after the collapse of the Soviet Union, the country's legendarily meddlesome and corrupt bureau-cracy makes doing business difficult for locals as well as foreign-ers. As well, some feel that the Russian media seem more subject to censorship than in Stalin's time. The country's badly managed attempts at capitalism and democracy have soured a majority of the population. *Privatizatsiia,* or privatization of Russia's industrial and natural resources, has resulted in such a pattern of grand theft that Russians have coined the term *prikhvatizatsiia,* or confiscation, to mock the process.

At a recent public relations seminar, a Swiss executive talked about his company's entry into Eastern Europe. He said it would be many years before one could assume local people would understand the professional standards we take for granted. He also suggested spending more time doing the work yourself than you would think you needed to do. In Budapest, for example, all the proposed news conference sites initially shown for our approval were much too small and had no provision for translators or television. You cannot manage a project like this from a desk in your home country. Nothing beats on-site knowledge.

10. **English is the universal language of global business. But, be careful!** Don't underestimate the language barrier. Most of the people you are dealing with will be listening and speaking in a second language, so each conversation takes place on two planes. You are thinking and speaking in English but your colleagues probably have to do the translation in their heads before they can comprehend and respond.

    Perhaps people sometimes pretend to understand, not wanting to interrupt the flow of the conversation for clarification. Maybe they think they do understand, but subtleties are lost. It is important to state things as simply as possible and be crystal clear in your communications. Get agreements in writing to see if your expectations match theirs. Interact frequently to be sure there's an easy avenue for questions. Get on a plane, make yourself available and find out firsthand what's going on. It is called "management by traveling around."

    On the other hand, be wary of business people who have traveled in the United Kingdom or the United States saying they speak no English. Even if they require a translator, they may understand more English than they let on and you should be careful not to discuss your negotiating strategy with colleagues in asides, thinking no one else understands.

11. **Take advantage of local resources to help you achieve your objectives and avoid cultural gaffes.** Several well-known public relations firms have set up offices in the former Soviet Union and Eastern and Central Europe. Look for those with proven experience and knowledge of local media—plus a staff that speaks the local language and understands the local culture.

You need someone who will catch you if your ad looks like it was created from a North American perspective, like the Coke print ads showing a glass filled with ice, when every North American who travels to Europe knows that Europeans don't use ice in their drinks; to alert you that Ukrainians want their country to be called Ukraine, not *the* Ukraine; or to remind you that in Hungary last names come before first and in Russia people wear their wedding rings on their right hand. That was important to a U.S. baby-care company that offended consumers when it pictured a young girl with a baby in their product promotions; scandalized viewers thought she was an unwed mother because she wore no ring on her right hand.

Another valuable contact is the U.S. Embassy—especially the press attaché at U.S. Information Service offices around the world. They have daily dealings with journalists and are pleased to give you advice and practical counsel on how to conduct business in their countries.

## Advice from PR Pros on How to Succeed in Their Markets

Here are some suggestions passed on by PR professionals, editors and business executives, all of whom are practicing PR in their local markets, to help you get the best possible results from your efforts as you go global:

### Asia

A major difference is the way news conferences are handled in Asia. For example, in Hong Kong and Taiwan it is a real show with all the key people sitting at the head table wearing corsages. The more senior people you have on stage, the more important the event. The setup is also very different. Theatre style is not very popular. Small tables for four where journalists can lean on something and have tea or coffee (obviously not served during the program) works very well, particularly in Taiwan. Because of their culture, Chinese journalists will rarely ask questions as a group, preferring to talk one-on-one with the speakers before or afterward. In Thailand a product launch involves two separate functions in one day, one for VIP guests with lunch, followed by the news conference. The odd thing is that all the journalists gather in a separate room at the same time as the VIP guests arrive and seem to enjoy themselves immensely at this informal gathering before the news conference. Again, the more keynote speakers the better. It may also be useful to know that the media here say they far and away prefer dealing with a company PR manager than an agency in most cases, because they feel they are getting directly to the source.

—Liz Dingwall Mueller, Hong Kong

## Australia

Even though Australia and the U.S. may appear to be very similar in terms of culture, there are some key differences. Aussies are not as intense when it comes to business presentations and face-to-face contact. That doesn't mean we're not serious about doing a great job. But we find some of the "show" associated with U.S. fanfare rather false instead of involving. So despite the fact that we follow the U.S. very closely in many trends, we tend to look to our English heritage for what is stylish, frowning upon flashy trappings. Also, American business people are much more direct about what they want and what they expect. Aussies, on the other hand, don't like to be seen as too bossy and we like to be friends with our business suppliers. So what we *don't* say may be as critical as what we say. We'll just not use your services again if we are unhappy rather than complain and cause a fuss. So you need to find the proper balance between not frightening us but also giving and getting useful feedback. As well, while Americans tend to idolize heroes, Aussies are known to "cut down tall poppies." So, for example, when Bill Gates was here there was as much talk about his being a boring speaker as there was about his brilliance in making Microsoft a worldwide brand name.

—Jo Roper, Sydney

## Canada

Consider whether your PR program or campaign is national or regional. We have a huge country and your approach would be different for each region. Nationally, you would aim at the larger media outlets (the networks and syndicated press), which are predominantly centered in Toronto. If you are looking at effectively reaching the entire country, you'll want someone with regional contacts to do the legwork for you. Use your professional network—the International Association of Business Communicators or Public Relations Society of America—to help you find them. Is it a national campaign to the English-speaking public only, or to the French as well? If so, you will have additional costs for translation, a francophone spokesperson and perhaps an agency that has experience in providing services for both the

English- and French-speaking markets. The cultural tastes of Quebeckers, for example, are very different from the rest of the country and, as a result, the way you communicate with this group might be quite different from how you present your story in the west. Also, Canada in recent years has become a nation of nations, with a great many people now speaking a Chinese dialect or Hindi.

—Bonnie Venton-Ross, Toronto

## France

If you want more media coverage in France about your company, provide journalists with background information on the history of your company and also how you are sharing the financial results of your business not only with shareholders but also with employees and society. Journalists here are very interested in cultural as well as economic success. So it is a good idea to brief them on how the company was built and what it is contributing to society overall—for example, establishing a foundation to support young artists.

—Henri Capdeville, Paris

The language of PR is highly culturally dependent. Any American operating here would have to be competent enough to read and write in French—or hire it done locally. Industry and government rules are quite different from the American scene, and for broadcast in particular the regulatory environment is very different. As a result, the rules and recipes valid in America have to be drastically adapted to fit the context here. Rules governing social and personal relations in France also are different from what an American is accustomed to. For instance, giving out one's home address or phone number would be misunderstood and it is not information expected on a news release. PR people here have many virtues but suffer from a lack of professionalism compared to their American colleagues. So as long as you adapt to "the French way," your ideas and talents would be welcomed and very useful here.

—Benedicte Barre, Paris

## Hungary

It is important for PR professionals to gather and weigh all advice from their clients and local colleagues—but then take care not to be overly influenced by such advice. The locals often try to manipulate journalists from behind the scenes rather than invest the time, energy and money that a professional campaign requires. Their results understandably often are mixed at best. U.S. PR professionals should make sure they are aware of relevant local laws, customs and attitudes but make their own decisions according to their best professional judgment.

—Peter Keresztes, Budapest

## Mexico

Before contacting the media, learn how it works in Mexico. It is very different than in the U.S. or Europe—much more personal interaction and less technology and specialized services, for example. If you cannot afford the time for this relationship building, get local help. Try not to go on your own "the American way." Also, always say no to media people who ask you to pay to get your news release published. It is much less common than it was, but it still exists—and if you do it once you'll have to do it forever.

—Ligia Fernandez, Mexico City

## South Africa

Firstly, it is absolutely imperative to join forces with a local PR firm experienced in the kind of campaign you are wanting. Contact an ad agency, your local attorney, the local office of a multinational company, even the editor of a major newspaper here to ask for their recommendations. Bigger is not always better. Small consultancies are known to go the extra mile. Secondly, in South Africa contacts are vital to getting your story in print. The media respond to relationships, which is all the more reason for collaboration with a local firm. Whereas in the U.S. journalists would be offended by gifts and junkets, here "social contact" definitely helps. If you are pitching a really big story that will take more than a few minutes in the telling, a lunch or coffee with a key journalist often works. The gift should be relevant to the story. Thirdly, when companies first started reinvesting in the post-sanctions era, any foreign company looking for a little coverage was pretty well guaranteed it. Now the story has to be sold as relevant to the local audience. It is also important to bear in mind that a significant percentage of the consumer market is functionally illiterate. However, smaller papers and especially free issues to local communities are widely read. South Africa as a fledgling democracy takes itself very seriously. All the mainstream papers and TV networks cover mainly politics, crime, the economy and any scandal involving famous people. There is not much space left for "soft" news. Here the sponsorship/advertising dilemma creeps in. Your story may be topical, but you will likely only get your brand mentioned if you are a sponsor or if your story is a must and there is absolutely no way they can cover it without mentioning who you are! But the papers are more sympathetic to publicizing events of non-profit organizations. The news media directory is usually out of date by the time it is printed and, in any case, caters mainly to advertisers. Local PR professionals usually keep their lists updated the hard way—by painstakingly phoning around on a regular basis.

—Fay Davids Kajee, Cape Town

## Sweden

Find the real decision maker when you have a PR proposal. Many companies have an "information secretary," but that may not be the right person to approach. It could be the managing director or the marketing director. Send a written proposal first—if you phone directly you may be considered too brash. Create a win-win situation with your proposal. Swedish companies have very tight PR budgets and will not go for any PR proposals that they cannot see a clear gain from. Come well prepared and act professional. After all, Sweden has always looked to the U.S. for role models in PR, management and advertising.

—Ullastina Ostberg, Stockholm

## Switzerland

Although it may sound simplistic, the best tip I can pass on to Americans coming to Switzerland to do PR is to contact a local PR agency skilled in collaborating with American companies. In Europe the best PR approach will differ from country to country. In Switzerland, for example, you will benefit from the local know-how you can get only from a local partner and adviser. Also, language is very important. Although business and media people generally speak English, an effective PR approach in Switzerland could well depend on a competence in French and German.

—Hans Bosshard, Zurich

## United Kingdom

Be sure to involve local people in the creative process. When you come over from headquarters and talk about rolling *out* a product or a campaign, the local people feel rolled *over*—like they've been hit by a steamroller rather than involved in a communications partnership.

—Russell Twisk, London

## Personal and Professional Growth

Your company or client probably is going global because expansion into international markets represents the only way to achieve long-term growth objectives. Yet resources can be scarce in many organizations. So your company's future in the global marketplace is up to the vision and skills of people like you.

Opportunities can be endless—not only for your firm's growth but also for your own. Immersing yourself in other cultures is a real learning experience. It also is a little like going through Alice's looking glass: You will never see yourself and your own country in quite the same way. With patience, a broad perspective, a willingness to learn and a healthy dose of can-do spirit, you can contribute to your organization's success at the same time you are traveling the world and expanding your professional skills.

# 10

# Crisis Planning

## How to Anticipate and Manage Emergency Situations

Emergencies. Crises. Catastrophes. Disasters. Terrorist attacks. Mismanagement. Fraud. There was a time when anything that went wrong was called a crisis, from an explosion in a factory to the sudden demise of the CEO to a product recall. Today, the word "crisis" seems insufficient to describe the depth, breadth, scope and ramifications of many bad situations. A parachuter's joke is: when your primary parachute doesn't open, you have an emergency; when the backup doesn't open, you have a crisis. PR consultant Jim Lukaszewski says victims make a crisis. "A crisis occurs when people, animals or living systems are involuntarily adversely affected by some organizational action. If there isn't life involved or affected, the incident may be important to the organization's or the CEO's well-being, but it isn't a crisis."[1] Joe Marconi offers another approach: "Crisis management is necessary when something negative occurs—a confrontation between companies or organizations and the media; companies and their competitors or rivals; companies and their stakeholders or customers; or negative activity in general."[2]

183

Into which category would you place the 2004 tsunami that devastated parts of Asia? What about the Enron and Global Crossing implosions? Out-of-control wildfires in California? Flooding in the Midwest? CBS's false reports regarding President Bush's National Guard service? The recall of your number-one product? Bombs exploding in the underground railway? Anarchy in the days following Hurricane Katrina? An energy blackout that covers several states? The downsizing of 400 people in your company?

And how do you handle or manage each situation? The world of 24/7/365 news media with satellite uplinks from their vans, battery packs, videocams, cell phones and on-the-spot gonzo reporters has taken away the ability for many organizations to get in front of the situation and manage the media and the message. Cell phone cameras have made the average citizen the first responder to news media, with the ability to send or upload images directly to CNN or a wire service. Cell phones themselves have made reporters out of your next-door neighbor. And the reliability on eyewitnesses—widely recognized as the most inaccurate of witnesses—creates distorted information.

Also distorted is the degree of importance given to these situations. A derailed train carrying toxic materials is now a local story and seldom gives rise to safer rails, less transport of toxic items and NIMBY (Not in My Backyard) activists. Suggested malfeasance among politicians or corporate executives is simply another day at the office. Terrorism happens all around us. The phrase "disaster fatigue" has entered the nomenclature to describe how each new incident receives less media coverage, less activism by private citizens and less anxiety. And William Wordsworth's sonnet, "The World is Too Much with Us" takes on new meaning.

In the aftermath of the 9/11 terrorist attacks in the U.S., a senior public relations person at one of the U.S. airlines told of the events of that day, and the days following, as it related to the airline's carefully constructed crisis response plan. "Our plan was virtually useless," he said. "The one thing we never anticipated was not being in control of our part of the crisis and not being able to communicate to our customers. All communication, all information was being handled by the authorities in the federal government because this was an attack on the U.S., not a single-plane crash, cause unknown."

Communication, always the vital element in any situation, can be wiped out as an earthquake, hurricane or tsunami rips away power lines, telephone lines, cell towers and gas lines or as your country is under attack. This is the new world of crisis planning.

## Creating a Plan for Any Occasion

In a workshop on crisis communication, PR consultant Raymond C. Jones listed as the most important prerequisite for an effective crisis plan is a CEO who understands:

- the serious damage that can be done by a poor public relations effort;
- the importance of trusting in and delegating to professionals;
- that an organization can actually emerge from a crisis with its reputation *enhanced,* if it responds well; and,
- that honesty is the best policy and that if you engage in gamesmanship with the media, you will lose every time.[3]

While the above list is timeless, there are important elements of a crisis plan that need continual updating and rethinking. Previous plans never took into account the crisis of an entire computer system going up in shreds from a bomb blast. Previous plans never looked at how you would communicate if the entire communication system were destroyed. Previous plans never thought about having to set up an entire business . . . from scratch . . . with no location, no furniture, no computers or telephones, no paper files, no staff.

So, perhaps the next most important prerequisite for an effective plan is the detailed list of probable and possible events that could become anything from a bad news day to a catastrophe. If your business location is near water, natural disasters such as a hurricane or a tsunami, or human disasters, such as an oil spill, should be on your list. If your business is in a tower, fire, terrorism, power outages should all be on your list. If you have a manufacturing operation, anything from chemical spills to sabotage to environmental issues should be listed. If you have operations in third-world countries, possible civil unrest and terrorism should be on your list. Also on that list should be the product recall probabilities, class-action lawsuits over a defective product, financial malfeasance, a charge of pedophilia against a volunteer, a federal investigation, an insensitive remark by a not-thinking-smart executive. Anything that can create a crisis.

The next step is to develop individualized plans for each eventuality. That may seem like a lot of work, but it is essential as no one plan will work for all situations. Crises don't happen the way you want them to or on your schedule. That carefully constructed scene in your head of having the media meet at a nearby location for briefings doesn't work if the nearby location is also in flames or under water and destroyed in the gas line explosion.

Another step is to work in concert with all the other departments who are looking at crises from their points of view. The information technology people are busy building/storing/saving backup systems across town or across the country. Human resources are looking at their databases to make sure they can have access to employee names, next of kin information, payroll data and benefits information. Corporate safety officers are working with myriad local, state and federal officials on the best evacuation plans and recovery efforts.

From your media relations viewpoint, you need backup files on media contacts, standby statements and executive contact information. You may need to run the postcrisis media operations from your home or another city or a different company location, so your plans have to account for that and for notifying the media how to find you.

Perhaps most important, you will need to adjust your thinking about crises: how they start, how they are perceived and how they could change your organization.

Carreen Winters of the MWW Group counsels that "to provide cogent communications counsel in crisis or otherwise, it is incumbent upon communications professionals to serve as a resource for real-time intelligence on the rapidly changing attitudes among the public and particularly the media, which play a key role in shaping and influencing public perception and reaction."[4] Consultant Fraser Seitel expresses it this way: "Public perception of 'who's winning, who's losing, who's at fault' is molded in the initial several hours."[5] Martin A. Kramer asserts that "fully half the battle in an adversarial television story is for the representative of the institution under attack to come across as caring and empathetic. And viewers form their verdict on that in the first 30 seconds of an interview."[6]

One thing all advisors agree on: You never get a second chance to make a good first impression. That adage is essential to remember as you set about making your crisis plans.

Also, in order to have a successful plan, your plans must be tested, tried and simulated in order to be the best they can be. "Regular training sessions and crisis simulations are critical to help sensitize your team to the various pressures that will be present during a real situation," says Jeff Braun of The Ammerman Experience.[7] As you develop a written crisis communication plan, a key point you will want to make clear to the top decision makers of your company or client is that the definition of a crisis is a relative thing. A few people speaking out to the media over a dress code can be big television news even though you feel the issue is trivial in light of broader, more pressing issues. Your prompt, matter-of-fact management of smaller issues will go a long way toward containing them so they do not develop into major media events.

## Strategic Questions to Test Your Crisis Plan

The following strategic questions were developed by Canadian publishing executive and adjunct professor Ralph Hancox to help boards of directors formulate clear, unambiguous and precise answers as they develop mission statements and strategic plans. They can serve as equally valuable guidelines for media relations professionals and your colleagues as you develop a crisis plan for your organization.

1. What are we going to do?
2. How are we going to do it?
3. How are we going to pay for it?
4. Who's going to do the work?
5. How will we treat them?
6. Who's going to consume what we do?
7. How will we reach them?
8. How will we treat our various publics (customers, clients, employees, industry associates, suppliers, regulators, etc.)?
9. What other people do we need to reach?
10. How will we organize and control all this?
11. What returns do we expect for our activities?

"From the Chair of the Board to the Shipping Room Clerk," paper presented by Ralph Hancox, Adjunct Professor and Professional Fellow, The Canadian Centre for Studies in Publishing, Simon Fraser University, Vancouver, Canada, to the 3rd McMaster World Congress on Corporate Governance, January 23–27, 2006.

## Things to Do During a Crisis

While there are countless ways to develop plans for dealing with the media (and other constituencies) during a crisis, you must have or know how to get the appropriate information about people, policies and events inside and outside of your organization. You must always be proactive.

1. **Know who is in charge.** Long before any crisis hits, there should be a clearly defined chain of command. The person in charge isn't always the CEO or the company attorney or the media spokesperson. The person in charge is the coordinator of

the many other people who are in charge of their responsibilities, from security to rescue, legal issues to media statements, employee evacuation to employee notification. Make sure everyone knows who is in charge.

2.  **Know who has the information.** Information exists by department, by type of crisis, by need to know, by the public's desire to know, by federal or state regulations. Make a list of the types of information needed and where it will have been stored in anticipation of a crisis.

3.  **Know who will speak on behalf of the organization.** The person in charge may also be the spokesperson but the spokesperson doesn't always have to be the person in charge. Whoever speaks to the public must be knowledgeable, calm, careful with words, optimistic. Selection of the "crisis" spokesperson should be done, if possible, long before a crisis hits.

4.  **Understand the feeding needs of the media.** Media reporting on your crisis will want facts when you don't have them, numbers when you can't speculate, estimates of damage that aren't yet available. And they will want them NOW. Give whatever you have: number of employees, list of products, the count of employees who have checked in, the offers of assistance you've received. In testimony after Hurricane Katrina, the former director of the Federal Emergency Management Agency stated that one of his big mistakes was in not giving enough briefings to the media about his agency's activities before, during and after the hurricane landing. Too late. In the absence of information, he and the FEMA agency were severely chastised for not responding quickly enough to the crisis.

5.  **Understand that "first beats better."** In the mad scramble to feed the dozens—hundreds—of news media who come down on a crisis, there is little effort to corroborate eyewitness accounts, rumors, innuendoes or speculation. "In a crisis, accuracy falls victim to speed every time. The victory goes to he who 'breaks' the story; who gets there before everybody else. If that means facts are slightly off or the wrong information is reported—so be it."[8]

6.  **Monitor the media.** Because the media are operating at mach speed during a crisis and are chasing all information, however incorrect it may be, it would be irresponsible to not pay attention to what is being said. "Monitoring the 'Net, the radio, cable, and the major media becomes a front-line crisis public relations responsibility."[9]

7. **Set up a plan for using your Web site during a crisis.** Dee Rambeau of DVCO suggests setting up a "dark site," a Web page that is ready to go but is not yet online. The site can be loaded with content that would be of importance to the public and of interest to the media, and can be turned on when the crisis hits; use the media to direct the public to the site.[10] If your site has a lot of regular exchange from customers, suppliers, shareholders, the public and other constituencies, it also can be a precursor to spotting potential crisis or issues that need attention.

8. **Communicate with employees.** Often the forgotten audience in a major crisis, employees can be your best line of defense and/or offense. "Acknowledging the scope of the disaster," and providing "truthful, sincere statements from top management even if that means admitting that plans for dealing with the crisis are still not finalized," will keep employees from speculating and spreading rumors. "It isn't business as usual, so companies really need to avoid pretending that it is."[11]

9. **Recognize that you have a potential problem.** When the flames are visible, when the water is lapping at the door, it is easy to know you have a problem. It isn't as easy when there are rumors of malfeasance, stories about an executive who has a severe drug problem or a stock price that starts to dip for no apparent reason. As an advisor to the senior staff and executives, you are the early warning system for potential problems. It might be a series of blogs discussing a report from an angry customer, or a reporter's story on lack of safety or security at your most important location—whatever it is, it's either going to be a problem, or already is a problem.

10. **Be accessible.** "Unfortunately, in a crisis, the first, and often overwhelming, reflex is to run and hide. You can't dig that foxhole fast enough. In truth, though, it's really time to put down the shovel. As counter-intuitive as it may sound or feel, this is the time to be more accessible than ever with the media."[12]

### Lessons Learned

George Stephanopoulos, chief Washington correspondent for ABC News and longtime advisor to President Bill Clinton, offered advice to political candidates running in the 2000 elections that applies equally well to organizations preparing crisis plans: "Know your weaknesses," he says. "Research all your own vulnerabilities before your enemies do."[13] Most misconceptions begin with a certain element of the truth. Look at how your policies and practices could be perceived by others, especially those who are not admirers of your organization or industry. If there is even a hint of a scandal, heed the advice of veteran journalist Bob Woodward, who said it is imperative to release the facts as soon as possible lest questions harden into "a permanent state of suspicion and warfare."[14] Ronald L. Levy, media expert and former president of North American Precis Syndicate, Inc., advises: "Be preemptive. The best time to avoid a media disaster is the same as the best time to avoid a fire or explosion in the plant—before it starts. Focus on the ultimate weapon of modern PR—the truth."[15]

It is important that you and your management recognize that incomplete and sometimes inaccurate media coverage is inevitable during a crisis. Perhaps all you can realistically hope for when you are involved in negative news is that the media get most of the facts right and portray your organization as being concerned and actively involved in fixing what went wrong.

### Helpful Hints on Communicating in a Crisis

The relationship between you and the publics you serve is never more tested than during a crisis. Here are some hints to help you maintain that relationship.

> Crisis communications is by no means a science, and the art of developing and enacting effective plans is particular to each company. But silence isn't a response and doesn't help a company tell its story. Reactions must be quick. They must show that the company is strong, stable and ready to act. By articulating a substantive position and communicating it in a timely way, a company has a better chance to influence how events unfold. While the presumption of innocence is the cornerstone of our judicial system, the competitive nature of our markets offers no such sanctuary.
>
> —Fred Bratman, President
> Hyde Park Financial Communications
> "Remaining silent during crisis can threaten credibility"
> PR Week, October 18, 2004, p. 6

Unfortunately, in a crisis, the first, and often overwhelming, reflex is to run and hide. You can't dig that foxhole fast enough. In truth, though, it's really time to put down the shovel. As counter-intuitive as it may sound or feel, this is the time to be more accessible than ever with the media,

especially under the added, and increasingly merciless, high intensity light of the Internet and the countless bloggers waiting to react and comment on everything you do.
—Interviewing: Are Media & Ethics Mutually Exclusive?
February 14, 2005
*www.imakenews.com*

Recognize that people are risk adverse and when upset will often fixate on negatives; be extremely careful in offering up the five "N" words—no, not, never, nothing, none—and words with negative connotation.
—Dr. Vince Covello
Keynote Address
U.S. Conference of Mayors Emergency,
Safety and Security Summit
Washington, DC
October 24, 2001

The biggest progress in crisis communication over the past five years has been the growing recognition that audiences are not all the same and are not blank slates. Their pre-existing knowledge, values and emotions matter, and it's very difficult to talk to them effectively without starting where they start.

["Metamessaging"] is the best I can come up with to describe all the content of crisis communications other than information content: how reassuring to be, how confident to sound, how to address emotion, etc. As a rule, crisis planners do not consider these questions explicitly; instead they rely on instinct. And their instinct tends to be system-atically wrong: over-reassuring, over-confident, inhumanly unemotional and intolerant of the emotions of others.
—Peter M. Sandman
"Crisis Communication: A Very Quick Introduction"
*The Synergist*
April 2004

# 11

# Measurement/ Evaluation

## How to Know if Your Program Is Working

Globally, the number of Web sites and blogs used as part of organizational communication increases exponentially each day. In addition, there are hundreds of thousands of daily, weekly and Sunday newspapers, and trade and consumer magazines worldwide. Add, to this, thousands of public and subscriber-based television and radio stations, and you can begin to see the scope of a media relations program for your company or organization. While it probably is not the intent of your particular media relations program to reach all of these media outlets, it should be your intent to know, insofar as possible, how many of your targeted media responded to your efforts to communicate about your organization and in what way and, more important, what action the targeted audience took in response to your message.

Measurement of the various media relations activities is generally the forgotten element of most programs. In fact, some handbooks on publicity do not even include a section on measurement or evaluation. Measurement should be as well thought out, as well planned, and as well executed as the rest of your media relations program. You should know if you want to measure:

- the relationship you have with reporters, editors, columnists and freelancers;
- the impact your messages have on the publics you wish to reach (Do they react to your messages the way you want them to? Do they understand your messages? Do they buy your products?);
- the number of people you reach via the media;
- the way your message is perceived by the public (Do they feel about your organization or product the way you want them to?);
- how many media used your message;
- which media used your message;
- an estimated value to the organization of your efforts (Was a boycott avoided? Did you receive favorable editorials? Did the people vote to support your institution?).

Organizations that have had a disaster also need to consider evaluating the spillover effect of that disaster onto subsequent public relations and media relations activities. Bad news stays in the public mind for many years and even generations and can heavily influence how the public feels about your company, organization, management or campaign. Innocent attempts at new, positive media campaigns can revive old, bad memories. For example, a story of a new method of cleaning up oil spills will trigger an editor's—and the public's—memory of the Alaskan spill, inevitably linking a good story to a bad one. A long-term, professionally administered measurement of current levels of this "guilt by association" attitude can help you determine when, how and where to launch new media campaigns.

## The Goal of Measurement

No matter how large or small your operation may be, every well-run media shop should have some method of monitoring and evaluating the results of its *output* in order to know its *outcome*. For many years, the rule of thumb on media measurement was counting clips and column inches. That was sufficient unto the day, the day before fragmentation of audiences, electronic media and satellite transmissions. Then, "air time" was added to the mix. Along came "impressions," which is another way to describe circulation and viewing-audience numbers. Then, "advertising equivalents" were touted as a great measurement tool. All of these efforts produce only abstract numbers. They measure output, not outcome, and give a false indicator of the value of media relations. Dan Burgess of Doe Anderson PR says, "I would argue that media placement is not necessarily a result; it's just on the way to a result."[1] Dr. Lloyd Corder adds, "There is still greater focus on doing the marketing than on proving it works."[2]

Changes in the media field itself, combined with increased sophistication in measurement techniques, have brought about changes in the way we measure our work. True measurement will show how a designated audience responded or how an activity changed as a result of the media relations efforts. Measurement begins with setting measurable objectives that are based on the organization's business goals and not on the process of media relations. If your media relations objective is "to get 1.5 million impressions," then you are measuring your process, not the company's goal of "increasing sales in the southwest market by 10 percent."

## How to Measure

### Do It Yourself

Perhaps the simplest way to begin measuring and evaluating is to create a log of activity. This isn't anything elaborate. Make a list of the media you deal with; each time you give them a story or issue a release, check off if they used it. Over a period of time you'll get a picture of who uses your material and who doesn't. You'll know which editors or journalists you need to talk with more frequently and which ones need less attention.

If your media relations activities are centered in a small geographical area such as a city, state or province, consider creating your own clipping/monitoring arrangement for both print and electronic media. Begin by subscribing to all the print publications you target; these publications could range from the daily paper to the business and financial publications to detailed engineering journals, trade newsletters or industry-specific magazines. Assign one person responsibility for reading the publications. She/he will become familiar with the style and arrangement of each publication and won't have to waste time wading through sections that would not normally carry your material. This reader also will be in a position to notice if certain publications are changing their style of coverage, if they increase or decrease coverage of your organization and other trends.

Reading shouldn't be an extra assignment to a staff person who already has a full workload. Reading should be a primary responsibility to assure that the reading is done in a timely manner so that results—and any ramifications—are on your desk as soon as possible. You also can create your own spreadsheet for clip information. Cells would include the name of the publication, date of publication, page number, headline, reporter's by-line and other data important to you. Or, you can design a clipsheet that includes space at the top for this information and space on the rest of the page for the actual clip.

Television and radio monitoring can be as simple or as complex as you desire. The easiest do-it-yourself method is to assign people within your organization to watch specific news programs and/or listen to radio newscasts and talk shows. With the exception of an all-news network, television has few lengthy news programs, and they generally fall into four primary time slots: morning, noon, evening and late evening. Although there are numerous newsbreaks and news updates throughout the day, your interest probably should be in whether your organization's story appeared during one of the lengthier, prime-time news shows.

Radio, on the other hand, has newscasts quite often. They can be every half-hour, every hour or even constant. There are, however, two prime times that may be of interest to you: morning and afternoon commuting times when decision makers, thought leaders and overall business audiences are commuting to and from work.

For both television and radio, the viewer/listener staff member has a relatively simple task of noting the name of the station (call letters as well as popular name), the name of the program and the time of day the item was mentioned. A one-line summary of the content also is useful, such as "Repeated announcement of new company president," or "Used announcement, mispronounced president's name," or "Information was correct, used film footage of office building."

Another way to check on coverage is to daily monitor online news sites and electronic newsletters, as well as retrieval services such as LexisNexis. Bookmark the sites and search for the key words from your release.

## Employing Clipping/Monitoring Services

If your activities are far-reaching or complex (for example, a nationwide or international campaign), you may find it advantageous to use clipping and/or monitoring services. What you gain in convenience and peace of mind, however, you might lose in money, as such tracking services can become costly. The best way to make sure you are getting full value is to define clearly, both within your organization and with the service, what it is you want monitored and/or retrieved. By starting with a well-thought-out program, you stand less chance of being disappointed later. For example, you may want only those clips that carry the name of your organization, such as the American Heart Association, or you may want to have clips that also talk generically of your product or service offering, such as heart disease information or heart transplants. There might also be variations of your organization's name, which should be noted by the clipping agency. Be clear about which publications should be scanned.

If your organization is considering launching a media relations or public relations campaign, you may wish to monitor other organizations' activities to help give you an idea of how your campaign might be received. For example, if your company is going to introduce a new method of installing solar heat units, you might want to see what the media are currently saying about solar heat generally and the installation of solar units specifically. You might want to determine the media's understanding of solar heating or the types of artwork or photography used most often. As another example, you might want to be aware of the public's attitude about care of the elderly before introducing a new senior citizen program.

As you can see, a tracking service can be as finite or as general as you direct. Certainly, such a service can be more thorough than you or your staff members because it has professionally trained people and technology to scan and retrieve items. These tracking agencies vary in pricing methods. Some may charge a flat fee for a specified number of clips; others may charge a monthly reading rate plus a cost per clip. The important thing is to check costs ahead of time and try to anticipate which system will be better for your organization.

Many of the agencies offer electronic clips as well, retrieving radio and television newscasts on a local, regional or national level. International tracking also is available but because of the costs, language translation and technology differences, you should be sure you want to avail yourself of this service. Agencies also track online news sites and can provide links or scanned copies.

Before purchasing audio or videotapes of your news coverage, think carefully about the possible uses you would have for them. For instance, do you really need six variations of the same product announcement? Or 10 radio spots naming your new president? Or 37 scanned clips of online pickups of your release on corporate donations? What use do you have for these clips? If your only purpose is for show-and-tell to a client, make sure the client knows what they are paying for.

One advantage of using a tracking agency is that the service can provide you with up-to-date data on circulation, viewing/listening audiences or Web hits. While this in and of itself doesn't prove audience action, it does define the scope of your media efforts.

## What to Do with Results

Few people know what to do with all the clips and monitoring data after they come in. There are several solutions to this dilemma, all of which clearly point to one thing: document your successes and failures (in order to learn from both) and let others in your organization know what is happening.

The simplest way to accomplish this is to organize your clips and the summaries obtained from electronic monitoring. Scan copies of the articles found by your reader or clipping service and/or the electronic media summaries they created and then e-mail the package to key executives who need to be informed on a daily or weekly basis of news coverage about the organization. A variation on this procedure is to write a synopsis of each article, combine these synopses and the summaries derived from electronic media into a one- or two-page brief, and circulate it to executives. Either method performs a highly needed service for your key leaders. They do not have the time to peruse all the publications that deal with your industry or service area. They look to you to perform that service. The clips or synopses do not have to be specifically about your organization, but they should be relevant to the business.

More important, the clips from print and online media and the TV/radio monitoring summaries should include an analysis of the coverage. For example, if you have announced the impending layoff of 4,500 people across the country, you and your executives will be anxious to know how the media dealt with the story. Did they treat it objectively? Were the editorials damaging or supporting? Were the explanations of the layoff repeated accurately? Was there additional pickup on the wire services? What type of photo coverage, if any, accompanied the stories? Viewing all of the clips, both print and electronic, and answering these types of questions will help you identify certain traits about the media, reporters and newscasters. You might notice that one reporter seemed to consistently misunderstand, and thus misrepresent, the story behind the layoffs while all others got the story correct. You might also notice that all the headlines or television leads were straightforward and not misleading or edgy. This information tells you—and those who helped you—if the material you assembled and disseminated to the media was easily understood. It tells you if the media have an understanding of the situation and if your story was handled fairly.

This type of analysis ideally should be done with each major news event. It also can be done over an extended period of time with an ongoing, low-key campaign. For example, a campaign might be created to increase public awareness of the many ramifications of drunk driving. Articles supporting this theme would be placed with general and specific media over a long period of time—a minimum of one year, although two to three years would be better. Remember, as with advertisements, the public begins to retain and act on a message only after seeing, reading or hearing it numerous times. Keep electronic files of your clips to show how many articles have appeared on the subject, how many people received that information through the media, which geographic regions used the articles the most, what type of headlines appeared, what types of audiences received the information, if the articles were completely rewritten or used almost in the original form, and how many additional articles were created by the media based on the information that you sent out.

The nice thing about a long-term project such as this is that the campaign can be changed along the way to counter any negative items that might be appearing or to take advantage of any special opportunities. For example, if the articles are being totally rewritten, then you need to look again at your releases to find out why. Are they not in the proper journalistic style? Are they full of typos? Did you fail to include contact information? If articles aren't being run in certain publications, find out why. Do they not fit the style and substance of the publication? Are they going to the wrong editor? Are you missing the deadlines?

The final report on a long-term project should talk about both the positive and negatives. It should tell what was accomplished by the campaign and explain both how the external audience benefited from it and what the internal media relations staff learned from it. Most important: a long-term campaign whose focus is on increasing public awareness needs to have both benchmark polling among the targeted audiences and follow-up polling at routine intervals to determine if the message is being received and if awareness is increasing.

Clips also can be used to spot trends in your industry or service area. If coverage of your organization changes, perhaps it is because of new industry-related activities in Washington from environmentalists or labor lobbyists. Perhaps something else has occurred to make reporters and editors look anew at your company.

Where to keep clips—if you keep them at all—can sometimes be a problem. For one-of-a-kind announcements, such as the opening of a new facility, an initial public offering (IPO) or a 50th anniversary, you may want to keep clips (or scanned copies) for archival purposes. For an on-going or annual effort, such as fund-raising, labor negotiations or corporate social responsibility programs, you may want to keep clips for a designated amount of time before tossing them out.

## Technology to the Rescue?

Certain types of new software can often help the beleaguered media relations person who is operating a one-person shop. Or not. For example, some software easily calculates ad-equivalent data, based on preselected advertising costs. However, ad-equivalent comparisons remain an abstract number, therefore they actually signify nothing. There is no comparison between an editorial piece on a new product and an advertisement about the same product. In an ad, you control the space, the time of the placement, the size, the words, the photography. In an editorial piece, you control nothing.

You might better invest in software that helps you provide qualitative data. Along with entering hard data (date of placement, air time, outlet, column inches, etc.), a user can enter self-selected subjective measurement fields such as number of messages in the article and story slant (positive, negative or neutral) on a numbered rating/ranking scale. The resulting information tells how the media used the story. It does NOT, however, tell you if the audience acted on that information. That's where polling comes in.

While media relations software can be of great help in keeping qualitative data on your program and process, it probably isn't the way to try to measure true outcome. Only by linking your media relations objectives with those of marketing, sales or promotions will you see true outcome measurement.

## Measuring Actions and Determining Attitudes

Measuring how people react to a media relations campaign is something best left to public opinion experts and pollsters. There are times when this knowledge will be essential for strategic planning, so it will be worth the time and money invested.

Simply put, you are trying to find out if the targeted audience acted in the way you wanted them to because of your media program. It could be that one of the objectives of your campaign to increase public awareness of the ramifications of drunk driving was to get the public to write to their legislative representatives to push for new legislation. To get feedback as to whether or not your objective was met would require the assistance of professional public opinion gatherers. On a more easily measurable level, you might just need to know how many people attended the open house of your new office building or the festival in the park as a result of your media efforts.

Additionally, you may want to do a content analysis of articles or broadcasts about your organization or related media event to determine if the information you have provided to the media generates positive, neutral or negative reactions. In turn, this information can guide you in developing continued or brand-new campaigns, such as during labor negotiations, bond referenda or rezoning talks. Continued use of content analysis during the media campaign will help you adjust your media processes, target audiences or media outlet preferences to achieve success. The important thing to note is that with content analysis you can measure beyond the number of column inches and numbers of clips—and determine the impact of your media relations program.

Using a combination of measurements for a long-term campaign can provide information that leads to astonishing results. Returning to the drunk driving campaign as an example, once you learn the answers to the following questions, you can then draw correlations between the number of drunk driving incidents in a certain geographic area before, during and after the media campaign. If the results are positive, you can share in the credit. If the results are negative, find out why and begin a new campaign.

- How many people are reading/hearing the desired message?
- In what geographic areas do these people reside?
- Which media are using the message?
- Is the public is acting on the message in the way you want them to?
- Is the campaign creating letters to the editor or other public response?
- Has your message been more effective in the past three months than in the three months prior to that?

Whatever the method used to determine results, you have evidence that your bottom-line approach to media relations is working.

## Media Audits

Unless you are dealing with only a few media outlets, you probably will want to consider a media relations audit every so often. For objectivity, the audit should be done for you, rather than by you.

The media relations audit works like this. An opinion research firm surveys editors, news directors and reporters in the geographic or topical area you specify. The questionnaire can be structured to deal with any aspect of news media relations you want it to. Generally, the survey asks the same questions about several different companies in order to avoid the "halo syndrome" where the editor might say good things about your organization because your company is the largest one in town. Asking several companies to participate can help cut down the costs.

The surveyors ask questions such as how responsive an organization is to media inquiries, whether the editor knows whom to contact for information at an organization, the quality of the news releases received, and the courtesy of the company in dealing with the media.

This type of audit actually measures the relationship you have with the media. So, when the audit comes back saying you have some journalists and editors who do not think you do a very good job, you know you have to start from square one to build a better relationship.

An audit also will help you continue to meet the needs of the media, which should be one of your primary functions. Audit results will help you refine the products you provide (news releases, accessibility to executives, response calls), give better interviews (by providing media training for your spokespersons and executives) and teach your staff how to be more responsive to even the smallest request.

## Summary

No matter the extent of your media operations, you should have built-in measurement techniques. After all, you have put a lot of work into creating a program that will tell your company's story to the public, offer your products to an audience or ignite attitude or behavior change. Surely you want to measure the impact of that story and relate how that helps your organization meets its goals and objectives. To do any less would be less than your best professional work.

# 12

# The Future

## Expanding Your Counselor Role

Not so long ago CEOs were celebrities and General Electric's Jack Welch was a poster boy for outstanding management. Yet in the early 2000s, Welch became a symbol for excessive greed after his retirement package was revealed in a messy divorce. Regulators and prosecutors began hunting down corporate chicanery with zeal and investigative techniques long used against organized crime and drug trafficking but seldom employed against white-color crime.[1] Several CEOs and CFOs faced judges, juries and jail. *The Wall Street Journal* created a special section with its own logo called "Executives on Trial." And the public's respect for business plunged to new lows.

In economic booms it is easy to turn CEOs into celebrities, and in downturns to denigrate them. As Matthew P. Gonring, vice president of global marketing and communications at Rockwell Automation, put it: "The journalism community that helped create these business heroes was just as swift to label them goats."[2] But many boards and executives have brought their current disregard on themselves. As management guru Peter Drucker told *Fortune* magazine, "Let me

203

quote J. P. Morgan, who said, 'The CEO is just a hired hand.' That's what today's CEOs have forgotten."[3]

Where were public relations counselors when the whistles should have been blowing? Two of our most important roles are to represent the opinions of all of our organization's stakeholders and to counsel management on how various scenarios will be viewed as decisions are being made. Shareholders have become increasingly skeptical that boards of directors are looking out for their interests—and PR people appear to have failed them in these instances as well.

Nonprofits have not been immune to high-profile scandal either. Even prestigious charities like the Red Cross and United Way have faced harsh criticism over executive salaries and perks and the improper use of donated funds. Other high-profile disgraces have involved child abuse in the Catholic Church and oil-for-food corruption at the United Nations.

Nor have the scandals been restricted to American shores. Global dairy giant Parmmalat SpA, the flagship of Italian industry, saw its founder resign in disgrace, suspected of being at the center of an €8 billion fraud. In Germany, a criminal trial resulted over a huge bonus

---

### What Keeps CEOs Awake at Night?

In preparation for its Spring 2003 Seminar in New York City, the Arthur W. Page Society asked Donald K. Wright, cochair of the Page Society research committee, to interview the CEOs of 16 member companies about the issues that are of primary concern to them. A summary of those issues:

- Reputation
- Innovation
- Reestablishing trust and confidence
- Challenges of successful marketing
- Personnel issues
- Achieving growth in a declining economy
- Potential ethical issues
- Civil justice reform (tort reform)
- Achieving company potential
- Global business opportunities

Source: "Report on the CEO Survey," *Journal*, Arthur W. Page Society 18th annual spring seminar, April 3–4, 2003, New York City.

for a CEO following the biggest hostile takeover in that country's history. In Europe they call debacles like these "Anglo-Saxon capitalism," referring to a corporate environment rife with ballooning executive pay, layoffs and unfriendly takeovers.

## Lessons to Be Learned

Corporate governance issues make front-page headlines, bringing dramatic media attention and widespread public interest to subjects that often had been buried in boardrooms or shareholder materials. Executive compensation has been a hot issue for decades. While the stock market was up and employment was high, it lay relatively dormant. Then, after so many people lost significant savings when the stock market plunged, and huge layoffs and outsourcing became the norm, awareness quickened and rage blossomed. Now executive compensation is the number-one negative corporate issue, at least in the United States, according to researchers at Governance Metrics International, an independent research firm in New York that scrutinizes corporate governance practices for institutional shareholders.[4]

Corporate reputation and governance issues offer significant opportunities for PR counselors because the solutions cross disciplines from public relations and legal to investor relations and finance, and they affect virtually all the organization's target audiences. They also remind us that integrity now stands high on the list of attributes people consider important as they evaluate organizations and their leadership. As the legendary business leader Warren Buffett says, "If you lose dollars for the firm by bad decisions, I will be understanding. If you lose reputation for the firm, I will be ruthless."[5]

What lessons can public relations professionals learn from abuses of power and the failure of those in responsible positions to speak up—especially when public relations professionals appear to have been conspicuously quiet in their role as advocate for the corporations' stakeholders? "Public trust sits at the core of every powerful business brand," points out Marilyn Laurie, former executive vice president of brand strategy and public relations at AT&T.

> It is the absolute core—the foundation, the prerequisite—of business success. It underpins employee pride and employee motivation that produce customer satisfaction. Destroy it and watch your shareowners run for the exit doors. More broadly, trust is the glue that holds together our entire economic system. Trillions of dollars of assets are traded every day based only on the good word of business people we've never met. And when financial

results are manipulated by more than a few bad apples, our entire market system shudders.[6]

Yet even several years after the massive corporate scandals first surfaced, most public companies continue to use legal accounting actions to smooth earnings and meet analyst estimates. Given the choice between hitting earnings expectations and missing them in order to improve long-term financial health, most U.S. companies would go for the short-term target, according to a survey of financial officers in 401 firms, conducted by professors at Duke University and the University of Washington. "The thing that stunned us was that they were so up front about making these real economic decisions to manage earnings," one of the professors told *The Wall Street Journal*.[7] And an article in *CFO* magazine in May 2004 said that nearly half—47 percent—of finance employees still feel pressure from their superiors to use aggressive accounting to make results look better.[8]

Average citizens may not understand the intricacies of accounting ploys, corporate corruption and insider trading. But they know what it means to the lives of employees and their families when corporations deliberately take money out of pension funds to puff up corporate profits and inflate management pay. They understand the pain to the typical family when health benefits are curtailed—or cut altogether. And they know that mutual funds, once considered the quintessential good investment for the small investor, have been stained by improper trades by some of the industry's most prominent and richest managers.

Public relations people do not have the option of operating in a moral twilight. How could we have continued to write news releases, annual reports, 10Ks and quarterly earnings statements when their content was as much fiction as fact?

## Symbols Communicate Loudly

So many executives and boards of directors have taken advantage of their privileged positions for personal gain that Tyco's $6,000 shower curtain and the Rigas family's flying Christmas trees on the corporate jet may seem like petty cash. But sometimes it is the relatively small things that disgust and infuriate the public, causing extraordinarily passionate responses. After all, PR people learn from the earliest stages of our careers that perception is reality and symbols have exceptional power.

The symbols keep communicating: The big guys take care of themselves while average workers and small shareholders lose. As Dick

Martin, AT&T retired executive vice president of public relations, described his experience: "AT&T's CEO was a symbol not simply in the sense that he stood for 'downsizing' or 'corporate greed,' as a barber pole signals haircuts, but in the sense that he actually evoked all the feelings of pent-up fear and anger that working people were experiencing. And no rational argument could change that." In fact, Martin says, "The hardest part of counseling CEOs is getting them to look beyond rational arguments to stakeholders' emotional concerns."[9]

This dire situation can be a defining moment for public relations. We are not alone in missing opportunities to right what is going wrong. Many legal, accounting, brokerage and banking firms acted no better. In fact, the list of blue-chip companies enabling the Enron fraud reads like a Who's Who of Business and Industry. But pointing fingers at others does not lessen our responsibility.

## Speaking Up for What's Right

Veteran PR counselor Chester Burger asks why no PR people have been identified as whistle-blowers, although they must have known or suspected what was going on. "Why were PR people omitted from the decision-making councils, as they surely were at Enron?" he queries. "Is this a consequence of their self-identification as communicators rather than as public relations counsel? Is this new self-identification as communicators related to the new and startling reality that in some corporations purchasing departments are selecting the PR firms? Not a very happy positioning, but isn't it logical?"[10]

It is one thing to navigate your way through blurred ethical boundaries. It takes guts, family support and a solid bank account to confront a CEO when you might be committing job suicide. And a convoluted reporting arrangement that has the senior PR officer reporting to the CEO through someone else adds even more barriers.

Nonetheless, the actions in the Enron, Tyco, Adelphia, World-Com, Quest, HealthSouth, New York Stock Exchange, mutual funds and other institutions were blatantly and obviously wrong. PR people ask for the proverbial "seat at the table," wanting to be involved in decision making and considered as respected counselors to management. Along with rights, that seat brings responsibilities: to speak up when things are wrong; to act to get them changed.

If it is an auditor's job is to catch malfeasance at the companies they oversee, then it is the PR professional's role to help keep it from happening in the first place—or to work to get it stopped if it starts. Weren't there opportunities to pass on concerns to the corporate

auditor or outside counsel during working sessions on the 10K, on a
road show or at the annual meeting?

## Accepting Responsibility

We make our most significant contributions when we act as counselors and crisis managers—and surely the debacles mentioned above
qualified for action in both arenas. A shocking number of firms have
paid multimillion-dollar fines that sound enormous until you remember the huge pay and perks of the people involved—and the fact that
many are permitted to "neither admit nor deny wrongdoing." Hardly
a reassuring message about their sense of individual responsibility.

What happened to the fundamental premise of crisis management (and decency) that we admit error and say what we're doing to
fix the situation? Obviously there still is a large leap between accepting punishment and accepting accountability. It will take much more
than new accounting standards, independent boards of directors and
corporate oversight laws like the Sarbanes-Oxley Act in the United
States to fix what's wrong in too many executive suites today. Actions
speak louder than words.

## Return to the Fundamentals

Full disclosure is not enough. Performance is what counts. We
need to help our organizations return to the fundamentals of right
and wrong, fairness and decency that most of us were taught by our
parents years ago. We need to adhere to the basics of trust, honesty
and genuine concern for customers, employees and shareholders.
John F. Budd Jr., chairman and CEO of The Omega Group, put it succinctly: "The egregious failing was a violation of trust, a moral issue
not a legal one."[11] This is an ideal opportunity for PR to make substantive contributions not merely to communications issues but to
business issues.

Harold Burson, founder of Burson-Marsteller, once described the
evolution of public relations this way: When PR was in its infancy, clients called on us to ask, "How should I *say* it?" As the profession
became more sophisticated, the question evolved to, "*What* should I
say?" At the next level it became, "*How* should we *do* it?" And at the
highest level it is, "*What* should we *do?*" As that question has
changed over the past few decades, so our function has changed and
grown as well.

Such breadth requires that we have a thorough understanding of our organization's business strategy and marketing plans, internal challenges and future opportunities, customers and competitors. We must regard ourselves as counselors and general managers, not just communicators. We need to become, as management consultant Harry Levinson put it, "organizational radar, taking soundings and helping to steer rather than expecting to be piloted."[12]

## Working on a Solution

A good first step to get back on the ethical tack would be to work with Human Resources colleagues to convene small discussion groups to solicit input from middle managers and employees, anonymously if necessary. They are among the most knowledgeable—and today, likely, most disillusioned—people in the organization. They have witnessed firsthand what goes wrong when executives shift their priorities from customer service, quality products and fair pricing. They are among the most likely to have practical solutions and useful ideas on what policies and procedures need changing.

Another important priority is to help boards and senior management see the need to restructure reward systems so that they are compensated for working for shareholders, customers and employees rather than for themselves. Suggest that options be replaced with phantom shares and ESUs (equivalent stock units) and require that they be held at least 10 years, or maybe until retirement.

Make the board's compensation committee as independent as the audit committee. Allow neither the CEO nor the head of Human Resources to attend meetings. Publish committee decisions in a 10Q-type public document readily available to shareholders. Encourage extensive discussion—even some dissension—in the boardroom when compensation issues are being debated. If everyone is in agreement, maybe all the boundaries have not been explored.

Multimillion-dollar annual salaries paid to a handful of executives are in no way acceptable, even when the stock price goes up. After all, the whole employee team made that happen, not just the CEO, CFO and COO. Executive pay should be half fixed and half variable, depending on results. When the stock goes down, executive pay should go down proportionately—and automatically, unless there are mitigating circumstances such as an unusually large capital or R&D investment program that will not show results for several years.

By law, employees should not be required to keep the major portion of their retirement and savings assets in company stock. Other than that, it's not the government but rather corporate boards and senior management who need to take command and control. It also is crucial to enforce the principles of ethics codes. Infractions must result in serious punishments that are publicized—even when the violators sit on the company's board, as was the case with Enron. How else will everyone—employees, investors, suppliers—know that the code's words have meaning and consequences? Ethics and honesty have to become an integral part of each organization's DNA. You do not debate ethics.

In the end, Arthur Page had it right all along. He was an AT&T vice president from 1927 to 1946, the first person in a PR position to serve as an officer and member of the board of directors of a major corporation, and the founder of corporate public relations as a strategic management function. Page believed that while well-thought-out communications programs are vital to an organization's success, they must be based on the reality of its performance and not on Madison Avenue slogans. Page summed up his philosophy in a single sentence: "Public relations is 90 percent doing and 10 percent talking about it."[13] This is wise counsel for CEOs and public relations counselors as well.

## Avoiding Surprises

There is an old saying among public relations counselors—and CEOs—that there is no such thing as a good surprise. The objective of effective PR counseling is to anticipate and identify developing issues early so your organization can help shape those issues instead of just react to them. This proactive posture guarantees a minimum of surprises, good and bad.

Important issues may surface in the community, the industry or within the ranks of your own organization. They can have a nationwide or global impact. They might involve employee matters, politics, health care, privacy or the environment. The possibilities are endless. Many are fundamentally "wallet issues," affecting people's financial and emotional well-being.

If an issue has the potential to some day affect your organization, it is your job to understand that issue and share your knowledge with the decision makers of your organization. PR counseling, though, goes beyond sharing information. As a PR counselor, you also should help your organization develop a position on emerging issues, as well as manage the business to avoid negative situations and capitalize on opportunities. Think of yourself as an ombudsman. In addition to being the eyes and ears of your organization, you sometimes have to be the conscience as well. Being an effective counselor is one of the most important and demanding roles of the media relations professional.

As a counselor, you need to be part of the decision-making process in your organization. You must:

- Have constant access to the CEO and other key executives.
- Be part of the strategic planning team for your organization's business activities.
- Have "a seat at the management table" when debate is underway and decisions are being made.
- Help management consider the long-term strategic and "image" implications of your company's response to an issue.
- Ensure that your company's policy-formation process gets the benefit of a broad perspective and variety of opinions, both inside and outside the organization.
- Have media relations and other communications functions included in your organization's business plans.

If you are being called in only after decisions are made, you are not practicing PR counseling.

## Building Your Credibility

While media relations professionals generally are well informed, you can increase your chances of recognizing important issues early by paying careful attention to all media, traditional and new, not just those that cover your business and industry regularly. As a media relations professional, you should:

- Read a wide variety of media—not just the business and trade press but also "alternative" press and publications devoted to subjects and ideologies outside the scope of your industry. Do key word searches on the Internet and visit opinion-leading Web sites and blogs.
- Read editorials consistently to be alert to new subjects and shifts in the opinions of thought-leaders.
- Monitor letters-to-the-editor sections in newspapers and magazines, especially in the more prestigious publications, as well as blogs, newsgroups, chat rooms, user groups and forums on the Internet. Emerging issues or changes in viewpoints on old ones often get their first public exposure in these arenas.
- Pay attention to better-quality TV and radio talk shows and interview programs, which are good sources of perspectives on issues.

- Maintain informal contacts with key media people. Seek their opinions. Get them to share their experiences with you.
- Build internal alliances and a strong informal network of source people within your organization. They can alert you to developing trends within your industry and markets, and changes in courses of action that are needed.

To get the attention of your senior management, you have to earn their respect through your performance. Top executives and other decision makers within your organization will find it difficult to take advice on media relations and other communications issues from anyone who does not have a thorough understanding of the business. You must constantly update your knowledge of the organization, its strategy, its position in the marketplace, and its growth and expansion plans. Demonstrate this knowledge for the management team by connecting it to the advice you give.

When you make a presentation to management or the board of directors on the importance of an issue, support your evaluation with facts—for example, opinion poll or research results, news media reports, speech excerpts from opinion leaders, and your operations colleagues' evaluation of its relevance to the business. Important issues—especially emerging issues—usually have many interpretations. Your own interpretation is part of the value you contribute as a PR counselor. To protect your credibility, though, you should make your management aware of other views on the same issue by different interest groups.

## Expanding Your Role

The evolution from communicator to counselor is so natural and so subtle that you may not be aware of the metamorphosis until it has occurred. One day you are responding to a journalist's question on why your organization has a certain policy on drug abuse in the workplace. While your lips are providing the answer, your mind is asking, "Why indeed?" Or you might be briefing a spokesperson for your organization before a major media interview, when suddenly it becomes obvious to both of you that a particular personnel practice is woefully out of date. So together you work out a plan to change it. Perhaps you are writing remarks on your organization's global marketing strategy for your CEO to deliver at a news conference when you cross the line from simply articulating someone else's policy to actually participating in policy formation yourself.

Your role has changed. Your responsibilities expand. As a stained-glass window diffuses the light that passes through it, enhancing the light by the addition of myriad beautiful colors, you find yourself contributing to your organization's policies and helping to shape its future. You have become an entrepreneur in the broadest sense, whether or not you run your own company, because you are truly breaking new ground. You have become a public relations counselor.

You still will spend time answering questions from reporters and preparing media plans. But more and more you will find yourself focusing on communications strategy, being a champion and agent of constructive change, and giving advice—on issues as complex as your CEO's responsibilities, as broad as your organization's business, as fundamental as its culture and values.

When President Kennedy asked Edward R. Murrow to become director of the U.S. Information Agency, Murrow responded that he would be happy to do so "provided it is understood that I shall be in on the takeoffs as well as the crash landings."[14] That is a position we all argue for—albeit perhaps not so cleverly. Too often the task of media relations people is to make the rough *appear* smooth, rather than to apply sandpaper carefully to make that objective a reality.

## Substance Over Style

As former Eli Lilly CEO Randall L. Tobias put it, too much emphasis on how and what we communicate

> is nothing more than a Band-Aid on some symptoms, not a cure
> for anything very important. Integrating what we speak and write
> is no substitute for integrated *behavior*—shared behavior that is
> single-mindedly focused on customers and their needs, as well as
> the needs of each of the other stakeholders of the corporation. . . .
> In my view, the activities of communications professionals are
> simply the means to other ends, and not ends unto themselves.
> For me, communications must be defined to include all forms of a
> corporation's behaviors toward all of its stakeholders. For me,
> integrated communications is just another form of cross-functional teamwork. It's silo-busting—doing away with fiefdoms—
> doing away with turf. Another way, in other words, for an organization to do the right thing. . . . I believe the most effective public
> relations organizations are the ones who are embracing change
> and leading the transformation of communications integration
> within their own institutions. As I define it, communications is
> the sum of all the activities that demonstrate—through actions—
> what a business really stands for.[15]

Presidential speechwriter, political analyst and author Peggy Noonan reinforces the importance of substantive policy rather than merely pretty words:

> Style enhances substance; it gives substance voice, it makes a message memorable, it makes policy clear and understandable. But it is not itself the message. Style is not a replacement for substance, and cannot camouflage a lack of substance. And where there is no substance, the style will perish. You cannot be eloquent about nothing.[16]

Barie Carmichael, partner in the Brunswick Group LLP, believes that every business has "inherent negatives" that must be evaluated and addressed. They might include how products are produced, where they are produced, and how they are used by customers—for example, under-age drinking and drunk drivers to the alcohol industry. The firm's analysis of crises in 2002 showed that fewer than 20 percent start from people or forces outside the organization. In fact, two-thirds of the headline-generating crises studied were small, internal and "smoldering" before they erupted publicly, so they might well have been averted with strategic leadership. Carmichael stresses that commitment to mitigate "inherent negatives" must start at the top and permeate the company. "Solve and remediate rather than defend" is the advice. The role of the PR counselor in the process? Identifying corporate blind spots and their business implications, partnering with stakeholders to achieve constructive actions, identifying vulnerabilities before your company's critics do it for you, and always speaking the truth.[17]

## The CEO Role Is Key

Clearly, substantive leadership starts with the CEO. Burson-Marsteller's research on CEO and corporate reputation demonstrates that in today's business environment, integrity is a major issue and the CEO's reputation is a key factor in a company's reputation. That is the bottom-line result of the opinions of 1,100 business influentials—CEOs and other senior executives, financial analysts, institutional investors, business journalists and government officials in the United States. This finding has not merely persevered since the first study was done in 1997, but it also has become more pronounced despite recent events that have tarnished so many reputations. In fact, the research shows that in 2001:

- CEO reputation counts for a staggering 48 percent of a company's reputation—and this percentage continues to climb. Similar surveys in the UK, Australia and Germany show a similar high correlation. In the Nordic countries, it is climbing but still somewhat less, at one third.

- Companies whose CEOs were rated "most admired" achieved a 13 percent compound annual shareholder return over a three-year period. Companies with CEOs rated less favorably delivered a negative return.

- A good CEO reputation had other benefits: 88 percent said it would influence whether they recommend a company as a good place to work, 94 percent said it would make them believe a company's position if it were under media pressure, and 92 percent said it would help them maintain confidence in the company even if its stock price were lagging.

Christopher Komisarjevsky, president and CEO of Burson-Marsteller, summarizes what this study teaches: "If the person on top is perceived to be credible, then financial capital, human capital and the 'trust' capital will follow. These intangible assets are priceless and

---

### Getting to Know the CEO

In an article in the Summer 2004 issue of *The Strategist*, James E. Lukaszewski, chairman of The Lukaszewski Group, suggested the following questions to test yourself on how well you know your CEO and understand your counseling role within his or her context:

- Do you know your CEO's favorite business book?
- Do you know your CEO's top priority every day?
- Do you know whom your CEO quotes as a business thought leader or model?
- Do you know what's on your CEO's desk?
- Have you met other CEOs your CEO admires?
- Can you help your CEO meet other CEOs?
- How frequently do you read publications like the *Harvard Business Review*, *Sloan Business Journal*, *Fortune*, *Barron's* and the Berkshire Hathaway annual report?

Source: James E. Lukaszewski, "Inside the Mind of the CEO," *Public Relations Strategist*, Summer 2004, p. 17.

must be invested in and sustained. According to the Federal Reserve, 47 percent of a company's value is due to intangibles such as reputation, talent and intellectual property."[18]

This thesis was reinforced in 2004 when Walt Disney Co. dropped off the top 10 most-admired companies for the first time in the sixth annual Reputation Quotient study conducted by Harris Interactive Inc., a market research company in Rochester, New York, and the Reputation Institute, a research organization based in New York City. As one respondent summarized the anti-Disney sentiment: "It's not Mickey Mouse or Disney World that comes to mind when hearing the name Disney, but rather CEO Michael Eisner and exorbitant executive compensation." Said another: "When I grew up, Disney was on a pedestal in my mind, pristine and untouchable. Now it's all about greed and ridiculous salaries. Next thing you know they will lay off Mickey and Goofy to further enrich the executives." Many other companies were targets of similar criticism from survey respondents, disgusted by super-size executive compensation, shabby treatment of employees and American jobs lost to outsourcing. In fact, in 2004 68 percent of survey respondents graded the reputation of U.S. businesses as "not good" or "terrible," compared with 74 percent in 2003.[19]

## Involvement Brings Responsibility

The access that our media relations responsibilities gives us—not only to top management but also to the decision-making processes of our company or client—brings with it a great obligation. We can take apparently random sequences of events and help translate them into an actionable agenda. We can ensure that our organization's decision makers have access to public opinion and attitudes so they can evaluate their actions against perception as well as reality. After all, every misconception begins with a certain element of truth. Much like products, public issues also have life cycles. We can help identify emerging issues early enough so our organizations can shape and manage them rather than merely respond.

Counseling is much more than offering advice. It acts as a strategic glue, bringing together input from all available external and internal sources to ensure a "catholic" rather than a "parochial" view. It is selectively sorting information and focusing only on events that are important and contribute to understanding. A good counselor will relate and interpret the facts; a great one will understand and enhance the meaning. Harold W. Burlingame, a retired executive vice president at AT&T, advises:

You should try to get yourself positioned as one who has a special sensing system and thus can anticipate problems in time to solve them before they erupt publicly. Public relations people need to be an integral part of the planning process if you are to help your organization anticipate and prepare for change. To be credible, however, you have to demonstrate a solid understanding of the business and appreciation for its operations problems. Without that knowledge you will have great difficulty being accepted as an equal member of the management team.[20]

## Business Problems Are PR Problems

Almost all the critical problems facing your organization are public relations problems in the broadest sense of the term. Like Rubik's cube, the solutions can be deceptively simple in appearance. But the cosmetic touches of a publicity program cannot obscure deeper blemishes in organizational policy or practice for long. You can help your top management look at each problem strategically, searching for well-thought-out actions that contribute to permanent resolution. You can apply a touch of healthy skepticism since, as Carl Sagan put it: "Skeptical scrutiny is the means . . . by which deep insights can be winnowed from deep nonsense."[21] You can reflect shareowner sentiment, customer concerns and employee expectations, for you are their voice within your organization just as you are its ears and eyes in the community and the marketplace. Instead of expending energy criticizing the media for inaccurate reporting, you can help your top management address the policies and practices that prompt investigative journalism and negative news stories.

You have an opportunity to use the unique window you have to public opinion—those constant contacts with the news media—to act as an early warning system for the decision makers of your organizations, to perceive not only what is going on around you but also what is coming. You can become a catalyst for change. Like truffle hounds—dogs used in France to root out delicacies from underground—you can search for signs of emerging concerns so your organization has a head start in addressing those that merit attention.

The length and breadth of the list may be awesome. Isolating and defining the underlying causes may be difficult, much like grappling with Jell-O. To be effective, solutions must reflect an objective analysis of the problem, rather than merely respond to the needs of your company or client. As Reader's Digest Association retired Chairman and CEO George V. Grune put it:

The combination of knowledge, judgment, instinct and skills will result in a solid working relationship with your senior management. They will come to rely on you as one who provides added value when they are making major decisions affecting the business—decisions on a wide variety of topics from expanding into new markets and launching new products to downsizing a department and laying off employees.[22]

## Achieving the Role of Counselor: Advice from Experts

The Vernon C. Schranz annual lectureship series at Ball State University brings the thoughts and vision of the most distinguished names in public relations to the attention of students, professionals and scholars. Organized by Professor Melvin L. Sharpe and his graduate assistants in the public relations sequence at Ball State, the lectures provide what Sharpe calls "a time capsule of the progress, problems and change that give us a clear picture of an evolving profession where credibility and social responsibility remain the constants." We searched the lectures for samples of insight from PR leaders as to how media relations professionals can make the transition from communicators to counselors.

> Unfortunately, we too often perceive our responsibilities as "explainers" rather than "influencers." We perform our functions with much the same tactics and techniques as those who preceded us, advances in communications technology notwithstanding. Every problem is reduced to a communications context—that's what we know best and best can do. We are busy all right . . . but are we effective? Is anybody listening? Understanding? People don't change opinions because you buried them in newsprint! We must force ourselves to resist orthodoxy . . . to think qualitatively . . . to fight the status quo as if it were cancer! We should never be satisfied. It can always be done better, done differently. Your left brain will bring you financial reward. But if you really want to make a difference, to stand apart from your public relations journeymen, trust—and use—your right brain!

> —John F. Budd, Jr.
> Chairman and CEO
> The Omega Group
> New York City

My plea to colleagues and to students preparing to enter public relations is—let's lift our eyes above the process and start thinking about the outcomes. Let's stop being the carpenters and start becoming the architects. It's one thing to know how to play the piano; it's something else to be able to move an audience with a Beethoven sonata. Therefore, we have to think carefully about what the goals of public relations practice are, and about what the goals of each of our client's activities are. The goal is not communication; communication is process. The goal is not influencing opinion; opinion is process. It isn't even changing attitudes. Although we may have to do all those things, they are a process. The goal is behavior. The outcome we're seeking is to influence the hearts and minds of men and women so they behave in certain ways. So they prove by their actions that we have achieved positive public relationships, not just gone through the process of public relations.

—The late Patrick Jackson
Founder, Jackson, Jackson and Wagner
Editor, *pr reporter*
Exeter, New Hampshire

Working my way up through the PR department, I always thought of the additional responsibility as gaining more leverage to influence what the company was doing. No matter how small the PR shop in the place you work, no matter how much you love this endlessly fascinating PR discipline, to me that principle still applies. The higher you go in the organization, the more you take responsibility to row the boat along with the rest of the senior team. The more you must recognize that you too are accountable for the business' decisions. Not the conscience of the business somewhere above the fray, judging those with "less noble" motives, although you will often struggle on matters of short-term business gains vs. long-term values. Not the one who just communicates what others decide. Your role as counselor is to bring the broad outside perspective, practical knowledge of stakeholders and unique communications support that helps those business decisions succeed. You get no credit for all the times you stop bad stuff from happening. But over time, despite the steep hill that PR may have to climb, you win the trust of the business. You have a great career. And you sleep well at night.

—Marilyn Laurie
Former Executive Vice President
Brand Strategy and Public Relations
AT&T
New York City

If you're going to get to the top in your organization in a policy-making role, you need an insatiable thirst for information. For starters, that means reading everything you can get your hands on. You can be useful to your boss only if you're on top of relevant developments—not just in your industry but all over the world. Writing is the universal currency of public relations professionals, whether you're rookies or seasoned. Make sure yours is clear and concise. Above all, write in a manner that gets the boss's attention. A five-page proposal might be a literary work of art, but it's a functional flop if it doesn't get read. So cut right to the chase. A half page of bullet points may not be nearly as eloquent as your five-page memo, but it's much more likely to get results.

—James L. Tolley
Vice President of Public Affairs (retired)
Daimler/Chrysler
Auburn Hills, Michigan

Source: Ball State University, 25th anniversary collection of speeches from the Vernon C. Schranz Distinguished Lectureship in Public Relations, Melvin L. Sharpe and DeAnna L. May, October 2003.

## An Integral Part of the Planning Process

Donald E. Procknow, retired AT&T Technologies vice chairman, added:

> Public relations people should not be used simply to write announcements of what we have decided—or, worse yet, to fancy up words someone else has written. We all benefit when public relations is brought in much earlier in the decision-making process. Public relations is a management tool just like any other in the company—a very, very important resource.[23]

Charles Marshall, retired CEO of AT&T Information Systems, called his public relations staff "not only the business' communicators, but the business' consciences as well." Paraphrasing the poet Robert Burns, he says we must help our organizations see ourselves as others see us to ensure top management is not insulated—even when hearing the public's or employees' views is painful. Further, he reminds us: "We cannot just react. We must be proactive. Your role is to determine how we want our various publics to view us, and then help us develop a game plan to make it happen. After all, you cannot make us look any better than we deserve to look."[24]

Marshall articulates a view held by an increasing number of CEOs who have given their public relations people a status in the corporate and nonprofit worlds comparable to operations, marketing, human resources, legal and finance staffs, because their skills are recognized as vital to setting sophisticated strategies and meeting ambitious objectives.

## The Teletype Case

An example of a direct contribution to the development of an organization's business practices by media relations professionals took place at the Teletype Corporation in Illinois. The public relations and marketing staff not only began working more closely together but also were integrated into the company's overall corporate business plan.

When John J. Pappas was named president of the corporation, Teletype had been in existence for almost 75 years and a part of AT&T for 50 years. The company employed about 5,000 people who designed, manufactured and marketed data communications products. Headquartered in Skokie, Illinois, Teletype had manufacturing facilities there as well as in Little Rock, Arkansas. In addition, it had a nationwide distribution and service organization. But it suffered from being a subsidiary of a subsidiary. Owned by Western Electric (now Lucent Technologies), which in turn then was owned by AT&T, Teletype rarely was considered news by the national business and trade press. Like Cinderella, Teletype people often stayed home and tended house while sister companies garnered the publicity by going to the ball.

AT&T knew that Teletype would play a key role in its future because of its data communications expertise. One sign of the company's new prominence was Pappas' appointment—it was the first time Teletype had been headed by a full executive officer from the parent company. That move spawned an active media relations program to generate wider media coverage of Teletype. National business and trade press reporters who cover the communications industry are veteran AT&T watchers, alert to reading between the lines for indications of a change in corporate strategy. Previously, no effort had been made to promote Teletype as a separate entity. Astute reporters read the signals and asked why. Publications such as *The Wall Street Journal, The New York Times, Electronic News, Telephony, Datamation* and *Telecommunications Report* covered the change.

From a strict media relations viewpoint, then, the plan was a success. However, it was becoming clear that Teletype's media relations, sales promotions and employee communications staff needed to better coordinate their efforts. As is the case in too many organizations, public relations and marketing were separated philosophically as well as organizationally. Each operated independently, rarely sharing plans or exposing their materials to each other's audience. They did not have management's blessing of their information plans, so they had no assurance their activities were supporting the corporate plan. Media relations responsibilities were split—sales promotions handled the trade press while public relations handled the local media.

Pappas created a task force composed of media relations, marketing and employee communications people to make recommendations to the corporation. Its objectives were to present a consistent image of Teletype in all media and to all target audiences; to ensure that everyone involved in producing media for Teletype understood the company's corporate objectives and had written, detailed plans to help achieve them; and to upgrade the professionalism of promotions and communications materials where necessary. The task was rooted in the economic imperatives facing all organizations in times of scarce and expensive resources. Its overall goal was firmly focused on helping to achieve the corporate mission: To increase sales and to position Teletype as a high-technology market leader.

After two months of analysis, the task force recommended new communications strategies that offered a coordinated, unified approach to Teletype's wide variety of promotional materials— whether they traditionally were perceived as public relations, advertising or marketing media. Included was a new definition of Teletype's current and future business—in effect, a new mission statement— based on interviews with its top executives. The strengths that the company brought to that mission also were documented, later to be translated by its advertising agency into a broad advertising campaign with the theme "Value sets us apart." Media relations activities were expanded and targeted news release lists were developed. Public relations and marketing responsibilities were delineated so the skills of both were allied to offer more specialized service to the media and better results to the company.

With its public relations and marketing functions reorganized to capitalize on each discipline's skills while at the same time pooling knowledge, Teletype was able to take full advantage of the visit to its headquarters of New York and Chicago financial analysts, investment advisers and portfolio managers. Pappas' keynote address became the basis of a news release that was picked up by the local media and trade press. Media relations staff in Little Rock got coverage in both local papers on Pappas' visit to the Arkansas plant to give the financial analysts' presentation to employees there. Reprinted in booklet form, his speech was distributed to employees, reporters, key customers and financial analysts around the country.

The Teletype case illustrates corporate America's belief that media relations and other communications skills can play an important role in increasing sales and contributing to business policy before it is made. That recognition has elevated these functions within most organizations to the point where they now are valued participants in top-level councils. As Pappas put it:

> You show me a market-driven organization and I'll show you a place where public relations counseling is an integral part of the planning process. CEOs should take advantage of all the expertise they can gather before they make decisions. Public relations is a valuable management resource. Media relations specialists in particular can offer insight into the shifting demands of the marketplace as a result of their contacts with reporters, who often reflect our customers' opinions.[25]

## The Denny's Case

In 1991, a group of African-American students was asked to prepay for meals at a Denny's Restaurant while a smaller group of white customers was not. The black group hired a civil rights attorney and filed a class-action suit in California against Denny's. That was just the beginning of the crisis that would lead to Denny's diversity turnaround. Two years later a group of African-American Secret Service agents complained that they were not served at a Denny's in Annapolis, Maryland. A second class-action lawsuit was filed, charging Denny's with racial discrimination.

Public relations played a major role in the resolution of this crisis and in the resultant dramatic turnaround in corporate culture at Denny's, demonstrating the value of involved and informed counsel when a company is facing a serious business challenge. In fact, the turnaround at Denny's was so sweeping that within four years, in 1998, Denny's parent company was ranked number two on *Fortune* magazine's list of "The Top 50 Best Companies for Asians, Blacks & Hispanics." And those high rankings have continued.

The problem Denny's faced was more than settling the class-action lawsuits; they actually were settled out of court in 1994 for a total of $46 million. The real issue was changing a corporate culture from one in which discrimination had occurred to one that embraced diversity in all of its manifestations and in which there would be "zero tolerance" for discrimination. Karen Randall, vice president of communications for Advantica Restaurant Group, Inc., Denny's parent company, was one of the key players in devising the strategy to create and communicate this new culture. James B. Adamson, Advantica's chairman and CEO, was told a turnaround in Denny's corporate culture would be good for business. "I really didn't care if it was good for business," Adamson said. "It's the right thing to do."

A corporate diversity officer was hired. Then a management team led by Adamson set six objectives: To provide every employee from cook to senior manager with racial sensitivity training; to change the workforce composition to include more minorities and women, especially in middle and senior management positions; to change the composition of the company's board of directors to include more minorities and women; to change patterns of franchise ownership so that more minorities and women owned Denny's restaurants; to seek out and use minority suppliers; and to improve the chain's reputation in the minority community.

It is significant that Advantica's strategy was one of changing the *company*, not just changing the company's *reputation* or what key publics *thought* of it. Adamson and his senior management team knew that some very basic practices within the company had to change. Communications was key to implementing change, but the change itself was about much more than communications.

Part of the strategy was to have top-down insistence that change would occur. Adamson was unrelenting in his insistence that Advantica and Denny's would not tolerate discrimination and would insist on a climate where diversity was valued. Another key was admitting Denny's had made mistakes—and then moving forcefully and openly to correct those problems. Denny's used research to develop its turnaround strategy and monitor progress. In 1995, the company held focus groups with white and black customers. The research indicated Denny's needed to get out its message of a changed company—based on a new leadership team and minority involvement in decision making through ownership of franchises and positions in management.

Advantica and Denny's met their objectives, and Adamson says the company has made important strides toward its goal of creating a corporate culture that respects diversity and will not tolerate discrimination. Evidence of success:

- In 1999 the Advantica board of 12 included three African Americans, a Hispanic and a white female, compared to one minority board member in 1993.

- African Americans returned to Denny's. Focus groups conducted in 1996, 1997 and 1998 showed a nearly 14 percent increase in blacks' visits to Denny's in 1998 over 1996.

- In 1999 almost half—45 percent—of Denny's senior management team was minority or female. Three women, one of them black, were among the 11-member senior management team, and minorities made up 28 percent of Denny's managers.

- In 1999 more than a third—36 percent—of Denny's franchises were owned by minorities, compared to none in 1993. By 2004 that figure had grown to more than half.

- In 1998 Denny's did more than $25 million in business with minority vendors compared to none in 1993.

- In addition to being ranked number two on *Fortune*'s 1998 listing of the best companies for minorities, Advantica also was featured on *60 Minutes* in a very positive segment on the culture turnaround and profiled in several other complimentary media pieces. Most significant, these changes have been long lasting; Denny's has remained in the top five of *Fortune*'s best companies for minorities through the *Fortune* listing in 2004.[26]

Throughout this difficult and complex turnaround, company executives remained calm, patient and good humored—so much so that Adamson approached Jay Leno about the changes at Denny's. Leno responded by picking up the phone himself and promising not to do any more jokes about Denny's and discrimination.[27]

## The American Century Investments Case

"How are my investments doing?" is the single-biggest question and ongoing concern most investors have about their money. Although there is a wealth of information available about investment performance, it does not tell an individual how his/her personal account has fared. Performance figures for any given security are readily accessible, but what an individual investor actually earns may differ materially based on when the investment was made, withdrawals from the account, additions and dividend action.

Given Americans' reliance on mutual funds to save for retirement, Kansas City-based American Century Investments made providing personalized performance information the centerpiece of an initiative to overhaul investor statements. While revamping account statements may seem mundane, no other direct-marketed (no-load)

mutual fund group had provided personalized performance disclosure before. The effort would demand scarce information technology resources, as well as a willingness to manage the risks in trying something new and highly visible, which was not legally required.

Corporate communications led this year-long project, marshaling the resources and commitment from business partners in I.T., finance, marketing and the executive committee to make personalized performance reporting a reality for all 1.8 million of the firm's investors. American Century's research confirmed that investors wanted personalized performance information. However, the obstacles to providing it were substantial. There was no industry-standard methodology for calculating performance. There also was the question of whether displaying results, some of which could be negative, would cause investors to panic and make ill-advised sell decisions. The operational and technology-related risks of such an undertaking created additional concerns. If the statements were late—or, even worse, inaccurate—the company's credibility would suffer, raising the specter of more serious legal and financial repercussions. Other companies had dismissed the idea of providing personalized performance due to the potential cost and the extensive computer programming involved.

The timing of the new statements also posed a challenge. The market was in a late summer correction, and there was a good chance the first statements introducing personalized performance would show negative numbers due to the market downswing. The company's decision was to proceed anyway, based on the belief that its long-term goal was to present a truer picture of investment performance regardless of market conditions. Later research would indicate investors found this approach demonstrated American Century's confidence and honesty, and that investors' needs were the company's top priority.

The overall goal of the program was to win investor loyalty and trust by being the first direct-marketed fund family to provide personalized performance statements. Related objectives included industry, regulatory and public recognition for American Century's pioneering efforts. The company relied on customer input and feedback to design the prototype statements so that they were easy to read, clear and communicative while providing more information than ever before. It also minimized implementation risk by relying on proven vendors and by building in extensive testing. As well, American Century communicated extensively about the initiative to key publics—especially customers—before, during and after the implementation. A media plan and materials also were developed, resulting in positive coverage of the new statement in key publications.

The result of providing personalized performance information to investors was overwhelmingly positive. Customers praised American Century for taking a risk in providing information that had been deemed too controversial and cost-prohibitive by other companies. Quantitative research conducted after the rollout found that overall customer satisfaction scores were high, and satisfaction scores comparing the statements to those of competitors had increased. *Kiplinger's Personal Finance* magazine listed the statement on its annual "Best List," saying, "The American Century group of mutual funds comes up a winner with a redesigned mutual fund statement you can actually understand. In addition to being investor-friendly, it features nifty graphics. . . . Even when you've lost money, it still looks good."[28]

## Earning the Right to Counsel

The right to offer candid counsel and expect confidence in your advice does not flow automatically from your role as the media relations spokesperson. It must be earned. To be credible you have to demonstrate a solid understanding of the business and appreciation for its operations problems. You must do as good a job of preparing a case to persuade your management, board of directors and other decision makers as you do when you are preparing a case to persuade the public.

You can take a lesson from the world of advertising. Look at the hard, creative work that advertising agencies put into researching and presenting an advertising program to a client. Then compare it with too many public relations presentations to top executives. Where are the opinion polls, the editorial analyses, the examples of competitors' actions, the evaluation plans and the clear and dramatic visuals? A presentation does not have to be fancy—and it should not be expensive. It should be complete enough to back up your case, whether you are trying to sell a new media relations program or a new recognition plan for employees. It must demonstrate a clear understanding of your organization's goals, both short- and long-term.

It also can be helpful to presell your programs to others in the organization who will benefit from them. They then are likely to support you in their own interest. All too often public relations people are in the position of selling not only programs but also the need for them. Make sure your priorities are the same as your top management's. Then work with others in your organization whose needs you are attempting to meet, and turn your recommendation into a joint solution.

In Bob Haldeman's book *The Ends of Power*, there is a story about Henry Kissinger that symbolizes the multiple roles of the media rela-

tions professional. Haldeman was very protective of access to President Nixon, and this was a continuing area of conflict between himself and Kissinger. One day Kissinger came into Haldeman's office saying he had to see the president right away. Haldeman asked why, and Kissinger pointed to a stack of pictures he had in his arm. "It's a Cuban seaport, Haldeman," Kissinger said, "and these satellite photos show the Cubans are building soccer fields. I have to see the president now. Who's in there with him?" It was an important meeting on the economy, and Haldeman thought Kissinger had taken leave of his senses. "Are you going to burst into the Oval Office and interrupt a critical meeting to tell the president the Cubans are building soccer fields?" Haldeman asked, incredulously. "Of course I am," Kissinger answered, as patiently as he could. "These soccer fields could mean war. Cubans play baseball. Russians play soccer."[29]

We too must be able to distinguish between "baseball fields" and "soccer fields"—and then, once we have made the determination, to understand the difference and recommend appropriate action. Only then will we have completed the circle that is—or should be—our job description: to work professionally with the media to *tell* our organization's story, and to take advantage of our daily contacts with reporters by listening not only to what they are *asking* but also to what they are *saying*. Whether you believe the media leads public opinion or reflects it, the opportunities are the same: Reporters are a key window to the world's view of our organizations, our products and our people. Reflecting their interests, anticipating their concerns, adapting our media relations efforts and suggesting new courses of action as a result of their input—that is what makes us valuable to our companies and clients. That is also what makes us true media relations professionals.

## Building Respect for Our Role

We sometimes complain that we do not get enough respect within our organizations. But so many of us who aspire to greater recognition do not fulfill management expectations. On occasion we are carried away more by mechanics and methodology than by substance and measurable results. We cannot afford to confuse motion with progress—or to do well that which should not have been done at all. We cannot claim authority merely from our place on the organization chart. Rather, we must prove we have skills that make us a valued part of the management team by using those skills to anticipate and then help solve the problems that keep our bosses and CEOs

awake at night. Only then will we forge the close ties with our CEO and other decision makers in our organizations that are essential for achieving our counseling role.

We live in an environment of such complexity that almost each activity we confront requires new thought and sensitivity in applying the old principles. As Chester Burger, a PR veteran and long-time counselor to many Fortune 500 companies, cautioned, "Perhaps too many of our corporate messages are being framed in exactly the same way they were presented a quarter-century ago. We seem to pretend that the cynicism and changed values of a new generation don't exist."[30]

We need to help our organizations and clients see the world through a wide-angle lens, so that even those things that are far away or on the sidelines come into focus. We have a responsibility to assimilate, interpret and clarify information we gather from the

---

### Checklist: How Involved and Valuable Are You to Your Organization?

Following is a checklist that the public relations directors of The Reader's Digest Association were given at their Global Public Relations Conference in New York City to help them evaluate their value as communicators and counselors to management. Test yourself to see how you measure up:

❏ Recognized by colleagues as having excellent communications skills.

❏ Knowledge of the company—mission, strategies, products, people, competitive strengths—to be a competent counselor to management.

❏ Member of significant committees and task forces within the organization.

❏ Close relationships with decision makers in all departments so your advice is sought by them.

❏ Always know of major news long before it breaks.

❏ Involved in counseling and planning as well as communicating.

❏ Offer advice—sometimes on own initiative—to CEO and other members of senior management.

❏ Advise senior management of upcoming PR opportunities and anticipate potential problems.

❏ Work with CEO and affected departments to create "just in case" communications plans when necessary.

media and our publics, and get it to the right person or group. We should be measured not by the amount of news coverage we generate or number of briefing papers we prepare but by our ability to mobilize the appropriate response within our organizations as well as externally. We need to be experts in influencing behavior.

We should ensure that our company or client has long-range plans reflecting both economic and social objectives, just as we provide guidance and discipline for making better decisions today. We should take care that our plans are operating like an architect's drawing: changes can be made and arrangements altered while the basic structure remains a strong, workable blueprint for action.

Beyond that, we should put the same effort into the long-term "storm warning" job as we do into the short-term activities. We must gain the confidence of the top management of our organization or client so that when we disagree with them they know it is *not* because we are argumentative or do not understand their goals but rather because we feel we would be abdicating our responsibility if we were to remain silent while they launch an unguided missile. We must gain their confidence so that we earn the right to offer counsel by persuasion, negotiation or exhortation. The trick is to rock the boat without making everyone sink. Yet we must retain our humility. Our value lies not so much in our knowledge as in our sources of information and our ability to come up with questions that ensure thoughtful evaluation and reasonable answers by other experts in the organization.

At the time of Anwar Sadat's death, Henry Kissinger wrote a moving obituary for *Time* magazine in which he described the characteristics that propelled the Egyptian president to the center of the world's stage. He was writing about great leaders in a lofty context, of course. Yet, the same qualities should be our ideal if we are to become effective organizational counselors. According to Kissinger:

> The difference between great and ordinary leaders is rarely formal intellect but insight. The great man understands the essence of a problem; the ordinary leader grasps only the symptoms. The great man focuses on the relationship of events to each other; the ordinary leader sees only a series of seemingly disconnected events. The great man has a vision of the future that enables him to place obstacles into perspective; the ordinary leader turns pebbles in the road into boulders. . . . But a statesman must never be viewed as starry-eyed. He must have vision and depth; he must also translate his intuition into reality against sometimes resistant material."[31]

## Managing for the Future

The environment in which our organizations and clients operate is not one filled with easy managerial decisions to make in isolation or at a leisurely pace. The competitive global marketplace has little tolerance for complacency. To succeed, our organizations must offer products and services that meet customers' expressed needs—not assumptions of those needs.

As counselors, we should help our organizations manage for the future by establishing programs that detect emerging public issues and demands early, analyze their ramifications, track and respond to them as they develop, evaluate the results, and modify activities based on this knowledge. We must demonstrate that we have a solid grasp of both our organization's objectives and the world in which we are operating, so that we can provide concrete assistance in articulating and dealing with the complex problems top management faces in relating to this ever-changing environment. Edward M. Block, a PR veteran and retired senior executive at AT&T, put it this way:

> Counseling is what got us into top management in the first place. And counseling is what will keep us there, not withstanding the great changes that now envelop our companies or the ever-changing fashions of management consultants and business school theorists who presume to tell top management how to stay the course. . . . Problem solving is what management is all about, and corporate management will always have a need for—and respect for—constructive advice and timely action initiated by public relations people who know the business from the inside out as well as the outside in. To whatever extent public relations may have been disenfranchised by other management disciplines or by the unintended consequences of reorganizations and restructurings, I think it's because we have come to be viewed as communicators rather than problem solvers. Communications is *overhead*. Problem solving is *value added where it really counts*.[32]

We should help our organizations view themselves in a larger context, ensuring that they are not isolated from the mainstream of cultural, political, economic and social thought. We should not only react wisely to changing circumstances but also, when appropriate, help create them. We should embark on a continuing search for the tools and talents required to help our companies and our clients deal with immediate issues and plan for future challenges.

Above all, we need to return the values most of us were brought up with. For years we used to advise our clients (and ourselves) not to say or do anything that we would not be comfortable reading on the front page of *The New York Times* or *The Wall Street Journal*. Now we think there's a much more fundamental test of acceptable behavior: Just ask ourselves if we would be happy if our parents or our children knew what we were doing.

Ronald E. Rhody, CEO of The Rhody Consultancy, stresses that we should be concerned not about what is legal but rather with what is right—in the service of all the organization's stakeholders.

> Successful companies are going to have to demonstrate an interest in "doing the right thing"—and doing so in the spirit of what their constituencies define as right and responsible. There is no reason this needs to be a negative. In fact, it can be a significant plus. In the long run this sort of approach, this commitment to "doing the right thing" wins the public support and trust that ultimately results in improved profits and stronger stock prices.[33]

It simply gets down to individual behavior and responsibility. Every action we counsel, every thing we do and every word we write is a litmus test of our integrity. Not our employer's or our client's integrity, but our own. We would never let our executives walk into a news media interview without preparing them for tough questions we expected from the reporter. By the same token, we cannot let our organizations move unprepared into next year—or into the next decade.

## Advice from Top Executives, Consultants and Academics

We asked experienced public relations executives, consultants and academics the question, "What skills and qualities are the most valuable for a media relations professional to develop in order to become an effective counselor to management?" Here are their replies:

> Management today is seeking out and depending upon public relations professionals who can see down the road and point out the likely outcomes of a course of action. This requires good risk management skills. It also is increasingly important to know both the business you are working in and the language of that business in order to understand the unspoken motivations and the backdrop for decisions that need to be made. As you learn to "read" the management group you are counseling, you need to understand the peer group of each executive, who she/he respects, etc. This will add rich perspective to the counsel you give. Today's public relations professionals need solid skills in working with the media and being able to build ongoing strong media relationships. This

clearly is on the list of top concerns of corporate management—and can be the ticket to credibility as a counselor to management.

—Ann H. Barkelew
Senior Vice President and Partner
Fleishman Hillard, Inc.
Minneapolis, Minnesota

Everything in my own long experience has taught me that a good counselor possesses at least three attributes that are not particularly well developed or rewarded in the other management disciplines: The first is an intimate understanding of the business, its culture, its goals or, as we used to phrase it, "The Big Picture." The second is a confident understanding of what a company's various publics are thinking or may think about the company's policies and actions. And the third is the assertiveness to make certain these perspectives are heard, understood and heeded when management seeks to solve problems that exist or head off problems that may emerge.

—Edward M. Block
Senior Vice President (retired)
AT&T
Key West, Florida

The effective counselor to senior management needs to bridge the quantitative demands of business to the more qualitative demands of key audiences—employees, customers, investors, communities. To build that bridge, communications counselors need a solid understanding of the business, strong communications skills, the confidence and courage to speak the truth, and the ability to build alliances to get things done—while keeping a sense of humor.

—Pat Brozowski
Vice President–Communications (retired)
FMC Corporation
Chicago, Illinois

Counselors to management must step beyond the narrow role of being merely a "wordsmith" and a disseminator of messages to media. They must become truly sensitive to all the trends and developments inside and outside of their organization which have the potential to affect its reputation. They also must be familiar with the full range of communication tools and technologies at the disposal of the organization—including the many techniques of advertising and marketing, and their potential interrelationship with traditional public relations approaches—so that they can help ensure that the public "face" of the organization is presented in a properly integrated manner. By developing this broad base of knowledge and skills, counselors can see "the big picture," integrate different aspects of communication to ensure that they work in harmony, appreciate the varying roles and problems of other professionals in the organization, ensure that communication efforts are tuned in to the concerns of both internal and external audiences, and above all demonstrate to senior management that they are genuinely useful contributors to management decision making. The good counselor is therefore a true "image police officer" (of the "good cop" variety) who helps to align corporate reality with desired corporate image, keeps everyone out of trouble, and builds positive ongoing relationships with all the people and groups important to the organization's future.

—Graeme Domm
Former Senior Consultant
Fenton Communications
Melbourne, Australia

My easy access to top management always stemmed from the ability to write effective speeches tailored to fit the personalities of the speakers. You can't write their speeches without knowing what's going on, and what you write for them to say often triggers policy. It happened this way for me from my first assignment as a 2nd Lieutenant in the Air Force writing for a general on through my career with three Fortune 500 companies. I not only wrote for the CEO but other top officers too. This is probably how I survived twenty-some years and five complete changes of top management at my last company, which held me an extra year beyond my retirement age.

—John W. Felton, APR, Fellow
President & CEO
Institute for Public Relations
Gainesville, Florida

Anticipating and managing issues that are pertinent to the viability of the business and can impact the corporate reputation are the proving grounds. Having a voracious appetite for knowledge about the company and its market will help you better identify ways to manage these issues and force those in public relations to demonstrate value in language and context common to business leaders. This is job one, and by performing it well we gain credibility to protect and enhance reputation in other ways.

—Matthew P. Gonring
Vice President–Global Marketing and Communications
Rockwell Automation
Milwaukee, Wisconsin

The most essential qualification for a corporate communications counselor is a thorough and detailed knowledge of the company's business, its strategy, and its financial issues and track record. This knowledge, together with the full range of communications skills and an understanding of the media and how to work with reporters and editors, make up the communicator's tool kit. In addition, there must be a rapport between the communicator and the CEO. This, on the communicator's side, is aided by tact, respectfulness and a willingness to take a firm stand. Back it up with facts and logic, and accept the boss's final word.

—Gale L. Griffin
Vice President–Corporate Communications (retired)
Bestfoods
Williamstown, Massachusetts

A principle espoused by Arthur Page, the first corporate public relations officer, is "Listen to the customer." The management pioneer Peter Drucker pointed to the number-one management objective: "Create a customer." Tom Peters, modern management's gadfly, recommended that every management strategy begin with a *listening* strategy. I've listened to these folks for so long they feel like friends, and I agree with my friends. The counselor learns to listen. Listen, interpret, initiate. That's the essence of counseling. Consider publics—employees, the news media, stakeholders of all stripes—to be "customers" who must be created and re-created constantly. You can only sell to customers your product, service or message if they understand, want and are ready to deal with you. You can only sell when you understand them. To understand them you must listen to them. That's why public relations begins with research. It is the listening strategy. The counselor to management will do well to consider management as a customer or potential customer to be created, which you can achieve if you listen well, interpret well (within the context of stakeholders to whom you have listened) and initiate. Listen a long time before you talk.

—E. Bruce Harrison
Harrison Consulting
Arlington, Virginia

First: Sharply honed minds capable of clear, logical thought and oriented to the solving of problems. At the very heart of public relations and public affairs, and at the heart of all the techniques we employ, is clear, insightful and foresightful thinking. Second: Flexibility, not only in terms of working long and hard when the need arises, but also in terms of the ability to recognize and respond to instantaneous changes. Third: An ability to communicate clearly in terms that can be understood without ever simplifying to distortion.

—Douglas G. Hearle
Former Vice Chairman
Hill and Knowlton
New York City

PR professionals first and foremost need to be business people who understand corporate finance, operations and strategic planning. It is not enough to be an accomplished practitioner of any one public relations skill, such as media relations, employee communications and the like—those skills should be a given for any senior professional. But, reading a balance sheet, understanding cash flow and why it's important, knowledge of SEC regulations that apply to your business/industry and the like will convey to your colleagues and to senior management—your CEO, company president, operating division heads—that you are their peer and speak their language. Add to this, an understanding of issues that affect or might affect your business and your industry, experience in operating divisions, broad and deep knowledge about what's going on in the world as well as in the business world, the ability to listen and to articulate complex ideas in understandable language, and the ability to inspire trust and support from your colleagues and your subordinates, and you will have at least a reasonable chance of achieving that enviable position of *effective* counselor to management.

—Carol B. Hillman
Strategic Planning Consultant
Framingham, Massachusetts

The skill that is most important to develop—and most misunderstood—is consulting techniques. The best public relations programming in the universe won't be accepted or utilized if practitioners can't persuade managers of its value. These techniques are not natural, but must be studied and learned. For instance, too often practitioners feel they must give specific *advice* on what to do in a situation (the *counselor's* solution)—when what is most often effective is providing the *options*, and letting the *manager* select the solution. That way, when the boss charts the course, but with guidance from the professional, chances are infinitely better something will get done.

—The late Patrick Jackson
Founder, Jackson, Jackson & Wagner
Editor, *pr reporter*
Exeter, New Hampshire

I look for people who excel in traits essential for counseling or taking a leadership role in public relations: personal integrity; lucid and compelling writing; the strength to tell the truth to powerful people; the ability to see the big picture and make the connections that help others see that picture as well; interpersonal skills that encourage confidence and candor in others; enjoyment of change; enthusiasm for technology; deep knowledge of and interest in the operations of the business; and no problem saying, "I made a mistake."

—Marilyn Laurie
Former Executive Vice President
Brand Strategy and Public Relations
AT&T
New York City

The practice of corporate communications is subjective and directly reflects a corporation's chief executive officer. The top communicator's success is based upon (1) developing the capacity (tactical skills and business knowledge) to accomplish what is required, (2) enjoying a personal chemistry between the communicator and chief executive, and (3) establishing a mutual trust between the CEO and communicator based upon competency, reliability and sincerity of commitment. Competency is the assessment that you are able to perform the actions necessary to fulfill a commitment. Reliability is the assessment that you are able to fulfill the commitment on time, over time, and as promised. Sincerity is the assessment that you are honest and not holding back on the commitment.

—Curtis G. Linke
Vice President–Corporate Communications
Deere & Company
Moline, Illinois

I believe good listening skills, courage and confidence are critical qualities of a PR person who is counseling senior executives. I've found that it is most important to be able to recognize the underlying concerns or issues (not just what's said out loud), not only from the CEO but from employees, customers and shareowners. Then, you need to have the courage to bring these perspectives or issues, good or bad, to the forefront. And, you've got to be confident enough to take executives out of their comfort zones by really serving as the voice of your constituencies. Don't think of communications as reporting on an organization. Think of it as driving the organization. After all, communication and leading a company are really the same thing.

—Maril Gagen MacDonald
CEO
Matha MacDonald LLC
Chicago, Illinois

In my experience, what a CEO looks for in a PR counselor boils down to three things: judgment, creativity and integrity. Judgment based on deep business knowledge, not political correctness. Creativity applied to solving business problems, not to crafting nifty slogans or cheap publicity stunts. And integrity to stand up for what is right, even at high personal cost. The PR counselor's role is to help the CEO bring the company's policies and practices into harmony with its stakeholders' needs and expectations. Sometimes that means winning agreement or, at minimum, acceptance. At other times it means getting the company to change its plans. But it always means having acute antennae and anticipating where corporate and public interests might collide. One of my colleagues called it "seeing around corners." It's an apt description because for the senior PR counselor the world is all corners, all roads are narrow, and all bridges have tolls.

—Dick Martin
Executive Vice President–Public Relations (retired)
AT&T
Summit, New Jersey

Here is what I believe it takes to use the skills we are assumed to possess as a key element in the management matrix required to maximize an organization's performance: First, work continuously to apply and improve your communicative and creative skills on a scale that ensures that managing public perceptions of your organization is consistent with the expectations of senior management. Second, develop a keen understanding of senior management accountabilities and priorities. Know the business as well as is humanly possible. Third, cultivate relationships with executive/leadership mentors, and absorb yourself in the wisdom and judgment available from the mentors. And fourth, square your communications planning perfectly with the organization's strategies, goals and priorities as defined by the senior management team of which you should be an integral member.

—Richard R. Mau
Senior Vice President (retired)
Rockwell International Corporation
La Jolla, California

The most important three skills are listening, honesty and the ability to bring solutions, not just problems. These skills work together like this: As the company's senior communicator, we talk with the media, investors and employees about their perceptions of our company. It's important to listen carefully to what they are saying, and not shut them out because they "don't get it," you're short on time or they may have a negative slant. Sometimes you'll even hear a positive! Assuming the comment is legitimate, a senior communicator should tell management—in an honest, straightforward and constructive manner—about the issues. But that's not enough. If it's a problem, bring a potential solution to the table. If it's good news, suggest a way to share it as positive reinforcement.

—Ruthellyn Musil
Senior Vice President–Corporate Relations
Tribune Company
Chicago, Illinois

Counseling is more than just being a professional communicator, although that's an important prerequisite. It requires always being on top of your game, both internally and externally, anticipating the good as well as the bad and being able to offer constructive advice in a timely manner. You must also have the ability to earn the trust and confidence of those in senior management who may look to you for sage counsel in achieving the goals of the company. Without that trust and confidence, your message, no matter how good, will likely fall on deaf ears.

—Edwin F. Nieder
Partner
Nieder & Nieder Associates
Los Angeles, California

Skills needed to counsel management? Nontraditional, very varied and too often unappreciated attributes: To balance—even break through—the comfortable, myopic mindset of too many senior executives, the public relations counselor must read widely (not just business books), troll for ideas everywhere and analyze pragmatically. A solid liberal arts grounding, ability to think outside conventional wisdom, convincingly argue a position and even gently educate others in the principles and possibilities of public relations are essential. Also important are understanding operational management and fostering personal chemistry with the CEO.

—Dr. Marion K. Pinsdorf
Senior Fellow in Communications
Fordham Graduate School of Business
New York City

Developed oral and writing skills are primary for PR counseling to management. As advocates for clients and their outside interests, you have to be convincing in your presentations. A broad perspective of the world through education, travel or experience helps. Loyalty to top management and to all employees on the staff—and knowing what to do when they are in conflict—also is important. Personal integrity is the glue that keeps it all together and humor helps you survive when things get tough.

—Magda A. Ratajski
President
MarassoCo
Virginia Beach, Virginia

First, it is critical to be able to look broadly across the functions of a business—legal, finance, marketing, business development, etc. If you understand their roles and objectives, you'll be able to put yourself in their shoes and better understand their needs and concerns. PR leaders are uniquely positioned to see the big picture and bring diverse interests together to seek solutions. Second is the need to back up your position with facts and data. Without research to support the work and its results, PR will never be taken seriously by senior management.

—Judi Servoss
Vice President-Public Relations (retired)
MediaOne Group
Denver, Colorado

To be an effective public relations counselor to management, you must first have management's confidence in your ability to handle the basics of the business. To most CEOs, that means media relations. Do you know members of the press who cover your company or industry or government department? Have you gained their respect by being available and knowledgeable? Do they trust you? Are you ready for a crisis? Do you get results? If you can handle reporters, you can handle management.

—Robert B. Sims
Senior Vice President (retired)
National Geographic Society
Washington, D.C.

When CEOs are asked who they listen to on important issues, there is a great deal of consistency. They tell me they want people who deal well with ambiguity. They want an individual who, while having a balanced approach to a problem, sees both sides—and has a point of view, with the confidence to back it up. At the top of our profession, we have moved from a skill-based profession to a strategic seat at the table, and now we are being forced to view our jobs from a policy platform. Business people first—and then communications becomes one of the tools to solve the issue. The ability to know what is possible, and probable, comes from experience and practice. Basic skills will always be necessary to get in the door.

—Kurt P. Stocker
Associate Professor, Emeritus
Northwestern University
Dean of NYSE Directors' Institute
New York City

Strong writers must have a good understanding of how research can be used to develop and evaluate consistent, integrated and accountable strategic communications campaigns. They also must possess the ability to develop and nurture professional relationships with internal and external customers; have the knowledge to align senior management's goals with external and internal communications needs; and have the talent and abilities to integrate public relations measures with the organization's business objectives. I'll take one additional step and suggest all of this will require solid undergraduate-level education—and perhaps graduate-level study backed up with appropriate professional development training—that focuses upon (a) a solid understanding of practical and theoretical aspects of communications and public relations; (b) a thorough background in liberal arts and sciences; (c) an awareness and understanding about technology, diversity, politics and culture; and, (d) an appreciation of the global business environment, ideally including the ability to read and speak foreign languages.

—Donald K. Wright
Professor of Communication
University of South Alabama
Mobile, Alabama
Director
Arthur W. Page Society PR Executive Forum

To bring real value to senior management, public relations professionals must be able to represent the "outside in" as well as the "inside out." That is, PR managers must not only communicate the company's messages to external audiences, you must also communicate how those audiences view the organization and its decisions back to the management. That will not make you popular with your peers and superiors but is an absolutely vital management role. Otherwise, your organization will operate in a vacuum, oblivious to the public's impact on its ability to function.

—C. Richard Yarbrough
Vice President–Public Relations (retired)
BellSouth Corporation
Managing Director (retired)
Atlanta Committee for the Olympic Games
Atlanta, Georgia

# Endnotes

## Chapter One

[1] Grant N. Horne, "Brawling and Squabbling Towards the 21st Century," Hall of Fame lecture, Arthur W. Page Society 15th annual conference, October 4–6, 1998, Naples, FL.

[2] Fraser Seitel, "1998's Six Public Relations Lessons," *Ragan Report*, January 4, 1999, p. 2.

[3] Lesley Stahl, *Reporting Live* (New York: Simon & Schuster, 1999).

[4] Robert MacNeil, *Breaking News* (New York: Doubleday, 1998).

[5] Don Hewitt, 21st annual Frank E. Gannett Lecture, The Freedom Forum Media Studies Center, New York City, December 10, 1998.

[6] "Slouching Toward Sanity," *American Journalism Review*, March 1999, p. 6.

[7] Anderson Consulting, "The End of Innovation?" *Outlook*, 1999, No. 1, p. 9.

[8] "Ten Reasons Why PR Is Entering a Golden Age," *PR Week*, March 29, 1999, p. 12.

[9] Dan Rather, "An Anchorman's Views of the News on Television," *Wall Street Journal*, August 5, 1982.

[10] Robert MacNeil, *The Right Place at the Right Time* (Boston: Little, Brown and Co. 1982), p. 129.

[11] Randall L. Tobias, "Communications in a Time of Change," remarks delivered at the Arthur Page Society annual spring seminar, New York City, April 4, 1995.

[12] Walter K. Lindenmann, "Measuring Relationships in Key to Successful Public Relations," *Public Relations Quarterly*, Winter 1998–99, p. 19.

## Chapter Two

[1] Lynne Masel-Walters, "Working with the Press . . ." *Public Relations Quarterly*, Fall, 1984.
[2] Dr. Amanda Hamilton-Attwel, "Developing a communication strategy." Client presentation, Magaliestruin, So. Africa, 2003.
[3] AT&T Archives, Short Hills, NJ.

## Chapter Three

[1] Alan Simpson, in a presentation at Arizona State University, Tempe, AZ, February 8, 2000.
[2] Robert J. Samuelson, Washington Post Writer's Group, *Arizona Republic*, June 18, 1999.

## Chapter Four

[1] "How to use audio news releases," *PR Week*, June 18, 2001.
[2] "What kind of story works best for an audio news release?", *PR Week*, February 28, 2005. "What to look for in an ANR vendor," *PR Week*, August 30, 2004.
[3] "What to look for in an ANR vendor," *PR Week*, August 30, 2004.
[4] Fraser P. Seitel, "News Release Requisites," O'Dwyer's PR Daily, October 20, 2003.
[5] Tina Koenig, "E-Media Relations—Same Routine or New Shuck?", *The PR Network*, April 30, 1999.
[6] Soni Dimond, *Life's A Pitch!* (Xlibris Corporation, 2004), p. 121.
[7] "Is It Really News," *Interviewing, www.imakenews.com*, July 13, 2005.
[8] "White Paper Boom is Boon for Back-to-Basics Public Relations, *PR News*, September 16, 2002.

## Chapter Five

[1] Larry Weber, "The Dawn of Experiential Public Relations," *Ragan's Public Relations Journal*, January/February 1999, p. 41.
[2] John A. Meyers, "A Letter from the Publisher," *Time*, November 14, 1983.
[3] Lesley Stahl, *Reporting Live*, (New York: Simon & Schuster, 1999), p. 256.
[4] "10 Steps to Becoming A Web Genius," *Ragan Report*," May 10, 1999, p. 7.
[5] John A. Meyers, "A Letter from the Publisher," *Time*, May 17, 1982.
[6] "The Hot Zines," *PR Week*, March 22, 1999, p. 12.
[7] Ibid., p. 13
[8] "The Los Angeles Times Reaches for the Top," *Washington Journalism Review*, July/August, 1982, p. 17.
[9] Marlin Fitzwater, *Call the Briefing! Reagan and Bush, Sam and Helen: A Decade with Presidents and the Press* (New York: Times Books, 1995).
[10] "Our Expectations of You: Your Expanded Role in Our Global Company," remarks by George V. Grune, The Reader's Digest Association's global public relations conference, New York, October 19, 1992.

[11] Ann Wylie, "Simplify, Simplify, Simplify," *The Editor's Worksheet*, May 1999, p. 2.

[12] "Title Fight," *Fortune*, June 21, 1999. P. 88.

[13] "Why Americans Hate the Media" *Atlantic Monthly*, February, 1996.

[14] Stahl, p. 405.

[15] "Time to Send Embargoed News Releases to Jurassic Park?", *PR News*, June 21, 1993.

## Chapter Six

[1] Joseph Heller, *Good as Gold* (New York: Pocket Books, 1979), p. 77

[2] David Wallechinsky, Irving and Amy Wallace, *The Book of Lists* (New York: Bantam Books, 1977), p. 469.

[3] John O'Toole, *The Trouble with Advertising . . .* (New York: Chelsea House, 1981), p. 112.

[4] Quoted by Eliot Frankel, "Learning to Conquer 'Mike' Fright," *Washington Journalism Review*, July/August 1982, p. 32.

[5] Ibid., p. 33.

[6] *The New York Times* staff, *Churchill in Memoriam: His Life, His Death, His Wit and Wisdom* (New York: Bantam Books, 1965), p. 160.

[7] Ann Wylie, "Simplify, Simplify, Simplify," *The Editor's Worksheet*, May 1999, p. 1.

[8] Quoted by Susan Astarita, "Handle the Press With Finesse," *Savvy*, June 1981, p. 58.

[9] *Newsweek*, April 19, 1982, p. 90.

[10] William Safire, *On Language* (New York: Time Books, 1981), p. 138.

[11] Chester Burger, "Truth and Credibility in an Era of Disbelief," *Reagan's Public Relations Journal*, January/February 1999, p. 13

[12] Materials provided by the Arthur W. Page Society, New York, NY.

[13] Robert MacNeil, *The Right Place at the Right Time* (Boston: Little, Brown and Company, 1982), p. 10.

[14] Bill Adler and Bill Adler, Jr., "He Keeps His Wits About Him," *Parade* magazine, excerpted from *"The Reagan Wit."*

## Chapter Seven

[1] "Classic Corporate Stonewalling: Dan Does It Well," *Interviewing*, September 24, 2004, *www.imkenews.com*.

[2] Lee Banville, "Jayson Blair: A Case Study of What Went Wrong at the *New York Times*," *Online NewsHour*, December 10, 2004, *www.pbs.org/newshour*.

[3] Kirk O. Hanson, "A Case for the Truth," *Journal*, Arthur W. Page Society 20th annual conference, September 14–16, 2003, San Diego.

[4] Ibid.

[5] "Ethics in Public Relations," *Public Relations Journal*, December, 1982.

[6] Louis C. Williams, Jr., letter accompanying "Lou Williams Seminars" brochure, Fall, 1992.

[7] Lanny J. Davis. *Truth to Tell: Tell It Early. Tell It Early. Tell It All.* (New York: The Free Press, 1999).

[8] "Honesty is Best Policy in a Crisis," *Jack O'Dwyer's Newsletter*, June 28, 1999, p. 2.

[9] Jeanne Mann, "Improving Relations with the Media: Two Views," *Business and Media*. Summer, 1981.

[10] "Quotes of the Day," *Ragan's Public Relations Journal*, March/April 1999.

[11] *Communication briefings*, November 1993, p. 2.

[12] John Rosica, "To Comment or Not to Comment?" *Ragan's PR Intelligence Report*, June 1999.

[13] Mike Sorohan, "Conference Workshop Examines CIA's Shroud of Secrecy," *Communication World*, February/March, 1999, p. 6.

[14] "The Business-Media Relationship," an AMA Research Study (AMA-COM), 1981, pp. 39, 43.

[15] Foreign Press Center brochure, Washington, DC, 83–220(27).

[16] Jim Brynes, AT&T's Media Relations Newsletter, March 6, 1990.

[17] Thomas L. Harris, *Viewsletter*, March 2005, p. 1.

[18] Erica Iacono, "Football hero endorses your company on cable TV—for $29,000," *PR Week*, June 27, 2005, p. 1.

[19] Ibid.

[20] Lansie Pearmain, "The Miami Papers—What Price, Truth?" *The Measurement Standard*, July 30, 2003. *www.themeasurementstandard.com*.

[21] Erica Iacono, "Advertisers' Efforts to Screen Editorial Tone Grab Media Attention," *PR Week*, May 30, 2005, p. 1.

[22] Ibid.

[23] Dr. Dean Kruckeberg & Ms. Katerina Tsetsura, International Index of Bribery for News Coverage, Institute for Public Relations, December 1, 2003. *www.instituteforpr.com*

[24] Paul Holmes, "Money Paid for Editorial Content Will Always Be Outweighed by the Cost to Its Credibility," *PR Week*, June 23, 2003.

## Chapter Eight

[1] *www.brainyquote.com/quotes/authors/d/david_ogilvy.html*

[2] "Art center hopes to paint Cincinnati in a whole new light," *PR Week*, August 25, 2003, p. 19.

[3] Material provided by W. P. Carey School of Business, Arizona State University, Tempe, AZ, October 2004.

[4] Material provided by International Association of Business Communicators, 2005 Gold Quill Winners, Jann George, The Phillips Group, Australia.

[5] "Publisher's Memo," *Business Week*, October 3, 1983, p. 10.

[6] "The Integrated Bug," *PR Week*, April 26, 1999, p. 16.

[7] "Packaged PR Is Key to Branding," *PR Week*, March 22, 1999, p. 18.

[8] "The Integrated Bug," p. 16.

[9] "The Voice of Marketing PR," *PR Week*, March 29, 1999, p. 18.

## Chapter Nine

[1] "What's Wrong with Multinational Public Relations?" *The Strategist*, Spring 2000, p. 34.

[2] G. Clotaire Rapaille, "Secrets of Communicating in a Multi-Cultural World," *Journal*, Arthur W. Page Society 17th annual spring seminar, April 4–5, 2002, New York City.

[3] "When History No Longer Repeats Itself," *Forbes ASAP*, August 25, 1997, p. 28.

[4] "Best Practices in Global Corporate Communications," *Journal*, Arthur W. Page Society 17th annual spring seminar, April 4–5, 2002, New York City.

[5] John M. Reed, speech to Arthur W. Page Society 21st annual conference, September 12–14, 2004, Chantilly, VA.

[6] John le Carre, "The Honourable Schoolboy," (Hodder and Stroughton Ltd.: 1977), p. 84.

[7] "Foreign-Born CEOs Are Increasing in U.S., Rarer Overseas," *The Wall Street Journal*, May 25, 2004, p. B1.

[8] "Rehearsing for the PR world tour," *PR Week*, January 31, 2005, p. 14.

[9] "Courage, Discipline and Perseverance: The Future of Internal Communication in a Global Economy," *Journal of Employee Communication Management*, January/February 2005, p. 45.

[10] Tom Miller, "International Media Relations: Language Barriers," *Newswise*, August 25, 2004, p. 3.

[11] Henry Erlich, *Writing Effective Speeches* (New York: Paragon House, 1992), p. 141.

[12] Mia Doucet, "When in China: Take Responsibility for Poor Communication," *Journal of Employee Communication Management*, March/April 2005, p. 33.

[13] "Speaking a Universal Language," *PR Week*, August 9, 2004.

[14] Leslie H. Gelb, "America and the World—A New Evolution of Anti-American Sentiment," *Journal*, Arthur W. Page Society 19th annual spring seminar, April 1–2, 2004, New York City.

[15] "A Comparison of American, Canadian and European Perceptions of the U.S.," news release from Harris Interactive, April 2, 2004.

## Chapter Ten

[1] Remarks given at the IABC International Conference, 2002.

[2] "Crisis Management and PR," *Public Relations: The Complete Guide* (Mason, Ohio: South-Western Educational Publishing, 2004), p. 270.

[3] Remarks given at PRSA Crisis Communications Workshop, May 8, 2001.

[4] "Navigating the Changing Landscape of Crisis Comms," *PR Week*, February 21, 2005, p. 8.

[5] "Crisis Media Battlefield Principles," *O'Dwyer's PR Daily*, December 16, 2002.

[6] "The Facts Are Necessary, But Not Always Sufficient," *PIOnet Newsletter*, April 2005.

[7] "PR Toolbox," *PR Week*, January 31, 2005.

[8] Fraser Seitel, "Crisis Media Battlefield Practices," *O'Dwyer's PR Daily*, December 17, 2002.

[9] Ibid.

[10] PRToolBox, *PR Week*, August 16, 2004.

[11] "Internal Comms in a Crisis," PR Week, September 24, 2001.

[12] "A Graduate Course in How NOT to Handle a Crisis," *Interviewing: Are Media & Ethics Mutually Exclusive?*, February 14, 2005.

[13] George Stephanopoulos, "The New Rules of the Road," *Newsweek*, February 8, 1999, p. 34.

[14] "Watergate's Shadow," *Newsweek*, June 21, 1999, p. 38.

[15] Ronald L. Levy, "Turn-around PR: Techniques of Geniuses," *Public Relations Quarterly*, Spring 1999, p. 17.

## Chapter Eleven

[1] Dan Burgess, "What Price, Fame?", *PR Intelligence*, January 11, 1999, p. 1.

[2] Dr. Lloyd Corder, "Answering the Age-Old Marketing Question: What Have You Done For Me Lately?", *Tactics*, May 1999, p. 12.

## Chapter Twelve

[1] "Lessons of the Scandal Trials," *Corporate Board Member/Special Issue: Lawyers,* July/August 2004, p. 74.

[2] "Making Public Relations Indispensable to the CEO," Matthew P. Gonring, *Public Relations Strategist,* summer 2004, p. 14.

[3] B. Schlender, "Peter Drucker Sets Us Straight," *Fortune,* January 12, 2004, p. 118.

[4] Gretchen Morgenson, "Companies Behaving Badly," *The New York Times,* March 6, 2005, section 3, p. 1.

[5] Quoted by Christopher Komisarjevsky in a speech delivered at Ball State University as part of the Vernon C. Schrantz Distinguished Lectureship in Public Relations, fall 2002.

[6] Marilyn Laurie, speech delivered at Ball State University as part of the Vernon C. Schrantz Distinguished Lectureship in Public Relations, October 14, 2004.

[7] Justin Lahart, "Corner Office Thinks Short-Term," *The Wall Street Journal,* April 14, 2004, p. C3.

[8] "It's Better (and Worse) Than You Think," *CFO,* May 2004, p. 29.

[9] Dick Martin, speech to the Public Relations Society of America's Minneapolis chapter, September 15, 2004.

[10] Personal e-mail to the author, October 22, 2003.

[11] John F. Budd Jr., "Needed: Not Rules But Religion," *Observations* newsletter, June 2002, p. 2.

[12] Harry Levinson, lecture delivered to AT&T-Pace University Executive Management Program, New York City. 1977.

[13] Materials from the Arthur W. Page Society, New York City.

[14] Alexander Kendrick, *Prime Time* (Boston-Toronto: Little, Brown and Co., 1969), p. 456.

[15] Randall L. Tobias, speech delivered to the Arthur Page annual spring seminar, New York City, 4 April 1995.

[16] Peggy Noonan, *Simply Speaking* (Ragan Books: 1998), p. 78.

[17] Barie Carmichael, presentation to the International Association of Business Communicators annual meeting, June 2004.

[18] Christopher Komisarjevsky, speech delivered at Ball State University as part of the Vernon C. Schrantz Distinguished Lectureship in Public Relations, fall 2002.

[19] Ronald Alsop, "In Business Ranking, Some Icons Lose Luster," *The Wall Street Journal,* November 15, 2004, p. B1.

[20] Conversations with the author.

[21] Carl Sagan, "A Gift in Vividness," *Time,* October 20, 1980, p. 68.

[22] George V. Grune, remarks at The Reader's Digest Association's global public relations conference, New York City, October 19, 1992.

[23] Donald E. Procknow, speech delivered to AT&T Western Electric public relations managers, Princeton, N.J., October 15, 1982.

[24] Charles Marshall, speech delivered at AT&T public relations vice presidents' conference, West Palm Beach, Florida, March 15, 1983.

[25] John J. Pappas, talk to Teletype Corporation Integrated Promotions Task Force, Skokie, Illinois, August 3, 1981.

[26] "50 Best Companies for Minorities," *Fortune,* June 28, 2004, p. 140.

[27] Materials and information supplied to the Arthur W. Page Society 1999 national awards program by Judy VanSlyke Turk, Advantica Restaurant Group.

[28] Materials and information supplied to the Arthur W. Page Society 1999 national awards program by Patricia Harden, vice president-corporate communications, American Century Investments.

[29] H. R. Haldeman and Joseph DiMona, *The Ends of Power* (New York: Times Books, 1978), p. 85.

[30] Chester Burger, "Truth and Credibility in an Era of Disbelief," *Ragan's Public Relations Journal*, January/February 1999, p. 13.

[31] Henry A. Kissinger, "A Man with a Passion for Peace," *Time*, October 19, 1981, p. 12.

[32] Edward M. Block, remarks to the San Francisco Academy, May 5, 1995.

[33] Ron Rhody, "Standing Upright in Perilous Times: The CEO, The Board & Us," *Public Relations Quarterly*, Spring 2004, p. 2.

# Index